THE NAVAHO

THE NAVAHO

Clyde Kluckhohn
and Dorothea Leighton

REVISED EDITION

Revisions made by
Lucy H. Wales and
Richard Kluckhohn

With a Foreword by
Lucy Wales Kluckhohn

Harvard University Press
Cambridge, Massachusetts
London, England

10 9 8 7

Library of Congress Catalog Card Number 74-21690
ISBN 0-674-60603-5
Printed in the United States of America

To Alfred Tozzer and John Collier

CONTENTS

FIGURES

TABLES

PLATES

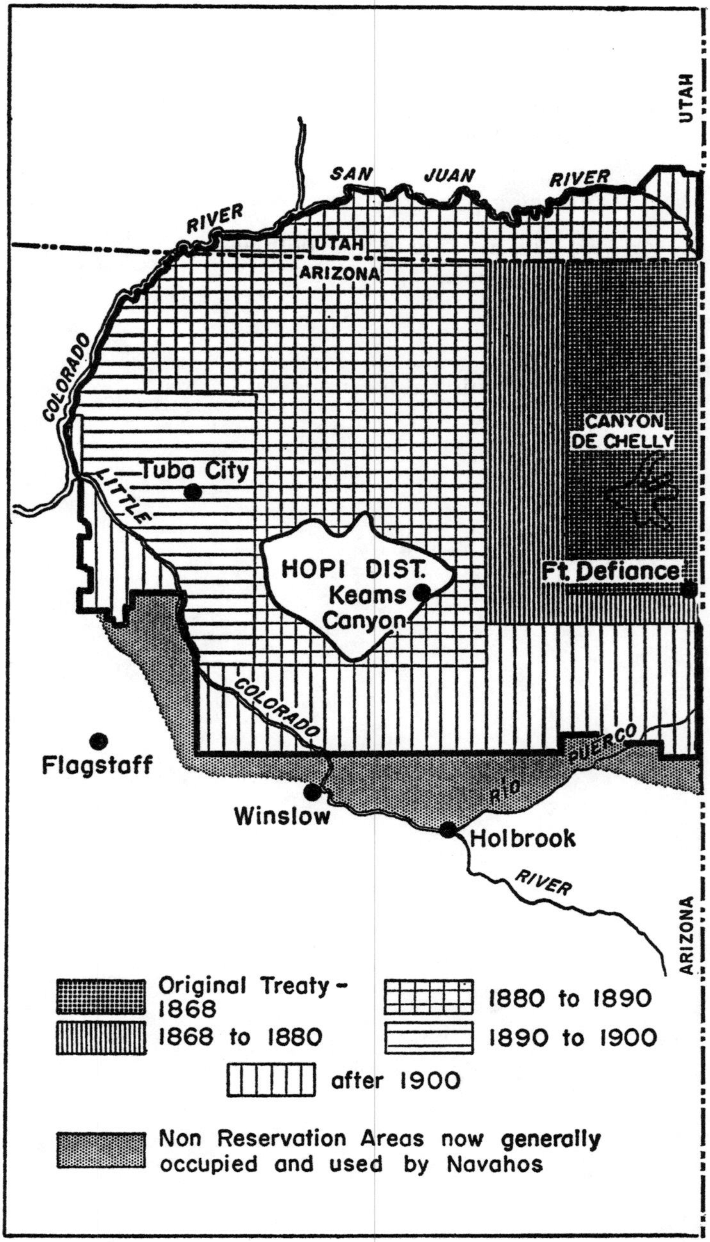
UTAH
SAN JUAN RIVER
RIVER
UTAH
ARIZONA
COLORADO
CANYON DE CHELLY
Tuba City
LITTLE
HOPI DIST.
Keams Canyon
Ft. Defiance
COLORADO
PUERCO
RIO
Flagstaff
Winslow
Holbrook
RIVER
ARIZONA
Original Treaty - 1868
1880 to 1890
1868 to 1880
1890 to 1900
after 1900
Non Reservation Areas now generally occupied and used by Navahos

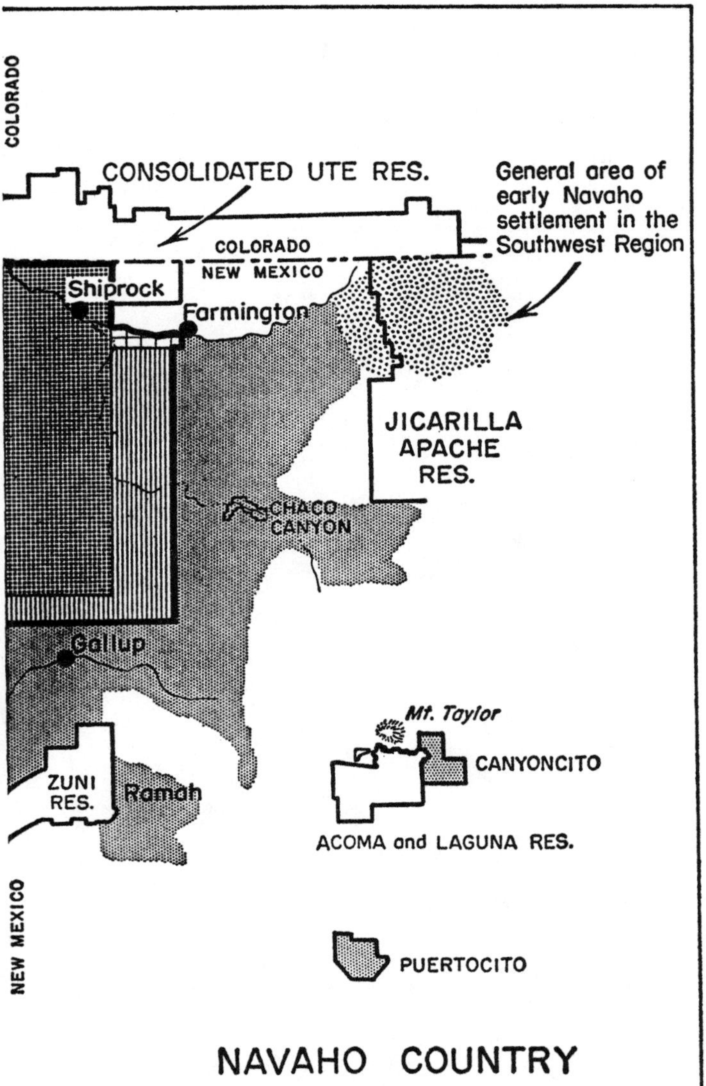

NAVAHO COUNTRY

SHOWING

GROWTH OF NAVAHO RESERVATION

THE NAVAHO

FOREWORD

The Navajo* Indians, whose reservation lands occupy approximately 25,000 square miles in the four-corners area of Arizona, New Mexico, Utah, and Colorado, are the largest tribe in the United States today. The population, estimated by Kluckhohn and Leighton in 1946 at 55,000, grew to approximately 90,000 in 1960 and to more than 120,000 in 1969. The growth rate would indicate an estimated population of 130,000 in 1974. The effects of this population growth are readily visible. Navajo communities are springing up around established centers (trading posts, government schools, chapter houses) throughout the Reservation, where no such communities were before. Hogans can be seen from the road; in 1940 they were usually out of sight. The increased population cannot be supported solely by the traditional activities of sheepherding and farming. Since the population can no longer live off the land, more services have been needed—schools, hospitals and clinics, jobs, better roads and transportation. These have been provided by

* When *The Navaho* was written in the early 1940's and when it was revised in 1962, "Navaho" was the spelling used by most anthropologists. The Navajo Tribe, however, has long used the *j* and in the 1960's the Navajo Tribal Council formally stated its preference. Today most anthropologists conform to tribal usage, and I have done so in this preface. But because *The Navaho* has been reissued by photographic processes, the *h* has been retained in the text of this edition.

a combination of federal, state, tribal, and private sources.

In many ways the Navajo of the 1970's are different from the group studied by Kluckhohn and Leighton in the early 1940's; yet in many other ways they remain the same. Areas where change is the most apparent include the economy, technology and material culture, health and education and political organization and administration. The changes in social organization and religion have been more conservative. In all areas, the Navajo have adopted new items and retained old items of a cultural inventory where suitable, and they have molded both to a distinctive Navajo way of life. This pattern of adoption and gradual change was in progress when Kluckhohn and Leighton did their field work; it is still going on.

The Navajo economy in the 1970's is far more dependent upon the job market than it was in the 1940's, although the trend was evident by 1960. The railroad was once the major employer for wage work, both on and off the Reservation, but the base for wage work has widened. The federal government is now the largest single employer of the Navajo (Aberle 1969:242). Many Navajos work in clerical and administrative positions at the Navajo Area Office of the Bureau of Indian Affairs in Window Rock. Tribal and state governments provide jobs in addition to those available from federal sources. Fairchild, General Dynamics, and EPI Vostron companies have established plants on the Reservation.

Other sources of income for Navajo families include the traditional ones. Families raise crops (corn, melons, and squash) for their own use. They herd sheep and goats. Cattle, which require less herding but need more acres per head, are increasing in importance. Arts and crafts provide family income as well. The Navajo Arts and Crafts Guild has helped with the distribution of these works. The price of silver has increased rapidly since 1960, dramatically since 1970, and the demand for American Indian jewelry has reached the point that major department stores are not only offering the jewelry but are advertising the wares in newspapers from coast to coast. How much the individual craftsman derives from this outlet, however, I do not know. Relief and welfare were important sources of family livelihood in the early 1940's and remain important today, but the focus has changed from federal welfare checks to a program sponsored by the tribe, with the guidance of the Bureau of Indian Affairs and the Public Health Service.

To fund programs and services for individual families, the Navajo Tribe needs income. The sources of tribal income have expanded in the last three decades. The improved road system across the Reservation has paved the way for tourism, an industry that was hardly envisaged in the early 1940's. Several Navajo tribal parks have opened, beginning with the establishment of Monument Valley Tribal Park in 1958, followed by the Lake Powell and Little Colorado River Navajo Tribal Parks (1962) and the Window Rock-Tse Bonito Tribal Park (1963). Kinlichee Tribal Park opened in 1964; the Anasazi ruins there (A.D. 800–1300) have been excavated by the Museum of Northern Arizona and stabilized by the Navajo Tribe. Grand Canyon Navajo Tribal Park opened in 1966. Guided tours are available: the Navajo Parks and Recreation Department pamphlet invites the visitor to see Navajoland on five-day package tours "featuring Navajo college students as driver-guides and pretty Navajo coeds as hostesses on sightseeing buses."

Tribal leases for mineral rights have been important since 1921, and with the ecology movement and energy crisis of the 1970's, leases are still important and are now controversial. Coal from the strip mine at Black Mesa is slurried across the Reservation to the western boundary near Page, Arizona. Extending 97 miles, the right-of-way brought in a lease income of approximately $14,933.45 for the first half of 1967 (NAO BIA 1967:17). The leases enrich the tribal coffers, but it is hard to herd sheep on a strip mine. There is air pollution from the Four Corners Power Plant south of Shiprock. Seven natural gas plants are planned for an area in the eastern Navajo Reservation in northwestern New Mexico. The Navajo residents in the area have voted overwhelmingly to oppose the projects (Fradkin 1973:2).

Tribal leasing involves more than gas and mineral rights. Business leases have been approved; a total of twenty-four business leases, five of them to Navajos, generated an income for the tribe of $109,400 in the first half of fiscal year 1968 (NAO BIA 1967:16). A supermarket opened in 1968 at Window Rock, providing a much-needed service to the central Navajo area. Navajos in other areas must travel great distances to non-Reservation towns or depend on the local trading post for their day-to-day needs (see Adams 1963; Aberle 1969).

Change since the 1940's is apparent in the areas of technology and material culture as well. Housing has changed. Cinder-block houses are being built with increasing frequency; 190 low-rent units were occupied in 1967, and 410 were under construction at that time (NAO BIA 1967:35). Yet a family group retains a hogan for ceremonial use, and the front door of a cinder-block house still faces east whenever possible. The availability of electricity across the Reservation has had its effect in the increased use of material goods. Furniture and appliances—beds, tables, chairs, bureaus, stoves, sewing machines, televisions, radios, washing machines, and freezers—are increasingly prevalent. Floors that once were dirt are now cement, often covered with linoleum. Dishes and pots and pans made of plastic, metal, and china, common in the 1940's all over America but not in the hogan, are now the rule rather than the exception for the Navajo. Transportation is by pickup truck rather than wagon, and the settlement pattern has changed according to where a truck can go or cannot go. Clothing has continued to change, and a great variety is seen: men in business suits or western shirts and jeans, women in dresses, blouses and skirts, or pants, according to current fashions available locally. Young women can, and do, wear jeans or slacks; even as late as 1958 this was considered outrageous, indecent, but it is now accepted for children and young adults.

Health services for the Navajo are improving. There is increasing use of the medical facilities available through the Public Health Service (the Department of Health, Education, and Welfare took over administration from the BIA in 1955), a change from the 1940's, when the level of distrust of anything Anglo was high. The Cornell-Many Farms project started in July 1955 was helpful in bridging the gap between Navajo and Anglo Medicine; both are used today. There are new Public Health Service hospitals in Gallup and in Tuba City, and clinics are held at the chapter houses. The first class of nurses in the new program at Navajo Community College was graduated in January 1973 (four girls were in this class, three Navajo and one Hopi).

Other public services are available to the Navajo. The Public Health Service and the Office of Navajo Economic Opportunity (ONEO) sponsor a popular Home Improvement Training Program. ONEO also sponsors legal aid services, programs for migrant agricultural workers, programs on employment and alcoholism, VISTA, and others (Bathke 1969:13). Overall, the picture is one of the Navajo Tribe, the BIA, and ONEO working in cooperation (and/or competition) to provide the Navajo with needed services.

The Navajo Tribal Education Committee has worked hand in hand with ONEO to use resources to the best advantage to meet the unique Navajo educational needs. ONEO has provided Head Start classes with Navajo teachers (seventeen kindergartens opened in 1968), and students can attend state public schools, federal day schools, BIA boarding schools, or mission schools, according to the wishes of their parents and the availability of transportation. An indication of the importance of education to the Navajo is the Rough Rock Demonstration School. D.I.N.E., Inc.

("Demonstration in Navajo Education"; *diné* is the Navajo word for "The People") was established as a nonprofit organization to receive funds and to direct the school; the school board is all Navajo. The first classes were held in the fall of 1966. The school is a unique example of Navajo community involvement in education: parents as well as teachers participate in the education of the children, and Navajo culture (including mythology, the kinship system, medicine and medicine men, and language) as well as American culture is emphasized. Courses are taught in both Navajo and English. English as a second language is taught for those who need it; courses in Navajo are offered for those who need to learn Navajo (see Johnson 1968).

Higher education is available to Navajo students at the Navajo Community College, which opened in temporary headquarters at the Many Farms High School, near Chinle, Arizona, in January 1969. In 1971 the Navajo Community College Press published volume 1 of *Navajo History,* written under the direction of the Navajo Curriculum Center at the Rough Rock Demonstration School (Yazzie 1971). Construction is under way for the new Tsaile campus of the college, at the foot of the Chuska Mountains. In addition, Navajo students today attend colleges elsewhere in the United States, many of them helped by tribal scholarships or by grants from the BIA. I remember the pride with which Clyde Kluckhohn greeted the first Navajo student at Harvard University—in 1959. Dr. Kluckhohn stated that there had been a few Navajo students at the University of New Mexico, but he knew of none at Harvard before 1959.

Political organization and administration have changed in emphasis since the 1940's. The major governing body of the Navajo Tribe, the Tribal Council, is still responsible for the major decisions affecting the tribe, as it was then. Established in 1923 with Henry Chee Dodge as the first chairman, the council was reorganized in 1938; membership increased from 12 delegates and 12 alternates to the 74 now serving for four-year terms (see Young 1961 for details). At the local level, however, chapters are now important. Established to provide a means of reaching Navajo communities with new ideas, the first chapter was set up at Leupp in 1927 (Young 1968:63; Shepardson and Hammond 1970: 37). With the support of BIA funds and materials and Navajo labor, local meetinghouses were gradually built across the Reservation. In the aftermath of the stock reduction program, however, and as BIA appropriations to the Navajo decreased after World War II (Jorgensen 1972:139; see also Brophy and Aberle 1966), many of the chapter houses fell into disrepair, and the chapter system languished. The Tribal Council revived the chapters in 1955, and by 1969 there were 100 chapters across the Reservation (Bathke and Bathke 1969:12). Today the chapter house serves as a town hall, the source of Tribal Council information for the local community, the locus of several tribal programs, and the like—chapters today are an important part of the political system. Organized to meet an imposed need, they illustrate the Navajo capacity for retaining what is essentially Navajo; owing to its decentralized nature, the chapter system is reminiscent of the nineteenth-century fragmentation of the Navajo political system structured around headmen. The local community today retains its integrity and its importance.

Changes in social life and religion have been less pronounced than changes in other areas of Navajo life. Members of extended families and matrilineal kinsmen still provide support and mutual aid when needed. This is more difficult for Navajos living in towns than for those in the more remote areas of the Reservation, but family ties remain strong and are highly valued. Many recent studies have been done on the social organization of the Navajo (see, for example, Aberle 1961; Downs 1972; Lamphere 1970; Levy 1962; Reynolds, Lamphere, and Cook 1967; Shepardson and Hammond 1970; Witherspoon 1970; and others).

Religious ceremonies are still held, and they are as important as ever. They are still scheduled to fit in with the other activities of the participants; many are now held on weekends. What is new since the 1940's is the increased membership in the Native American Church. The use of peyote on the Navajo Reservation was banned by the Tribal Council in June 1940, and for many years members of the Native American Church were arrested for practicing their religion. The struggle to allow peyote continued through the courts, and peyote is now legal on the Reservation; despite harassment, the number of peyotists among the Navajo has continued to rise; by 1965 there were approximately 35,000 peyotists, between 35 and 39 per cent of the Navajo population at that time, and the present estimate is at least that percentage, or larger. In addition, several evangelical Christian denominations recruit members from among the Navajo. Religious affiliation and the increased medical facilities available on the Reservation, however, do not seem to diminish the desirability and efficacy of the Navajo curing ceremonies. All are considered necessary.

In sum, the Navajo today are a vital, effective, and growing people; they call themselves "The People"—and, as a tribe, their administrative activities are so varied that the computer at Window Rock has trouble keeping up with the work load. Though today's problems are complex, it is the Navajo, not the government in some form, that takes the lead in trying for adequate solutions. When Kluckhohn and Leighton wrote *The Navaho*, the reverse was true. They set out to evaluate the whole Indian administrative program with special reference to the effect of its policy on Indians as individuals, to indicate the direction toward which this policy was leading, and to suggest how the effectiveness of Indian administration might be increased. In short, Kluckhohn and Leighton attempted to use the tools of anthropology and medicine to clarify what was viewed as "the Navajo problem" and to bridge the gap between

The People and those who were engaged in administering the Navajo area in the Southwest. In the process, Kluckhohn and Leighton provided a valuable ethnography of the Navajo in the early 1940's; many aspects of Navajo culture remained unchanged when the work was revised, and many remain unchanged today. Most of the 1962 revisions, however, were woven into the text; as Levy pointed out (1963: 732), the changes were hard to detect. The following key to what was revised and what was left alone should remedy this situation.

Preface. The last two sentences were omitted: "The book was written in the years 1942–1944. Unless a specific year is mentioned, 'now' or 'today' refers to the 1942–1944 period." In the 1962 revisions, the words "now" and "today" were avoided where possible in favor of specific years. Where general terms were used, however, they refer to the period through 1959.

Introduction. Population figures were revised from 55,000 in 1946 to 90,000 in 1961. To conform with current accepted usage, "Navajo Service" was changed to "Navajo Agency." The rest of the introduction remains as originally written.

Chapter 1. This chapter is nearly untouched. In the discussion about the governmental policy sympathetic to the Navajo which was evolved in the early 1930's, "fifteen years" was changed to "thirty years," and "two generations" to "three generations." The last paragraph in the chapter was revised to include material on the Indian Claims Commission, established in 1946.

Chapter 2. Although the geography of the Navajo Reservation has remained relatively constant, the use of the land has been changing since 1946. Revisions in Chapter 2 can be identified by such phrases as "since the war," "since 1940," "in the postwar years," or "recently" followed by statistics through 1958. Data were added concerning road construction (1951–1958), tribal income from oil and gas leases, range capacity, and soil classification. Data on population, infant mortality, median age, Reservation acreage, and population density were revised through 1958.

The order in which the material is presented on the sources of Navajo livelihood was maintained as originally written. Statistics were revised, however, and new material on postwar changes was added at the end of the appropriate paragraph. As a rule of thumb, the last sentence or paragraph in each section is new to the revised edition (note the identifying phrases).

Table I, Navaho Income by Sources, was added, and material on the Civilian Conservation Corps (CCC), which employed many Navajos in the 1940's, was deleted. Because of the change in relief assistance as the tribe took over some of the responsibility from the Navajo Agency, material concerning per capita income for 1940 through 1957 was added, as well as family income statistics for 1957. The increase in Navajo automobiles was noted (and "fifteen years ago" was changed to "thirty years ago"). A list of enterprises within the Tribal Program was added. Other material remains the same.

Chapter 3. There were but three changes in this chapter, two of them minor. A heading was changed by one word ("Hogan Group" replaced "Indian Group"), and the last sentence of the section "The Local Group or Community" was recast to include a cross reference to Chapter 4. The third change should not have been made. Within the hogan, women traditionally do sit on the north side (as stated in the 1946 edition, and as corrected in this edition), men sit on the south. In the 1970's, that requirement is maintained for ceremonials. Although research on the social organization and kinship system has been done since the 1940's, the chapter remains true to the picture of the Navajo as seen by Kluckhohn and Leighton in the early 1940's.

Chapter 4. By the time the 1958 statistics were available, the postwar changes were not only evident across the Reservation but were especially marked in the relations of the Navajos with those around them. The revisions in this chapter reflect this rapid expansion of contact. Wage work increased during the war years (in response to the war), and it continued after the war. Two paragraphs on the Gallup Inter-Tribal Indian Ceremonial were added; minor changes took note of the increase in contact between Navajos and Anglos at day schools and trading posts. The increase in missionary activity on the Reservation was also noted in new material. General dating was added to by twenty years, and contact "for the past two generations" became contact "for the past three generations." Statistics on the Navajo Agency budget were revised as of 1958, as were the acreage figures (from 350,000 in 1946) and population (districts varied in population from 1,100 to 6,400 in 1946) for the eighteen districts. Since range riders and wartime rationing were obsolete by 1960, a sentence was deleted.

Several statements were added at the ends of paragraphs concerning Navajo education, to reflect the growth not only in numbers of students but in appropriations from the Navajo Tribe and the Federal Government. Nineteen day schools were closed in 1944–1945, sixteen in 1945–1946, for lack of funds; statistics for 1958 concerning the types of schools were substituted. New data on school salaries for 1960 were added. In the 1970's most of these data are obsolete, but to bring them up to date would be a vast project in itself.

Literacy has increased among the Navajos, and consequently certain statistics were updated. Data from the 1930 census was deleted (71 per cent of the tribe spoke no English and only 10 per cent spoke it "reasonably well"), and a table showing the enrollment in the various types of schools on the Reservation was added. The "present school program on the Reservation" is described in the past tense and the date (1961 instead of 1946) was changed. Minor changes were made in the rest of the education section ("war years" became "past twenty years"; "range riders" became "local sub-agents"). A statement that "the scholarship program for developing professional and sub-professional Navaho teachers could be worked out much better" was deleted (which followed "Some things need more thought and action," p. 151).

The statistics in the section "Medical Services and Navaho Health," especially those for tuberculosis, were revised (there were an estimated 2,500 active TB cases on the Reservation in 1946); sulfanilomide and other antibiotics reduced the incidence of trachoma from 5 per cent in 1946 to 3 per cent in 1958. Statistics on Reservation hospital facilities were revised as of 1958, and material on the Navajo-Cornell Field Health Project at Many Farms was added.

Concerning law and order, the 1946 edition noted that "the Navaho Police Patrol is headed by a white man, but all policemen are themselves Navahos." The difficulties faced by tribal policemen in the 1940's included not only a wide area to cover and poor transportation but also resentment of "white-made law," and of white sanctions that differed sharply from Navajo means of dealing with offenders. The revised statistics note the increase in financial responsibility of the Navajo Tribal Council (starting in 1953) and the cooperation with the Federal Government in terms of trial and punishment in certain cases.

Material on the Navajo Tribal Council was revised as of 1961 (Young 1961:378–390), and the change from the "absence of women" in 1946 to the "comparatively small number of women in responsible positions" was briefly noted. Two paragraphs speculating on the growth of the Council's usefulness were replaced by material concerning the growth in The People's awareness of and participation in the world around them since 1946.

New data were added to the section "Tribal Courts." The statement on federal jurisdiction was revised to include eleven major crimes (embezzlement was added to the list of ten cited in 1946). The statistics given in the 1946 edition for 997 convictions in 1942 were for disorderly conduct (391 cases), liquor violations (148), and adultery (110). These statistics were replaced by data from 1958. Other material in this section was retained.

In the 1946 edition the section "The Government and The People: Present Problems" specifically pertained to the 1935–1945 decade. The section was entirely rewritten by Richard Kluckhohn.

Most of the material in the section "Navahos Working in the White World" was retained. The present tense was changed to the past tense, and the increasing acceptance of off-Reservation work was noted.

The section "Navaho Attitudes toward Whites" was changed to indicate the increase in trained and educated Navajos in the 1946–1960 period. A statement that "it is too early to estimate the effects the 3600 returned veterans will have upon tribal life" was deleted, as was a statement concerning the laws of disfranchisement of Arizona and New Mexico.

Certain comments were added to reflect the change of attitudes (Navajos are now willing to invest for future return), and a statement concerning the unpopular stock reduction program was deleted. The excerpt and translation from the government report were retained as written in 1946.

Chapters 5 through 9. No changes were made in Chapters 5 and 6. One minor change was made in Chapter 7. The increase in ceremonials noted in 1946 was said to be the result of more money available on the Reservation, "on account of soldiers' allotment checks" and the availability of jobs. Since allotment checks were less important as a source of income in 1960 than in 1946, that phrase was deleted. Chapters 8 and 9 are unchanged.

To update all the topics covered in *The Navaho* would have required far more time and research than was available. The topics I chose for comment here were those with which I am most familiar or on which material was available; many more topics deserve equal space and time. Any reader interested in learning more about the Navajo should consult the bibliography provided below and also *The Navajo Times* (available by subscription from Window Rock, Arizona, and in some libraries across the country).

In preparing this foreword, I gratefully acknowledge the help of certain people who prefer to be nameless, and I thank Dorothea Leighton and Terry Reynolds not only for bibliographic help but for encouragement when I needed it.

Lucy Wales Kluckhohn
June 1974

BIBLIOGRAPHY

Aberle, David F., "The Navaho," *Matrilineal Kinship,* ed. David M. Schneider and Kathleen Gough (Berkeley: University of California Press, 1961).

The Peyote Religion among the Navaho, Viking Fund Publications in Anthropology, No. 42 (New York: Wenner-Gren Foundation for Anthropological Research Inc., 1966).

"A Plan for Navajo Economic Development," *Toward Economic Development for Native American Communities: A Compendium of Papers Submitted to the Subcommittee on Economy in Government of the Joint Economic Committee, Congress of the United States, 91st Congress,* 1st Session, Joint Committee Print (Washington: U.S. Government Printing Office, 1969), 2 vols., continuously paged, pp. 223–276.

Adams, William Y., *Shonto: A Study of the Role of the Trader in a Modern Navaho Community,* Smithsonian Institution, Bureau of American Ethnology, Bulletin 188 (Washington: U.S. Government Printing Office, 1963).

Bathke, Alice, and Jerry Bathke, "They Call Themselves 'The People,'" *The University of Chicago Magazine,* 61, No. 5 (1969), 2–17.

Brophy, William, and Sophie D. Aberle, *The Indian: America's Unfinished Business* (Norman, Okla.: University of Oklahoma Press, 1966).

Correll, J. Lee, *Historical Calendar of the Navajo People* (Window Rock, Ariz.: Navajo Tribal Museum, 1968).

Correll, J. Lee, and Editha Watson, *Welcome to the Land of the Navajo: A Book of Information about the Navajo Indians,* Prepared by Navajo Parks and Recreation (Window Rock, Ariz.: The Navajo Tribe, 1969).

Downs, James F., *The Navajo,* Case Studies in Cultural Anthropology (New York: Holt, Rinehart and Winston, Inc., 1972).

Fradkin, Philip, "Gas-From-Coal Plants Will Change Life-Style of Navajos," *Los Angeles Times,* Sunday, October 21, 1973, Part II, pp. 1–3.

Johnson, Broderick H., *Navaho Education at Rough Rock* (Rough Rock, Ariz.: Rough Rock Demonstration School, D.I.N.E., Inc., 1968).

Jorgensen, Joseph G., *The Sun Dance Religion* (Chicago: University of Chicago Press, 1972).

Lamphere, Louise, "Ceremonial Cooperation and Networks: A Reanalysis of the Navajo Outfit," *Man,* 5, No. 1 (1970), 39–59.

Levy, Jerrold, "Community Organization of the Western Navaho," *American Anthropologist,* 64 (1962), 781–801.

Review of *The Navaho,* by Clyde Kluckhohn and Dorothea Leighton. *American Anthropologist,* 65 (1963), 732–733.

Navajo Area Office, Bureau of Indian Affairs (NAO BIA), Annual Report of Activities, 1967 (Window Rock, Ariz.) Mimeographed.

Reynolds, Terry R., Louise Lamphere, and Cecil Cook, Jr., "Time, Resources, and Authority in a Navaho Community," *American Anthropologist,* 69 (1967), 188–199.

Shepardson, Mary, and Blodwen Hammond, *The Navajo Mountain Community* (Berkeley and Los Angeles: University of California Press, 1970).

Witherspoon, Gary, "A New Look at Navajo Social Organ-

ization," *American Anthropologist,* 72, No. 1 (1970), 55–65.

Yazzie, Ethelou, ed., *Navajo History, Vol. 1* (Unrecorded History), written under the direction of the Navajo Curriculum Center, Rough Rock Demonstration School, Chinle, Arizona (Many Farms, Ariz.: Navajo Community College Press, 1971).

Young, Robert W., *The Navajo Yearbook, VIII* (Window Rock, Ariz.: Navajo Agency, 1961).

——— "The Role of the Navajo in the Southwestern Drama" (Gallup, N.M.: *Gallup Independent* in cooperation with the Navajo Tribes, 1968).

PREFACE

This book was written as a part of the Indian Education Research Project undertaken jointly by the Committee on Human Development of the University of Chicago and the United States Office of Indian Affairs. The immediate objective of the project was to investigate, analyze, and compare the development of personality in five Indian tribes in the context of their total environment—sociocultural, geographical, and historical—for implications in regard to Indian Service Administration. The ultimate aim of the long-range plan of research of which this project is the first step is to evaluate the whole Indian administrative program with special reference to the effect of present policy on Indians as individuals, to indicate the direction toward which this policy is leading, and to suggest how the effectiveness of Indian administration may be increased.

The results of the project are being reported in monographs on the several tribes and in shorter reports on special phases of the research in all the groups. Tribal monographs already published are *The Hopi Way,* by Laura Thompson and Alice Joseph (University of Chicago Press, 1944) and *Warriors without Weapons,* a study of the Pine Ridge Sioux, by Gordon Macgregor (University of Chicago Press, 1946). Studies of the Papago and Zuñi tribes are in preparation.

Such research necessarily depends in part upon information previously available. The sources of the present book lie largely in published literature about the Navahos and in the field work, still largely unpublished, carried on by the writers and others for some years before the Indian Education Research Project began. To these have been added the field work of the project and many conferences with professional students, administrators, and teachers who have had first-hand dealings with the Navahos.

The task of the writers, then, has been to synthesize their own materials with those in the literature and those supplied in oral conference. Since there is an exhaustive bibliography of the Navahos up to 1940 (Clyde Kluckhohn and Katherine Spencer, *A Bibliography of the Navaho Indians,* New York: J. J. Augustin, 1940), bibliographical references in this book have been limited to publications which have appeared since 1939 or are directly quoted herein. Detailed documentation of all statements has not been attempted because it would have created pages where footnotes outweighed the text, pages which would have pleased only the specialist. For a relatively complete tabulation of printed materials the reader may combine the list of references at the end of the book with those included in Kluckhohn and Spencer's bibliography.

Authority for assertions is to be found partly in the literature, partly in the field notes of the writers and of their colleagues who have generously supplied unpublished data. (See Acknowledgments.) A few facts are drawn from oral statements made in conference by Indian Service personnel. Interpretations have also been importantly influenced by these discussions and by administrators' criticisms of the book in manuscript.

Children of The People, also published by the Harvard University Press, is a companion volume by the same writers. Each book is a separate study, though the two supplement each other. *Children of The People* deals primarily with the individual (studying children especially) and with the formation of personality. *The Navaho* deals primarily with the situational and cultural context of

Navaho life. While each book stands by itself, two approaches, differently emphasized in the two books, are necessary for the deepest understanding. The Navaho way of life may be learned only by knowing individual Navahos; conversely, Navaho personality may be fully understood only insofar as it is seen in relation to this life-way and to other factors in the environment in the widest sense. Understanding of Navaho culture is dependent upon acquaintance with personal figures, but equally these personal figures get their definition and organization as individuals when the student is in a position to contrast each one with the generalized background provided by the culture of The People.

In this volume the accent will be heavily upon Navaho life today. The past will be treated to the extent that seems necessary for a comprehension of contemporary problems or of the characteristic attitudes with which Navahos face these problems. Greater attention will be given to Navaho dealings with the government than might be appropriate in another sort of general book about this tribe.

C. K.
D. L.

INTRODUCTION: "THE PEOPLE" AND THIS STUDY

The Navahos form the largest Indian tribe in the United States. Today they number about 90,000. This fact alone gives them a claim to the interest and attention of the general public, for in 1868 there were hardly more than 15,000 of them—some authorities say only 8,000. This increase is the more startling because their linguistic and cultural cousins, the Apaches, have done little more than maintain their numbers during the same generations.

"Navaho" is not their own word for themselves. In their own language they are *diné*, "The People." A case can be made for translating this expression as "men" or "people," but since there are no articles in Navaho, the translation used in this book is formally permissible and is better semantically. A number of interpreters habitually use the English rendering "The People." Technically, *dine'é* ("tribe," "people," or "nation"), an old plural of *diné*, is the more correct Navaho term, but actually simple *diné* is heard more frequently. This term is a constant reminder that the Navahos still constitute a society in which each individual has a strong sense of belonging with the others who speak the same language and, by the same token, a strong sense of difference and isolation from the rest of humanity.

"Navajo" is, of course, a Spanish word, and this spelling is followed in government publications. The anglicized spelling with an *h* instead of a *j* is followed in this book because it has become standard anthropological usage and also because the *j* is apt to be mispronounced by those who are not familiar with Spanish or with this particular tribal name.

The exact origin of the term is by no means certain. The view that "Navahu" was a place name used by Tewa-speaking[1] Pueblo Indians and that it might be translated "large area of cultivated lands" has been widely accepted in recent years. This interpretation gains plausibility from the fact that the seventeenth-century Franciscan friar Benavides speaks of the Navaho as "the Apache of the great planted fields." Some scholars claim, however, that the Tewa word really means "to take from the fields." There is also some support for deriving "Navajo" directly from the Spanish in the sense of either a clasp knife or razor or a large, more or less worthless, flat piece of land.

In recent years the Navahos have become the nation's foremost Indian problem. The social and economic assimilation or adjustment of so large a minority group could never be, at best, a simple matter. Their rapid increase in numbers continues, and the adjacent areas can no longer absorb the overflow. Moreover, the resources of their own ancient lands have been shockingly depleted by erosion. How are The People to make a living? Today, too, the Navahos are facing, for the first time in their completeness and full intensity, these difficult questions: How are The People to live with white Americans? What alien ways must they learn if they are to survive? How much of the old pattern of life can they safely and even profitably preserve?

Until a little while ago these questions hardly seemed pressing. The Navahos were so many, their country was so vast, that only the few who spent some time in boarding schools in cities or who happened to be drawn perceptibly within the web of white economy were deeply troubled. But today almost every Navaho has reason to feel uneasy. They all know that they can no longer move freely to new and uncrowded ranges. Every day the demands of different, and to a large degree antagonistic, ways of life press upon them.

In some very real senses this book is not about The People only but about two much wider issues that must concern all men everywhere. The first is the more specific: How can minority peoples, especially those which have a manner of life very different from that of the Euro-American tradition, be dealt with in such a way that they will not be a perpetual problem to more powerful governing states, and in such a way that the human values which minority peoples have discovered will not utterly disappear from the heritage of all humanity? This is no academic query. The United States, Great Britain, and others of the United Nations have inescapable responsibilities in all parts of the world to all manner of "primitive" and partially industrialized peoples.

The second and more general problem is in many respects the most crucial of our age: How shall we apply technical knowledge without disrupting the whole fabric of human life?

It is believed that every reader will agree, after finishing this book, that he has been reading about many of the most central dilemmas of world society, seen in microcosm. The very fact that they are seen in microcosm makes possible a canvas small enough to be manageable and to permit convincing workmanship of detail. Moreover, the fact that the Navaho Indians are in our American world but not yet of it guarantees the relevance of the data and at the same time affords the opportunity of studying them with considerable detachment, since it is not our own immediate interests and prejudices which hold the center of the picture.

In an endeavor to meet the highly critical situation of the Navahos since 1933, the government has drawn on the resources of many physical and social sciences—ecology, agronomy, animal husbandry, medicine, education, and others. Whatever its defects, the government program has been without a doubt one of the closest approaches yet achieved to an intelligent, planned, and integrated application of scientific knowledge to the practical affairs of a whole people. In some ways the results of this experiment have been gratifying, but in others they have been disappointing in terms of the knowledge, skills, and resources expended. Where was the flaw?

The central hypothesis of this book is that the incomplete success of the program has been due in an important degree to lack of understanding of certain human factors. It was necessary to know the physical needs of The People, to discover means of conserving their land and of improving their techniques of agriculture and livestock care. This knowledge was imperative, but it was not enough. Consideration of the human needs of the Navaho and comprehension of the problems of human relations were wanting in an important measure. Also lacking was an understanding that Navaho psychological processes and assumptions differ from those of the white men on which the administrators unconsciously based all their plans. Hence these plans often failed because of intangible factors which, being largely unknown to the administrators, were unpredictable.

For example, government technicians developed a stock-reduction program which was probably, at the purely rational level, in the best interests of the Navahos. But the Navahos did not see it in rational terms; they saw it in emotional terms. Large herds were not just sources of meat, wool, and money to them, but symbols of prestige and of the sort of life that is right and proper. They became frightened, angry, and suspicious. Practical and realistic as they are in many ways, they could not be persuaded that if they had fewer and better sheep they might actually be better off. They even seemed to find satisfaction in general resistance to anything else that was proposed by the government which had thus tried to alter the established routine of their economic and social life.

The writers of this book believe that the Navajo Agency has been too exclusively concerned with material things, with externals. Issues have been seen too little in the light of the life experience and patterned attitudes of the individual Navaho. All the so-called "intangibles," the human factors, have been left too much out of account. Though the policy-making group in the Indian Service has certainly been aware of these factors in theory, too often administrators have forgotten that to change a way of life you must change people, that before you can change people you must understand how they have come to be as they are.

Obviously, the partial failure of the government's program cannot be traced wholly to lack of understanding of the psychological and cultural factors involved. There are also the stubborn and irreducible facts of natural resources; there are legal difficulties; there have been sheer historical accidents which no amount of psychological knowledge could have foreseen—and which could not have been controlled if they had been foreseen. But it is the claim of the writers that some failures might have been avoided or tempered had there been available more information on typical Navaho attitudes. If the ways in which The People —as contrasted with whites—react to external situations had been investigated as carefully as the situations themselves, the results could have been much better.

For facts never speak for themselves. They must always be cross-examined. And every different human society has its own techniques of cross-examination. In many, probably in most, cases the same fact has a different meaning to a Japanese, a German, an Englishman, an American. Meaning is derived only partly from the external reality. It also derives from the premises, goals, categories in terms of which the facts are consciously or unconsciously evaluated.

This is what is meant by "culture" in the technical anthropological sense. A culture is any given people's way of life, as distinct from the life-ways of other peoples. There are certain recurrent and inevitable human problems, and the ways in which man can meet them are limited by his biological equipment and by certain facts of the external world. But to most problems there are a variety of possible solutions. Any culture consists of the set of habitual and traditional ways of thinking, feeling, and reacting that are characteristic of the ways a particular society meets its problems at a particular point in time.

More than anything else, this book is a description of those aspects of Navaho culture that bear most immediately upon the government's capacity to help The People strike a working balance between human needs and fluctuating resources. The focus is upon the normal problems of Navaho existence today as determined, on the one hand, by the situational factors of geography and of biology (the location, climate, size, and quality of Navaho lands; population density and health conditions) and, on the other hand, by the traditional ways which the Navahos have developed for meeting the dilemmas posed by the external situation.

The writers have tried to steer a steady middle course between "economic determinism" and "psychological determinism." In recent times one group of students of human affairs has loudly proclaimed that everything is due to situational factors, especially technology and economic pressures. Another group—which has lately become increasingly fashionable—says in effect: "Tools and economic systems are but the expression of human personalities. The key to the world's problems lies not in new techniques of distribution or in more equitable access to raw materials, or even in a stable international political organization. All we need is a saner method of child training, a wiser education." Each of these "explanations" by itself is one-sided and barren. Probably the tendency to oversimplification in these two directions corresponds to what we find in contrasting schools of historians, who, ever since Greek times at least, have seen history either as the interaction of impersonal forces or as a drama of personalities. Either conception has a strong appeal to human beings who crave simple answers to complex problems, but neither alone tells the whole story; we need both.

The central aim of this book, then, is to supply the background needed by the administrator or teacher who is to deal effectively with The People in human terms. Only such items have been taken from the literature, from field notes, and from other sources as were felt to bear directly upon this problem. Since the evidence has been so carefully screened from this point of view, the book has no pretensions to being a complete description of Navaho history, life, and customs. The ethnographer will find many gaps.

But the volume is more than a handbook for those relatively few persons who deal with Navaho Indians. It attempts to suggest partial answers to some questions which are vital in dealing with any minority group. How can technological changes best be reconciled with human habits and human emotional needs? How can recommendations made by technicians who have carefully studied a given external situation be most effectively explained to the people whom these recommendations are designed to benefit? What dangers must be foreseen and what errors avoided if facts are to be so communicated to a people of a different tradition that they will be understood rather than distorted? How can knowledge of a people's history, of its hopes and fears, of its unspoken assumptions about the nature of human life and experience, give a responsible administrator some idea of what to expect from a particular policy and how to present the policy in ways which will evoke coöperation? These are large questions, and no single book can provide full solutions even for a single specific case.

But the explicit suggestions and the implications of the discussion of the Navaho case will have meaning for all persons who have to deal with others in practical ways, whether they are teachers, administrators, or welfare workers. They will also have meaning for anyone who is interested in human beings. Readers are asked not to approach these pages with any single-minded conviction that they deal only with strange folk and strange ways. Navahos are human beings. They have had to face all the perennial problems with which mankind must somehow deal. The solutions which The People have worked out through countless generations of trial-and-error learning must have some message, some meaning, to other groups of our common humanity who have met the same issues in different contexts and worked out other answers. The effects which the special Navaho situation and the traditional Navaho solutions have had upon personality development illumine processes which are in some sense universal. To the teacher or administrator working with people who have a social heritage different from his own (whether the society be Indian or Asiatic or another "ethnic minority" in our country) the lessons which may be drawn from these materials doubtless have an application of special practicality. But this book has something to say to anyone who cares about human life.

THE NAVAHO

1. THE PAST OF THE PEOPLE

BEFORE THE DAWN OF HISTORY

There are many indications that the Navaho and the various Apache groups originally came from the north. The People have such a tradition. Certain words and phrases in their language suggest a more northern environment. Further, and more conclusively, linguistic analysis places the Navaho and Apache tongues with the Athabascan languages spoken also by a group of tribes in the interior of northwestern Canada.

When and how the Apaches and Navahos arrived in the Southwest are still matters of speculation. The date may be as early as the period around the year 1000; it may be later, or even earlier. It seems unwarranted to assume either that they did or did not arrive at one time or in a single group. Certain clues suggest that traits of Intermontane and Plains cultures had been added to whatever social heritage had been brought from the northern homeland. The Plains traits at least, however, may have been taken over in the Southwest as part of a general Plains Indian influence that seems to have moved westward and to have had its effects upon Pueblo towns as well as upon the Navahos. Certainly no known archaeological sites in the Plains area suggest specifically Navaho relationship, whereas some archaeologists have seen in quite early cultures of the Great Salt Lake and Fremont River regions in Utah a first blending of the way of life of hunting, Athabascan-speaking peoples with Puebloid influences. A case has been made for the view that ruins of hogan type in western and central Colorado, some of which would appear to have been built before A.D. 1000, were the dwellings of precursors of the Navaho or the Apache or closely related groups.

In New Mexico, archaeology is just beginning to fill in the picture of prehistoric Navaho life. Navaho archaeology is very difficult, partly because the hogan dwellings usually were not constructed of stone and so have not withstood the ravages of wind and water. Even so, dwelling arrangements and pottery and other artifacts which are plainly Navaho have been uncovered. The earliest known hogan site, which Hall dated by the tree-ring method, shows that Navahos were living in the Governador, New Mexico, region at least as early as 1540. Nearby sites excavated by Keur give a fairly full record for the ensuing two centuries and show that many Navaho artifacts had already attained a relatively stable pattern. Yet they show resemblances to considerably earlier cultures of the region which in turn may be connected with others of eastern affiliation. Competent authorities agree only on the fact that Navaho culture was already highly composite before the historical period.

These complex origins of Navaho culture make it difficult to be positive about any single specific trait. For example, some specialists believe that the Apaches and Navahos learned the rudiments of agriculture from the Plains Indians on their journey southward, but there are grounds for believing that they knew little of agriculture before they reached the Southwest. It is now the general belief that the Navahos learned to weave in the Southwest, but Reichard has pointed out very specific similarities between Navaho weaving and that of the Salish peoples of the Puget Sound region.

Of one thing we may be certain: the Apache and Navaho intruders were greatly influenced by the town-dwelling Indians of the Southwest. In Navaho myth and folk tales, these Pueblo tribes appear as wealthy, sophisticated peoples, rather awesome in the power of their religious ceremonials. It seems certain, too, that when the Navahos arrived in the Southwest they had no ceremonials as complex as those of today.

In sum, we must think of a comparatively simple culture being enriched during the prehistoric period by contact with other tribes, especially the Pueblo Indians. Furthermore, there must have been a whole series of gradual adaptations and adjustments to the physical environment of those portions of what is now New Mexico (and perhaps Arizona) to which the intruders came from the country farther north.

THE SPANISH-MEXICAN PERIOD [1626–1846]

The first known reference to the Navahos in a European document is in the report of a Franciscan missionary in 1626. A few years later Friar Benavides, another Franciscan, wrote a more extended description. By this time The People were already agriculturalists. No longer were they a migratory people, dependent upon hunting and upon the gathering of wild plants, seeds, nuts, and fruits. Their adoption of the techniques of cultivation had made them at least partially sedentary. But Benavides does not mention livestock or weaving among the Navahos of his day.

The Rabal documents, which were reports to the Spanish Viceroy of Mexico covering the period from 1706 to 1743, give us our first detailed accounts of the Navahos. The People lived at this time in small, compact communities located away from the fields on the tops of adjacent mesas.[1] Agriculture was the basic economic pursuit, but sheep and goats (and horses and cattle in lesser numbers) had already been obtained from Europeans by trade, by raid, or indirectly through the Pueblo Indians. Woolen blankets and dresses for women were woven. Men dressed in buckskin.

In the later eighteenth and early nineteenth centuries

references to the Navahos become much more numerous. But, since they occur almost entirely in reports of Spanish and Mexican government officials, they deal mainly with warfare. Skirmishes, Navaho raids and Spanish reprisals, punitive campaigns on the part of the Spanish or Mexican governments, are described so continually that the reader of these scanty historical records is likely to interpret them in unconscious accordance with the common folklore about American Indians. The Navahos, it should be noted, were primarily raiders, not fighters. They were interested in taking food, women, horses, or other booty; they waged war chiefly in reprisal. They were no match for the military cultures of Plains Indians such as the Utes and Comanches. To these Indians war was the apex of living. To The People war was one important practical pursuit, carried out partly through ritual techniques.

In another respect the Spanish documents are probably misleading. There are suggestions of a kind of tribal solidarity which we do not know from the period of fuller records. Leaders are mentioned to whom is ascribed control over the "nation." Upon these "generals" the Spaniards and Mexicans relied to restrain raiding parties against white and Pueblo settlements.

Only in passing was anything set down in Spanish-Mexican documents which did not concern warfare or trade. For example, in 1713 there appears a tantalizing reference to "the great dances of the Navaho." Otherwise the chroniclers content themselves with characterizing Navaho religion as "heathen." By the mid-eighteenth century the Spaniards had established missions in the vicinity of Mount Taylor, but they were not long maintained. Small groups of The People did have sustained contacts with Europeans and seem to have been partially Christianized. In the process, however, they became largely dissociated from their own tribe, so that to this day their descendants in the Canyoncito and Puertocito areas are called "The People who are enemies."

The extent to which European ideas reached and were accepted by the Navahos during the Spanish-Mexican period cannot be determined with certainty. It is known that young Navahos were taken as slaves to Santa Fe and other settlements and that some of them escaped and returned to their people, bringing with them some knowledge of the Spanish language and presumably also some familiarity with European concepts as well as techniques.

What is certain is that major alterations in the Navaho way of living occurred between 1626 and 1846. These were partly due to intensified contacts with the Pueblo Indians during this period. After the Pueblo Rebellion of 1680, Indians from Jemez and other pueblos took refuge for some years among The People. In the eighteenth century numerous Hopis fled from drought and famine to live with the Navahos, especially in Canyon de Chelly. These Pueblo Indians not only taught the Navahos their own arts, such as weaving and the making of painted pottery, but also acted as intermediaries in the transmission of various European technologies, which were acquired by The People in part through direct contacts.

By the time English-speaking Americans had their first dealings with The People, the Navahos were herders and weavers as well as agriculturalists. They had firearms and other objects of metal. Indeed if they had not already begun to work metal they were about ready to learn. But the greatest revolution in Navaho economy was that consequent upon the introduction of domestic animals and the associated trait-complex of saddles, bridles, branding, shearing, and the like.

Horses enormously increased the mobility of the Navahos for tribal expansion in warfare and in trade. Greater mobility in all these activities enlarged the range and frequency of their contacts with many other peoples. In the eighteenth century, for example, we find the Navahos trading and fighting with the Pawnees in western Nebraska. The People could now rove widely, and they learned much. Moreover, the character of social relationships within the tribe was altered. The horse made it possible to supply hogans and outlying sheep camps with food and water from considerable distances. More frequent visits and the gathering of substantial numbers at ceremonials and meetings of a "political" nature became relatively easy for the first time.

But the horse did not make the Navahos into "nomads." Navaho "nomadism"—at least during any historical period—is a myth, and it is most unfortunate that through popular writings this myth has become so deeply rooted in the notions which educated people have of the Navahos. The very fact that clan names are mainly place names suggests that sedentary groupings were the rule. The horse made the Navahos mobile, to be sure, but the shiftings were confined, in most cases, to well-defined areas. Once a family had moved into a new region, one or more dwellings would be built in places which became fixed centers of family life for many years. While actual buildings were often destroyed or abandoned because of deaths or for other reasons, the new ones erected would seldom be very far off. Within the range claimed by a particular family group, the number of desirable sites was limited by the necessity for protection from the weather and the scarcity of wood and water.

Since agriculture was always the basis of the subsistence economy, it was necessary that at least one dwelling be close to the fields; during a large part of the year some of the family were anchored to plant, protect, and harvest the crops. Because the sections which could be farmed profitably by floodwater irrigation and with Navaho tools were few in number, this factor also narrowed the choice of possible home sites. And so, while some members of the family made extended journeys to hunt, to collect pinyon nuts or plants, to obtain salt, or to trade, and while individuals or whole families would move with the sheep into lower or higher altitudes at certain seasons, the Navahos were never "nomads," for they always had fixed abodes.

The myth of nomadism has probably been reinforced by the undoubted fact that many families have "winter hogans" and "summer hogans" at some distance apart. For example, the population of the Dennehotso Valley is much greater in summer than in winter because the supply of wood for fuel is inadequate during the cold months. On the other hand, the farming opportunities are so much better in the valley than on the wooded tablelands that many families regularly shift back and forth between summer and winter establishments, which are in some cases as much as forty miles apart. But they are no more "nomads" than well-to-do New Yorkers who commonly migrate twice yearly over greater distances than do the Navahos.

Sheep and goats, which had been brought into the Southwest by the Spaniards, provided a larger and more dependable food supply, and this was a fundamental condition of Navaho population increase. Furthermore, livestock animals, wool and mohair, hides, and woolen textiles revolutionized Navaho economy in another way: they supplied a steady source of salable or exchangeable wealth, permitting the acquisition of metal tools and other manufactured articles. Surpluses were now more than occasional, and they ceased to be disposed of mainly by intra- and inter-tribal gift and exchange. As the bounds of trade were thus widened, a whole new series of demands for goods from the European world was gradually created. Finally livestock formed the basis for a transition to a capitalistic economy, with new goals for individuals and for family groups, a new system of social stratification and prestige hierarchy, an altered set of values.

THE AMERICAN PERIOD [1846–   ]

In his proclamation to the inhabitants of New Mexico in August 1846, when the United States took possession of the southwestern territories acquired from Mexico, General Kearny promised protection against the depredations of marauding Indian tribes. In the winter of the same year came the first military expedition against the Navahos. The history of the next fifteen years is a record of numerous military operations, of the establishment of army posts within Navaho territory, of the arrival of the first civilian agents to the Navahos, of a succession of Navaho raids and "incidents," of unsuccessful attempts to bring peace and stability by negotiation. Treaties were entered into with local headmen whom the whites believed to be tribal "chiefs." When the agreements were violated by members of other groups not under the jurisdiction of these leaders, the American authorities, totally misunderstanding the nature of Navaho social organization, judged the tribe to be hopelessly perfidious.

During 1862 the Navahos and Apaches took advantage of the army's preoccupation with the Civil War to increase their raids upon Rio Grande settlements. An alarmed government ordered Colonel Kit Carson into the Navaho country in June 1863, with specific instructions to destroy all crops and livestock. The land was systematically pillaged; fleeing bands of Navahos were pursued; some Indians were killed in various engagements, and others were taken prisoner. Word was sent out that all The People were to surrender at Fort Defiance. Finally, in early 1864, substantial groups began to give themselves up. On March 6 of that year 2,400 persons, 30 wagons, 400 horses, and 3,000 sheep and goats began the "Long Walk" of 300 miles to Fort Sumner, 180 miles southeast of Santa Fe. Only children and cripples rode in the wagons. By the end of April 3,500 more, in three separate parties, had made the same long march. Eventually 8,000 Navahos were in captivity at Fort Sumner, while a number of bands remained at large, hidden in the depths of the Grand Canyon, on the top of Black Mesa, north of the San Juan River, and in other inaccessible spots.

Probably no folk has ever had a greater shock. Proud, they saw their properties destroyed and knew what it was to be dependent upon the largess of strangers. Not understanding group captivity and accustomed to move freely over great spaces, they knew the misery of confinement within a limited area. Taken far from the rugged and vivid landscape which they prized so highly, they lived in a flat and colorless region, eating alien foods and drinking bitter water which made them ill.

Fort Sumner was a major calamity to The People; its full effects upon their imagination can hardly be conveyed to white readers. Even today it seems impossible for any Navaho of the older generation to talk for more than a few minutes on any subject without speaking of Fort Sumner. Those who were not there themselves heard so many poignant tales from their parents that they speak as if they themselves had experienced all the horror of the "Long Walk," the illness, the hunger, the homesickness, the final return to their desolated land. One can no more understand Navaho attitudes—particularly toward white people—without knowing of Fort Sumner than he can comprehend Southern attitudes without knowing of the Civil War.

When The People went "home," late in 1868, there were more privations and hardships to undergo. The old equilibrium of the society had been destroyed. Buildings had been razed and flocks removed. The People had to start all over again in their struggle to make a living. Eventually the government issued seed, tools, and some livestock, but there were many delays and for some time large numbers of Navahos existed on rations issued at Fort Wingate and Fort Defiance. To add to this distress came several years of severe drought, during which many Navahos shifted from place to place in misery.

When stable conditions were finally reëstablished, there followed a period of relative prosperity and rapid growth of population. But the generations since Fort Sumner have experienced more disillusionment and bitterness in their relations with whites. Soon The People were forced to surrender to the advancing railroad much of their best winter range land and many of their finest watering places. The areas later added to their Reservation as a compensatory measure were notably less desirable. Many of the early agents were ignorant and corrupt politicians. Promises were not kept. Even the establishment of the first schools about 1870 added to the rancor, for Navahos soon observed that their children, after many years in boarding school far from home, emerged fitted neither to live as white men nor to return to their places in the tribe.

Although there were several trading posts on the Reservation by the early 1870's, it was the building of the railroad across New Mexico and Arizona in the 1880's which brought intoxicants, diseases, and other disrupting forces of white society to The People. The gradual but steady increase in white population in surrounding areas came to mean economic exploitation and a mounting general pressure upon the Navahos. There have been many and serious misunderstandings on both sides; but even those Navahos whose direct contacts with whites are limited or negligible have a heightening sense of a net being drawn ever tighter around them, of being at the mercy of a more powerful and often unfriendly people. As more of their own number became bilingual and conversant with white ways, informed individuals spread bitterness among the tribe by quoting chapter and verse as to the deceit and trickery of the white rulers. In 1920, for instance, when Navaho tribal funds were allocated for the building of a bridge which was obviously intended for the use of white residents of Utah and Arizona, a wave of indignation swept over The People. Only during the last thirty years has a sympathetic governmental policy been evolved. Even recent administrations have found their serious practical problems complicated by the bewilderment, cynicism, and resentment bred by three generations of treatment that was often vicious, almost always stupid, and always based on the attitudes towards "backward peoples" current in white society at the time.

From 1868 to the present, the persistent theme in Navaho history has been the struggle with the whites for land. The treaty of 1868 set aside a total of about 3,500,000 acres—much less than the area which had been occupied by The People for generations. This Reservation, half in Arizona and half in New Mexico, has been extended from time to time, often through the efforts of white sympathizers with the Navaho, until it now includes about 15,000,000 acres, reaching north into Utah to the San Juan River and west of the Hopi Jurisdiction to the Colorado River.

But lands have also been taken away and use-rights thrown in doubt. One complication dates back to the building of the Santa Fe Railroad in the eighties, when all odd-numbered sections (mile-square tracts) on each side of the right of way to a depth of 40 miles were granted to the railroad. Thus a "checkerboard strip" was created in the region which had the heaviest concentration of Navaho population. On many of the sections Navaho families had lived or run their sheep for years. In 1908, owing to the efforts of white friends, about 3,500,000 acres were added to the Reservation; but white livestock operators of New Mexico and Colorado cast jealous eyes on parts of the Navaho range and brought political pressure to bear, so that in 1911 about the same acreage was restored to the public domain. These lands were opened to non-Indian stockmen, even though they were already fully occupied and stocked with Navaho herds. Further confusion was created when Arizona and New Mexico selected certain lands to be leased or sold for the support of public schools. Subsequently difficulties arose from conflicting Indian homestead allotments and white homestead claims, and confusion reached a climax.

Some clarification was achieved in 1934 when the Arizona Navaho Boundary Extension Act provided for the exchange of white-owned land within the Arizona part of the Reservation for land selected from the public domain. Similar action in New Mexico has been blocked by powerful political interests.

The Federal Government stepped in after the war, and in 1946 the Indian Claims Act was passed, establishing the Indian Claims Commission. One of the earlier cases before the Commission concerned the control of grazing on the Reservation range; compensation for lands taken during the mid-nineteenth century is another case which is in progress before the Indian Claims Commission. Any decision will not, however, alter the problem which confronts The People and the Indian Service: that of making self-support possible in an overpopulated region upon comparatively unproductive, deteriorated lands. The practical issues have been distorted by cultural bias on the part of both the Navaho and the white people of the surrounding country, heightened by strong emotional convictions.

2. LAND AND LIVELIHOOD

Set a stretch of sagebrush interspersed with groves of small evergreens (pinyon and juniper trees) against a background of highly colored mesas, canyons, buttes, volcanic necks, and igneous mountain masses clothed in deep pine green, roofed over with a brilliant blue sky, and you will have a generalized picture of the Navaho landscape. The sagebrush-pinyon-juniper-greasewood combination is characteristic of elevations of 5,500–6,500 feet. At higher altitudes the varying greens of pine, oak, aspen, and fir replace sagebrush gray as the main background color. Lower altitudes have the bleakness of desert flora except when relieved by lone or clumped cottonwoods along intermittent watercourses. At all elevations the landscape is seasonally brightened in years of favorable moisture by a profusion of wild flowers. Even the desert is yellow with the bloom of dodgeweed or spotted with stalks of white yucca blossoms and red and yellow cactus blooms. Not that, winter or summer, one misses color in the Navaho country. One is seldom out of sight of brilliant rocks, worn by wind, water, and weather into fantastic forms. The most typical hue is a carmine very like the red of the Navaho rug.

If tablelands covered with pinyon and juniper and cut by sage-floored valleys are the most typical of all landscapes, still within a few hours by automobile one can always see quite different worlds. There are splendid yellow-pine forests; there are also treeless wastes. The canyons cut deep into red or orange or red-and-white-banded sandstone masses and the wind-sculptured buttes of passionate colors have made the country of The People world famous. Variety and color are the keynotes.

Beautiful as this land may be, it does not favor the survival of large numbers of people who have limited technologies and remain isolated from the main arteries of commerce. The Navaho country only tenuously fringes a railway and major automobile highways. Within the Navaho domain, distances are great even on a map; but communication cannot be estimated by the geographical miles.

In the prewar period the Roads Division of the Navajo Agency* maintained nearly 1,300 miles of primary roads, about the same mileage in secondary roads, and 700 miles of truck trails. Of these, the road engineer stated that not over 150 miles could be kept open for traffic under extreme weather conditions. In such regions as Navaho Mountain, all travel by road is impossible for several months of the year because of snow. Mud blocks traffic for days or weeks during the spring thaw and again during the summer rains. One torrential summer rain can ruin anything short of a surfaced highway. Sand is as bad in dry periods as mud during rains. To gauge correctly the difficulties of travel by either Navahos or whites, distances must be measured in terms of bad roads and intervening canyons or other obstacles, rather than in terms of miles on a map.

Since the war, however, the need for improvement in the Reservation road system has been recognized, and through the Long Range Program authorized by the 81st Congress (Public Law 474) the conditions have been improved. During the period 1951–1958, a total of $13,870,180 was appropriated for road construction, and 371 miles of road were improved. Road maintenance is also necessary, in large part for school operation, and during the fiscal year 1958 a total of $392,000 was appropriated for the maintenance of 2,791 miles of Reservation roads. Even

* The Navajo Agency is the current designation for the local agency of the U. S. Office of Indian Affairs, which administers the affairs of the Reservation.

this is low, however, by contrast to State maintained roads situated outside the Reservation: an average of $140 per mile as opposed to the States' $500 per mile of primary roads and $300–$400 for secondary roads.

In such a terrain, one might expect to find minerals and other resources. The Reservation does indeed have potential resources in marketable timber, coal, oil, helium, vanadium, and other minerals, but only recently have these potentialities begun to be realized. The tribal income from oil and gas increased from nearly $50,000 in 1935 to nearly $30,000,000 in 1958. Individual Navaho income from uranium and vanadium (first noted by the Navajo Agency Branch of Realty in 1952) increased from $2,-692.10 in that year to $595,666.00 in 1958.

Yet for a folk who make so much of their living by agriculture and livestock, the environmental hazards are enormous: the ruggedness of the country, its depleted soils, treacherous frosts, and scanty and undependable water supply.

Variations in climate are connected more with altitude than with northern or southern position. The Navaho land is all part of the Colorado Plateau, an intensely dissected rocky region of elevations that range from about 3,500 feet above sea level to more than 10,000 feet. Altitude is the principal determinant of temperature and length of growing season, of rainfall and the character of the vegetative covering. Nights are cool in the height of summer throughout most of the area, and heavy snows are the rule for a month or more of the winter.

Although most of the Navaho area lies between 5,000 and 7,000 feet, one must, from the standpoint of livelihood, distinguish four types of topography and three distinct climates. Topographically there are flat alluvial valleys (such as those of the San Juan River and the Chinle Wash), broad, rolling upland plains, rugged tablelands, and mountains. In roughly half of the total acreage (at lower elevations) a warm, arid "desert" climate prevails;

perhaps two-fifths must be assigned to an intermediate "steppe" climate characterizing the middle elevations; the remainder is mountainous, with a cold, subhumid climate.

None of these situations is really favorable to agricultural production save where irrigation water is available. To be sure, there are many live streams in the mountains—one range also has lakes—and springs, seeps, and natural rock reservoirs are more frequent than the casual traveler suspects. But in general flowing water is rare. Rainfall is scanty in most parts of the Reservation. In nearly half of the lands of The People, it averages eight inches per year and occurs principally during July, August, and September. High temperatures during summer and sub-zero weather during winter, high winds, frequent sand storms, and high evaporation rates are characteristic. These liabilities also affect the steppe regions, where average annual rainfall is better than 12 inches. In the mountains rainfall averages 22 inches, but the brief growing season of ninety days is often interrupted by killing frosts, which are known to have occurred during every month of the year.

Nor are these the only perils. In years when the figure for total moisture would indicate adequacy, the precipitation may have come too early or too late, or in the form of snow, or as a sudden downpour which washed out seeds or young plants. Then there are the droughts. Practically every year in most regions there are two periods (April through June and October through December) when there is little or no precipitation. Cycles of longer droughts also seem to be expectable. Every three to eight years during the last fifty there have been periods of twenty to twenty-five months without measurable rain or snowfall in many sections. Such periods are sometimes broken by a single month or two with rainfall, followed by another protracted dry spell. Thunderstorms of some violence are frequent in summer, when lightning kills livestock (and occasionally humans) as well as igniting forests and dwellings. Crops are sometimes destroyed in the fields by hail.

1. Navaho family return from hoeing their corn

2. Flocks go down for water in a deeply eroded wash

Soils reflect influences of the climates under which they have developed. Desert soils are high in salts, high in mineral plant foods, low in plant matter, highly erosive, subject to movement by wind, and in general extremely unstable. Steppe soils are similar, but not quite so salty, high in mineral plant foods, slightly higher than the desert soil in plant matter, subject to rapid water erosion but not affected so severely by wind. The subhumid soils are more stable than those of desert and steppe.

These same hazards apply to the livestock industry. Inadequate or irregular rainfall limits the growth of edible plants and water storage for the animals. Desert vegetation (principally grasses and browse plants) is sparse, grows very slowly, produces only a small margin for grazing use, is easily injured by overgrazing, and requires long periods for recovery after depletion. Steppe vegetation is composed of grasses, sagebrush, and pinyon-juniper; it will ordinarily produce more forage than the desert but cannot safely be overgrazed. The subhumid zone produces yellow pine timber, oak, and associated grasses and shrubs. The mountain area is summer range and with proper use yields good forage.

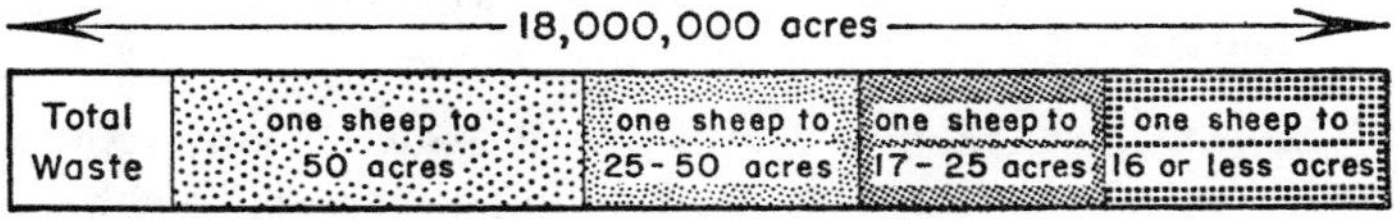

Fig. 1. Range Capacity of Navaho Lands

In the early 1940's, of the total Reservation, nearly 12 per cent could be described as complete waste; 30 per cent would support profitably less than one sheep for each 50 acres; 20 per cent would support one sheep for each 17 to 25 acres; only 20 per cent would support a sheep on less than 16 acres. (See Figure 1.) Range resource figures for 1958 indicate a much smaller amount of good grazing lands: only approximately 5 per cent will support one sheep on less than 16 acres. Nearly 50 per cent will support one sheep per 30 to 65 acres.

This predominance of poor-quality lands has been greatly accentuated during the last seventy-five years. A natural erosion cycle which probably began in the late 1880's has caused part of the trouble, but land destruction seems to have been accelerated by uncontrolled and abusive land use, primarily overgrazing associated with overpopulation. Whatever the causes, the wasting of grasslands by gully-cutting has been catastrophic. The loss of much of the vegetative cover has likewise resulted in a great wastage of the scanty rainfall, for there are not enough plant roots to hold it, and it runs rapidly down the slopes, carrying valuable top soil with it.

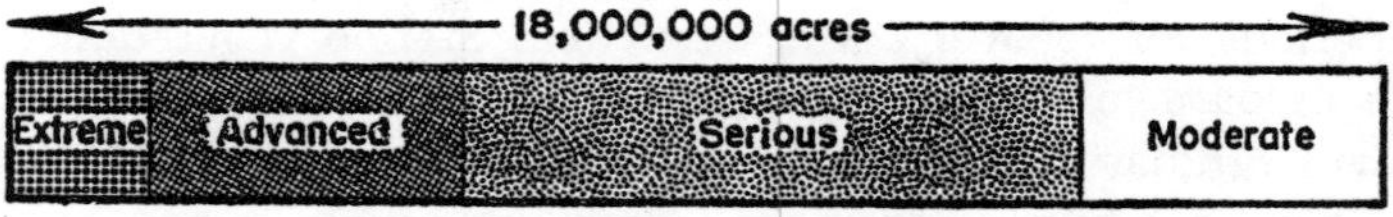

Fig. 2. Degree of Erosion of Navaho Lands

Extreme—three-fourths to all of top soil removed
Advanced—one-fourth to three-fourths of top soil removed
Serious—up to one-fourth of top soil removed
Moderate—most top soil remains but this land also includes much bare rock

Erosion has taken a heavy toll of Navaho land. As of 1945, up to one-fourth of the productive top soil has been removed from 45 per cent of the lands set aside for the subsistence of The People, and between one-fourth and three-fourths of the productive soil was gone from 23 per cent. In 10 per cent of the Reservation, over three-fourths of the top soil, and in many areas even some of the subsoil, was washed and blown away. (See Figure 2.) At present, the soil may be classed as follows: 15 per cent total waste, 23 per cent as poor, 29 per cent as fair, 22 per cent as good, and only 11 per cent as excellent. While important progress in the control of soil erosion has been made during the past two decades, the total productivity of the Navaho lands has probably been reduced by at least half since 1868.

This erosion has far-reaching effects. The Navaho country delivers only 2.5 per cent of the water which the Colorado River carries into Lake Meade above Boulder Dam but supplies 37.5 per cent of the silt which has threatened the dam's effectiveness. The completion of the Glen Canyon Dam will change this situation. But what looks at first like an exclusively Navaho problem is still one of critical importance to large numbers of white people as well.

THE LAND IS CROWDED

Since 1868 when the original Reservation was established The People have more than tripled in number. By 1940 they totaled almost 50,000, of whom it was estimated that between 9,000 and 13,000 lived permanently off the Reservation proper. By 1958, The People numbered approximately 85,000.

Figures for 1942–1944 have indicated a Navaho increase in number greater than that for the country as a whole—2 per cent per year, as compared with 1.1 per cent for all Indians of the United States, 1.4 per cent for the whole population of Arizona, and 0.9 per cent for the entire United States. The increase for the 2,371 persons in the Many Farms area was at the rate of 3.1 per cent, but this is undoubtedly due in large part to the clinic and health facilities there. The U. S. Public Health Service uses a figure of approximately 2.30 per cent for the annual net increase in Navaho population.

Such an increase may well be attributed to the high birth rate—38.7 per 1,000 as compared with 25.00 for the United States, all races. Yet the Navaho infant mortality rate far exceeds that for the rest of the country—in spite of tremendous decrease in recent years. In 1952, the Navaho infant mortality rate was 110.2 per 1,000 live births, that for the United States 28.4; provisional figures for 1957 show a Navaho rate of 74.7 as opposed to a United States rate of 26.3. In spite of such a high infant mortality, The People are comparatively younger than the general population—57 to 58 per cent are estimated to be less than 20 years old, in contrast with the general population of the United States of which more than 50 per cent are over 30 years of age. In terms of median age, the 18.8 years for Reservation Indians is nearly ten years younger than that for rural whites (28.2 years).

The determinants of Navaho population increase are undoubtedly manifold. Perhaps The People's varied origins, so heterogeneous from both biological and cultural sources, have resulted in an outstanding manifestation of that phenomenon known to biologists as "hybrid vigor." At all events, there can be no doubt that the fecundity of the tribe is but one symptom of a generally radiant vitality. They want to live. They want children, many children. The birth rate appears to be appreciably higher in western areas, where livestock economy, plural marriages, and matrilocal residence prevail.

Navahos have long since swarmed beyond the boundaries of the original Reservation, which has been increased in area repeatedly. Reservation lands now include 15,088,227 acres, an area just a little larger than the states of Connecticut, Massachusetts, and New Hampshire combined. An additional area, estimated at some 3,500,000 acres, or somewhat larger than Connecticut, is occupied by Navahos living off the Reservation on individually owned allotments and leased lands, many of them in the "checkerboard strip." Thus a total of over 18,000,000 acres is in Navaho hands.

Larger still is the territory which, in spite of the white "islands" within it, may be properly designated as "Navaho country." This vast, but arid and unfriendly, domain stretches in irregular outlines from the Jemez Mountains of New Mexico westward to the Grand Canyon in Arizona, and southward from the southern mountains of Utah and Colorado to depths of from ten to eighty miles below the Santa Fe Railroad and Highway 66. The old Southwestern saw, "Let's give the country back to the Indians," is no longer a pleasantry to many stockmen of the Navaho country. The People are taking the country back.

Yet even this vast domain is not enough for The People. Already the land is crowded. The density of population estimated by the Navajo Agency—2.1 per square mile—sounds low but is actually more than twice that found in adjacent rural areas peopled by whites. The density is not constant but ranges, for example, from 1.8 in Coconino County to 16 for McKinley County. If even the low living standards of prewar years were to be maintained and the absolutely essential soil conservation measures carried out, agriculture, stockraising, and government employment (the major wage work during the war years) combined could not support The People. The development of new means of livelihood has become a necessity.

The People's traditional remedies for such a situation—raiding and migration—are no longer open to them. The lands surrounding their island are fully occupied and already overused. In cold-blooded terms, the Navaho problem is this: There are already too many people for the resources; the people are increasing steadily and the principal resource (land) grows steadily less productive. How are The People to live?

SOURCES OF NAVAHO LIVELIHOOD

Contrary to the impression of many Easterners, the Navahos do not make a living mainly through weaving rugs or making silver for sale to tourists. As Figure 3 shows, arts and crafts form only a minor source of Navaho total income. In the prewar years, agriculture, livestock, and wage work have been far more important in the Navaho economy.[1] Since the war, wage work has come to contribute the major part of Navaho total income—79.9 per cent in 1958.

LIVESTOCK

For the year 1940, 44 per cent, or nearly half, the total income of The People came from livestock. Three-fourths of this income resulted from sales of livestock. The major part of this commercial income represented sales of lambs and sheep and of wool, the remainder coming from cattle, horses, pelts, mohair, and butchered meat. (See Figure 4.)

The importance of livestock in the total Navaho economy can, however, be easily misunderstood from these data. In 1940, Navahos on and off the Reservation owned about 432,000 sheep, 71,000 goats, 16,000 cattle, and 38,000 horses. But they were far from evenly divided among The People: 2,500 out of the 9,500 Navaho families owned no livestock at all; about 4,000 families owned less than 60 head of sheep; at the other end of the scale, 110 families owned more than 500 head each. Hence it is obvious that a high proportion of the tribe's total livestock income—and indeed of the total income—was concentrated in a small number of well-off families. Since the war, there has been a great change: by 1957, more than half of all Navaho families owned no livestock.

AGRICULTURE

Agriculture in the 1940's was estimated to be the source of about one-seventh of all Navaho income. Not more than 40,000 acres are now devoted to agriculture, and of these only some 18,420 acres were in 1952 in irrigated tracts with an assured supply of water. As noted on Figure 3, however, this distribution of total income, even in 1940, could not be taken without serious qualification, for estimating the value of foods consumed is difficult and unsatisfactory.

Agriculture is still the basis of the subsistence economy, as it has been for at least three hundred years. Almost every family raises some of its food, and many families live for weeks at a time chiefly from the produce of their gar-

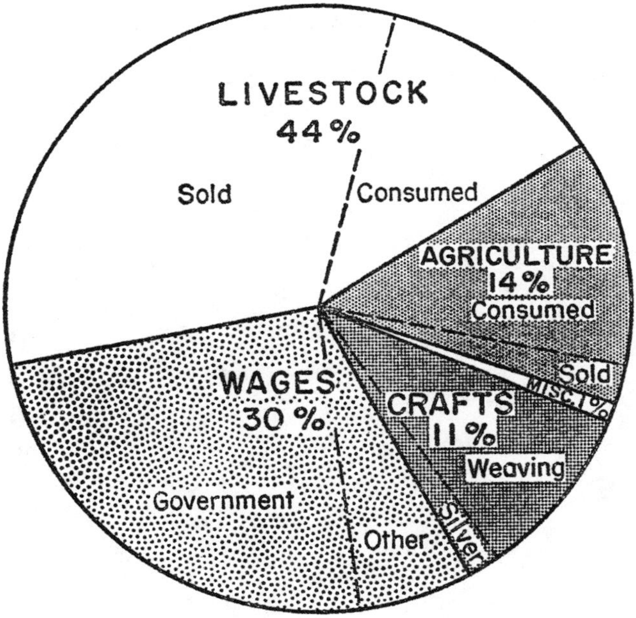

Fig. 3. Estimated Sources of Navaho Income, 1940

Note: "Income" as used here includes the estimated value of products used as well as those sold. It should be emphasized that this diagram represents income for all Navahos and is therefore overweighted toward livestock, since the few large and many moderate family incomes come chiefly from livestock. The value shown for agriculture is probably too small because most of the products are consumed, and estimates may well be too low. Subsistence incomes from hunting and from collecting wild plants are left out altogether.

dens and fields. There is considerable variation between parts of the Reservation in the amount of "income" from agriculture, but throughout the Reservation it has been the mainstay of life for all save the most prosperous families. In the postwar years, the decrease in the number of families with agricultural cash income has been steady—11,177 in 1946, 9,078 in 1951, and by 1956 such figures were no longer available. Agriculture and livestock com-

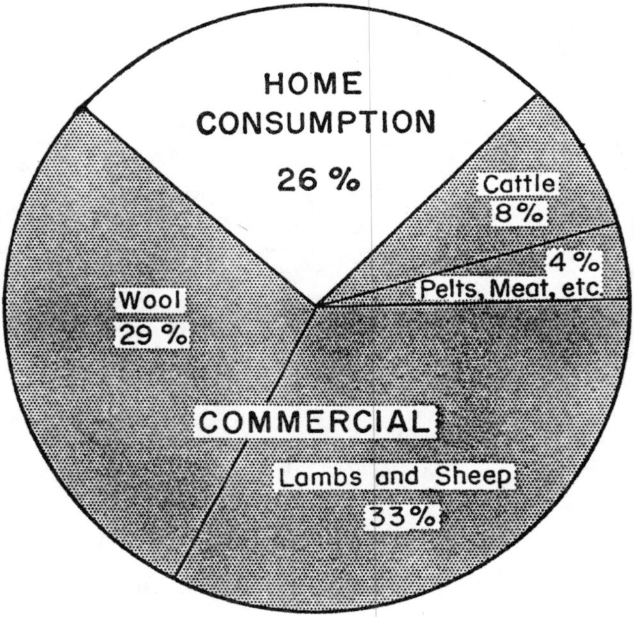

Fig. 4. Estimated Navaho Income from Livestock, 1940

bined to make up 58 per cent of the total Navaho income in 1940; by 1958, however, only 9.9 per cent of the total income derived from this source.

Still, maize and squash are the staple crops, with melons a valued addition, and in some areas, beans, wheat, and oats are important. On the ditch-irrigated farms along the San Juan River, as many as 42 different crops were being raised in 1945. As part of the Long Range Program, many new areas are being irrigated.

In 1944 the total number of acres planted by Navahos under the jurisdiction of the Navajo Agency totaled about 38,000. Acres harvested were as follows:

Maize	18,320	Alfalfa	3,818
Other Cereals	1,085	Other Forage	1,335
Potatoes	713	Wild Hay	418
Beans	1,501	Grapes	535
Squash	942	Tree Fruits	9,118
Melons	615	Garden	417

Trustworthy figures on average yield per acre were unavailable, but there was general agreement among competent judges that the average Navaho farmer obtains less from his farm land than the average white farmer in the Southwest would obtain. This is partly because adequate machinery is lacking, but even more because crop rotation, use of fertilizer, planting at the right time, and proper techniques of irrigation have been neglected. One experienced observer says that most Navahos earn only about $20 per acre from irrigated land as against the $100 per acre of their white neighbors.

WILD PLANTS AND ANIMALS

Livestock now eat most of the wild plants which furnished food for The People in the old days. Even so, almost every family will have a few dishes of wild greens during the summer, and the poorer families still occasionally utilize certain wild seeds as cereals. The fruits of several species of cactus are gathered to make confections.

There are, however, a number of plants which furnish cash income as well as food. Herbs are gathered and sold for ceremonial purposes and for use as household medicines; some of the rarer species can be sold within the tribe for high prices.

The important wild plant resource is the pinyon nut, of which a sizable harvest is gathered every three or four years. Four-fifths of these nuts are sold to traders and go eventually to the New York market, where they are salted and packaged for sale like peanuts. In 1936 a single trader paid $18,000 for the nuts. In such a good year they furnish a poor man with a cash crop that is comparable to the fall sales (surplus animals) of well-to-do livestock owners.

Game counts for little in the Navaho economy nowadays. It furnishes a few meals for the family during the year, and in some seasons rabbits and prairie dogs may tide a family over until it can produce or purchase other meat. Furs—coyote and wildcat skins and, in some areas, beaver—account for only a minute proportion of commercial income ($3,770 in 1940). This too has greatly decreased in recent years.

LUMBER AND MINERALS

Many of the mineral resources on the Reservation (coal, oil, helium, vanadium, and copper) are leased to white operators and so provide a small amount of unearned income.* A major contribution to Navaho economy, however, is in the wage work they afford.

A few Navahos own and operate small coal mines, but the income forms only a tiny fraction of tribal income. Much of the wood cut on the Reservation is consumed as fuel or in building, but the Navaho sawmill has become an increasingly valuable source of income for The People, not only in terms of log production but in terms of wages, for 95 per cent of those employed at the sawmill are Navahos.

* Increasing mineral exploitation, and the discovery of uranium have considerably increased the tribal income from this source in the past fifteen years.

ARTS AND CRAFTS

Of all Navaho products, rugs are perhaps the most widely known. Yet they accounted for less than a tenth (9 per cent) of Navaho income in 1940. This was mostly commercial income, since of all their woven products, only saddle blankets are in wide use among The People themselves. Much weaving is done for credit with the traders.

Baskets and beads form a small part of the income from arts and crafts, but the chief item other than rugs is silver jewelry, which accounted for about 2 per cent of the total income in 1940. This income is concentrated in a very few families. Adair estimated the total number of silversmiths in 1940 at six hundred, over half of them in the Smith Lake region south of Crownpoint. About 14 per cent of these smiths were professionals who worked at their craft the year round and earned from $400 to over $1,000 per year. Others worked intermittently. Most of the smiths made jewelry for their fellow tribesmen, who customarily supplied the raw materials and usually paid in livestock, blankets, or agricultural products. The fact that one-third of the smiths cited by Adair had known their craft for less than five years indicates that the increasing demand for Navaho silver may make silver work a more important source of income in the future. The Arts and Crafts Guild, operating as a tribal venture, has helped to promote a market for the crafts, and to stimulate the production of fine rugs and jewelry. Yet as a source of total Navaho income, it has declined in the past fifteen years.

WAGE WORK

By 1940 about a third of all Navaho income was in the form of wages. On the Reservation the government was the chief employer of Navahos, supplying 84 per cent of wages in 1940, 33 per cent to regular employees and 51 per cent for temporary or irregular work. Since the war, however, the railroad has become the chief employer, supplying 26.4 per cent of the wages. The contrast is shown in Table 1.

TABLE I

NAVAHO INCOME BY SOURCES, PER CENT TOTAL*

Source 1940–1958	Year 1940	1958
A. Reservation Area		
1. Payroll–Federal Government	24.6	12.2
2. Payroll–Tribal	0	6.6
3. Payroll–Mine/mill	0	4.7
4. Payroll–Natural gas	0	0.8
5. Payroll–Tribal Public Works	0	2.5
6. Arts and Crafts	9.0	1.3
7. Stockraising and Agriculture	58.4	9.9
8. Oil, gas, uranium leases	0	5.6
9. Miscellaneous–Construction	8.0	2.4
Total	100.0	46.0
B. Off-Reservation		
1. Railroad wages	0	26.4
2. Ordnance Depots	0	3.0
3. Agricultural wages	0	3.4
4. Non-Agricultural wages	0	2.5
5. Miscellaneous	0	2.5
Total	0	37.8
C. Unearned Income		
1. Social Security–C.A.	0	6.4
2. Other welfare and benefits	0	4.8
3. Railroad compensation	0	5.0
Total	0	16.2
Grand total	100.0	100.0

* Navajo Yearbook, Report No. VII, Fiscal Year, 1958, p. 108.

Wage work is varied in composition. Navahos are on the government payroll as interpreters, teachers, day-school assistants, matrons, advisers, maintenance workers at agency plants, road and irrigation employees.

Other Reservation wage employment has come from traders, who use Navahos as interpreters and handy men; from missionaries, whom they serve as interpreters and guides; and from some of the more prosperous Navahos, who employ their tribesmen during the lambing, shearing, and harvesting seasons.

Fees for performing ceremonial rites should also be mentioned as a source of individual income. The sum total probably does not bulk large in cash terms, but to many families the income in livestock, goods, and cash earned by one or more of their members is of considerable importance, and the prosperity of certain families is based primarily upon the substantial fees charged by famous Singers.

Work off the Reservation has also been varied. Navahos have for years worked for white ranchers on a seasonal basis or during the seasons of heavy work. In ever increasing numbers they have been going as seasonal laborers to the best fields of Colorado, to Arizona mines, and to ranches as far away as Texas. Since 1940 the large ordnance depots near Gallup and Flagstaff have employed many Navahos. In 1944, Navahos earned $785,000 in planting, weeding, and harvesting irrigated crops at Bluewater, New Mexico. It is interesting to note that while the increase in income from stockraising and agriculture was 67.5 per cent, that from Reservation wages was 87.5 per cent. The increase from all categories of wage work was 2.133 per cent, for the period between 1940 and 1958.

RELIEF

During the war years, the Navajo Agency supplied relief in the form of rations, intended to supplement an inadequate budget rather than to furnish complete support. In 1947 the Navajo Tribe assumed some of this responsibility and voted the appropriation of $143,000 to assist destitute Navaho families. The Bureau of Indian Affairs has also provided assistance, and in 1958, a total of $210,302 was made available for those ineligible for relief from other sources. The Welfare Program of the Navajo Agency has grown in the past years, and has concerned itself largely with child welfare.

AVERAGE INCOME

In 1940, the total income of the Navaho was estimated at $4,027,530, or $81.89 per capita. Per capita estimates for other years run from $45 to $98. During the later war years tribal income probably totaled $10,000,000.

These figures should not be accepted without qualification, for the economy of The People is still on a subsistence rather than a commercial basis, and there is reason to believe that barter, irregular wages, and gifts have not entered sufficiently into the computations on which the estimates are based. For example, the contributions to Navaho income of hunting and plant collecting are not easily converted to money terms without the danger of distortion due to inevitable guesswork, and it is probable that the data given above are too exclusively commercial and understate the role of wild products.

Furthermore, some allowance must be made for "indirect income" in the form of health, educational, and other services which are supplied by the government to a greater degree than among whites in many rural regions. Navahos on the Reservation are free from land-tax obligations, but other taxes, such as income and sales taxes, apply to them as to citizens of the surrounding area.

Nevertheless, the above estimates give a sound indication of the low Navaho standard of living. It is instructive to set against the estimated $82 Navaho income the per capita income for the United States as a whole in 1940—$579. For the state of Arizona, per capita income in that year was $473, and for New Mexico it was $359. Even the lowest state in the nation, Mississippi, which is like the Navaho country in that it is largely rural and has an important minority group, had a per capita income two and a half times as large as that of the Navahos—$205. These estimates are, of course, not strictly comparable with those of Navaho income, but the gap is startling even when the services which Navahos receive from government are taken into account. This is indeed a "scarcity culture," in which the margin between eating adequately and going hungry, between "good clothes" and "old rags" is a narrow one for the vast majority of families.

Since 1940, however, the estimated average per capita income has increased to $467, an increase of 470 per cent. Nonetheless, in 1940, the average per capita income in the states of Arizona and New Mexico was respectively 6 and 4½ times that of the Navaho. By 1957, the Arizona per capita income was 3.7 times that for the Navaho, and the New Mexico figure was 3.4 times that for the Navaho. The national average per capita income was 4.5 that of the Navaho.

Still more revealing and suggestive than per capita income figures, which are at best a very rough index, is information on family income among the Navaho. In 1942 (the only year for which such data are available) the median family income among the 9,500 Navaho families was about $450. In 1935–36, the only recent year in which income distribution was studied for the country as a whole, the median income among all families was $1,160. For farm families it was $965. In the South, where income is the lowest in the nation, the median for all families was $905. In the region which includes the Navaho Reservation, median family income was $1,040. With all due allowance for probable errors of comparison, it is obvious that in a peak year the median Navaho family income was about half of the median farm family income in a depression year.

There are a few wealthy families on the Reservation, and about 1 per cent of all Navaho families had incomes of $2,000 or over in 1942. About 16 per cent had incomes over $1,000. But half the families received less than $400.

Recent data indicate a large increase in the family income, but Navaho income ($2,335 per family) is still far lower than the national family average ($6,130) reported by the Department of Commerce in 1957. In spite of the increase, the Navaho remain among the least privileged groups in the nation.

NAVAHO TECHNOLOGY

Before The People had white contacts, their artifacts were very simple in comparison with those of other American Indian groups. They had none of the famous architectural skills of the Mayas of Yucatan and Central America. Navaho huts were comfortable but rude; while the construction involved hard work and a little cleverness in one or two matters of jointing, it showed no trace of sophisticated engineering. Navaho stone-carving was crude in the extreme when contrasted with that of the early Indians of the Mississippi valley. The People completely lacked the metallurgical knowledge and the subtle dyeing techniques of pre-Columbian Andean civilization. Pottery, weaving, and silversmithing have been their only crafts of any complexity. Of these, true Navaho pottery was a rough cooking ware. For a relatively brief period around 1680 painted pottery was made, and this technique survived in a few areas until quite recently, but these decorated pots were merely inferior imitations of Pueblo models. Weaving techniques also were almost certainly derived from the Pueblo Indians only a few centuries ago.

Silversmithing was learned even more recently. Woodward's data show that the Navahos started to work silver at some time between 1853 and 1858. Techniques were probably learned from whites, either directly from Mexicans or indirectly through other Indian tribes. Much about metal-working may have been learned from the smiths at Fort Sumner during the captivity in the sixties. Of design, Woodward says:

> The ancestry of Navaho silver ornament forms has its roots in the silver trade jewelry distributed to the tribes east of the Mississippi River after 1750, and in the Mexican-Spanish costume ornaments and bridle trappings of the late eighteenth and early nineteenth centuries.[2]

The silver distributed to eastern Indians goes back to the traditions of the great English smiths. Thus modern Navaho silver blends English and colonial traditions with Spanish and (ultimately) Arabic. This explains why the solid, simple pieces in the classical Navaho tradition often remind connoisseurs of antique English silver.

Some "primitive" groups, like the Eskimos, have a deserved fame for the ingenuity of the devices they have developed to face a severe environment. The People seem, by contrast, singularly uninventive. While the Navaho Indians came to surpass the Pueblo Indians as weavers, this superiority was gained not by technical advances but by the aesthetic imagination of the Navaho. As far as is known, the wedge weave is the only variation from ordinary Pueblo tapestry-weaving technique. The writer (C.K.) has seen only one mechanical device that was apparently a Navaho invention: a box arrangement used as a very rough-and-ready hay-baler in Canyon de Chelly.

Today The People use the white man's manufactured objects widely. Almost all their implements except their rawhide lariats and hobbles, occasional bows and arrows, rocks for grinding corn and medicines, and a few crude handmade objects such as troughs hollowed out of logs are of white manufacture. Ceremonial articles, however, are made by The People themselves. The houses of "medicine men" contain buckskin pouches for keeping ritual equipment, wooden composite fire drills for kindling ceremonial fires, and other archaic objects.

Pottery and basketry are now made exclusively for ceremonial purposes, and even here The People are relying more and more on the pottery and basketry produced by other Indian tribes. Most everyday containers in use at present are tin, enamelware, glass, or china bought at trading posts. When unbreakable metal vessels of European manufacture became available at not very high prices, it was no longer worthwhile to make pottery, and the craft grew obsolete. The utilitarian need for baskets was similarly extinguished. As baskets and pots grew to have only ceremonial uses, both crafts became surrounded with so many ritual restrictions that most women either were afraid to undertake the manufacture of them or were simply unwilling to go to all the bother.

A survey among the 665 Indians (131 biological families) of the Dennehotso area made in 1934 shows how widely white manufactured articles are distributed. In this group there were 38 wagons, 71 sets of harness, 99 saddles, 39 ploughs, 43 drags, 9 sewing machines, 17 trunks and 16 suitcases (for storing ornaments and family treasures), 6 tents, 2 automobiles, and numerous axes, hammers, and knives.

While the bulk of the material objects used today by The People show European derivation or influence, their way of life and their religion are much less altered. This is in full accord with the common anthropological finding that these latter are much more resistant to change. The ancient methods which have persisted are mostly the ones associated with ritual activity. Women seem to change more slowly than men: in women's costume, their ways of preparing food, and their commercial craft more of "old-fashioned" ways have been preserved. This has come about partly because of the nature of men's activities, and also because the white people's custom of dealing with men as the heads of households has made them the accepted intermediaries of their tribe with white society.

The really astonishing thing is the degree to which The People have taken over parts of white technology with so little alteration in the distinctive flavor of their own way of life. Most Indian groups which have accepted so many European material objects have tended to abandon their own customs and become a rather degraded sort of "poor white." The Navahos show, on the one hand, a general lack of emotional resistance to learning new techniques and using foreign tools, and, on the other, a capacity for making alien techniques fit in with their preëxistent design for living. This is in sharp contrast to the ways of some neighboring tribes. Certain Pueblo Indians, for example, still thresh their grain in the fashion familiar to us from Biblical descriptions, even though they know about combines and can well afford to buy them.

WEAVING AND SILVER WORK

Most persons, if they know nothing else about Navahos, realize that they weave rugs. At first their textiles were made as wearing apparel and were valued as outer wraps by other Indians and by Mexicans, but by 1890 they were producing mainly a coarse rug for commerce. Although several revivals of old designs and of vegetable dyes have occurred since then, the product remains commercial. The Navahos prefer to wear Pendleton blankets made in Oregon, which they also use together with sheep and goat pelts for bedding. The People use their homemade textiles only as saddle blankets.

Experimentation in weaving has been almost exclusively limited to design. Unlike their teachers, the Pueblo Indians, who have never departed from their original simple, banded patterns, the Navahos have used their lively imagination to elaborate patterns, and they have utilized the commercial dyes introduced by the traders to produce riotous color combinations.

All of the weaving is done by women. A Navaho family makes all the tools the weaver needs, save for her metal-toothed tow cards. A spinning wheel and a more complex type of loom would doubtless be impracticable when families move so frequently.

The silversmiths have adopted innovations somewhat more freely and now obtain both tools and materials almost entirely from white traders, who market most of the finished products. It is true that silver mining and smelting could hardly be expected, but the forging of their own tools would be quite possible. Here again the creativeness of The People is as artists, not technicians, in making new designs for stamp dies or for casting, in evolving new forms and arrangements.

The smiths are almost all men, but about half of the smiths interviewed by Adair received help from their wives. The women are apt to do the lighter work, such as setting turquoise.

Most of the silver work is hammered, but the more difficult cast work is highly valued. Only half of the smiths known to Adair knew how to do cast work.

AGRICULTURE

Floodwater farming is the common type, but ditch irrigation is practiced in a few regions. For the most part, The People have tried to take over the white agricultural techniques with which they are familiar, in so far as they have been able to purchase factory-made equipment. Close to the railroad and to centers of white influence, metal ploughs, barbed-wire fences, and the like are the rule today, although in more remote regions like that of Navaho Mountain digging sticks and brush fences are still common. Even where white techniques have been followed, however, The People still have much to learn about their application. The income per acre from irrigated land is probably much less than that obtained by nearby whites working under identical climatic conditions. Dry-farming income shows a comparable differential.

The old sunwise and other ceremonial ways of planting have almost disappeared, but most Navahos still use the Indian method of planting corn in hills rather than in rows. Planting dates are determined by various means—at Navaho Mountain, for instance, by the position of the Pleiades—and simple folk rites continue to be a basic part of agriculture.

ANIMAL HUSBANDRY

The techniques of animal husbandry have been derived first from the Spanish-speaking peoples of the Southwest (for whom many Navahos have worked as herders) and more recently from government stockmen, although there are a few minor variations which are distinctly Navaho. White influences have come to predominate more and more in recent years. Now one seldom sees undocked sheep, or flocks in which ewes and rams are herded together throughout the year. Most herding is done by children, however, and adult Navahos often herd on horseback—a practice disapproved by most white experts. Furthermore, the flocks are usually corralled for too many hours during the heat of the summer days.

Navaho sheep average about 6 pounds of wool when sheared, and only 57 lambs survive for each 100 ewes, while sheep owned by whites in nearby regions average 8 pounds of wool and produce 70 lambs per 100 ewes. Part of the trouble comes from the practice of using children for sheepherders, which means that, instead of utilizing distant ranges and moving the flock frequently, the flock is kept near home and brought back to the same corral every night.

The following description of herding methods used by

one moderately successful middle-aged Navaho shows also the mixture of sound observation and magical belief which characterizes Navaho methods of livestock care.

> Early in the morning we take the sheep out of the corral. I sing a song and open the gate. When the sheep are half out my song is half finished. When they are all out I stop my song. They eat grass all day. They mustn't eat loco weed or they go crazy and run all around. If they eat sagebrush, I mustn't give them water or they will get blown out. At first they hold their heads and tails up and I must keep them quiet for one or two hours. Then when their stomachs are big, I punch them until they throw up. [Don't some people put needles into their stomachs?] Yes, sometimes they put a knife in to let the air out but that is not good. The flies get on the cut and generally they die. They get blown up if they eat milkweed in the spring even without water. But oats don't get blown up. This tears out their guts. If you open them up you find their guts are torn. Then there is owl-foot weed. If they eat that they throw up and die. When you are out herding there are songs for the protection of the sheep and to make them increase.[3]

On the whole, Navaho livestock enterprise is uneconomic. Because of terrain and available forage, because of herding practices, and because sheep provide wool as well as meat and can be slaughtered and consumed more easily and quickly than cattle, sheep are usually more suitable to Navaho economy. But other animals are not used to the best advantage. Goats are valued for their milk and their intelligence in the flock, but too many of them are kept. Cattle are owned by only an occasional family except in a few parts of the Navaho country, and their number and distribution are not at the optimum. Indeed, probably half of the total carrying capacity of the range has been used by nonproductive stock: excess horses, old cows and steers, and goats.

HUNTING

In the old Navaho life, the hunting of certain animals was a matter of ritual, some of which persists today. In most parts of the Reservation guns are used, but in certain isolated localities bows and metal-tipped arrows are still in use. Deer and antelope are hunted according to ritual, but some Navahos today shoot them with a rifle. Steel traps are in use for prairie dogs, coyotes, and occasionally for wildcats, but native traps are used to catch birds for ceremonial purposes.

TRANSPORTATION

Travel by horse over trail and wagon road is still the usual form of transportation. The Navaho country is perhaps the only part of the United States where one may see great numbers of farm wagons, including covered wagons. Buggies are seen now and then. Cowpuncher saddles in all their luxuriance and variety are highly prized. Some Navahos use bits and bridles of Mexican type, but bridles beautifully ornamented in silver appear less and less frequently.

Thirty years ago, Navaho-owned automobiles were rarities. Fifteen years ago, perhaps one family out of every fifty owned a car. At present, more and more own automobiles. Very few are bought new; most originate in the interesting jalopy marts at Gallup and Flagstaff. Navaho men do most of the driving, even of wagons; only most rarely does one see a Navaho woman driving a car. Navahos—as compared with Hopi Indians, for example—make poor automobile drivers and mechanics. But The People are good-natured, patient, and persistent in tinkering with broken-down machines; by sheer trial-and-error methods some are able to keep ancient models in circulation. All too often, though, they show supreme neglect of such necessities as grease and battery water.

REGIONAL VARIATIONS IN ECONOMY AND TECHNOLOGY

In view of the numbers of The People and the size of their country, it is hardly surprising that the words "always" and "never" may seldom be used with any exactness. Regional and local variations in many features of the way of life are numerous and multiform. In large part, these reflect differences in the intensity of contacts with whites in accord with the location of the area, type of terrain making for greater or lesser isolation, etc. Moreover, sustained contact with the Ute and Piute Indians on the north has produced modifications of a different sort from those of the southern and eastern regions, where various Pueblo tribes or Jicarilla Apaches have been the neighbors of most influence. Additions of Indians from other tribes to The People have given a special character to certain areas. Thus the Navahos of the famous Canyon de Chelly and Canyon del Muerto are considered by The People of other regions to show a Pueblo cast to their ways, due to the coming of the Hopi mentioned in Chapter 1. Finally, there are local variations which may be traced merely to historical accidents. Silversmiths, for instance, are numerous in the Smith Lake region south of Crownpoint, but there are very few in some other parts of the Reservation. The making of baskets has disappeared in many regions. Similarly, various areas are characterized by minor preferences in the architecture of dwellings and in favorite ceremonials, and by other cultural variations.

Other differences are due to climates, soils, and topography. Along the northern, western, and a portion of the southern boundary of the Reservation stretches a broad C-shaped belt where the environment favors a livestock economy and where, except for a few localities, farming is of decidedly secondary importance. This type of economy also is characteristic of the eastern Navaho country, though in the "checkerboard" sections factors of land ownership and competition with non-Indian operators pose rather different problems. In most of the great central and eastern portion of the Reservation, conditions permit the development of considerable cropland, most of which is in small tracts conveniently located for receiving flood waters or sufficiently high to enable utilization of the increased rainfall in dry farming. These more favorable conditions have fostered an economy in which livestock and crops are about equally important. In a few restricted areas (Shiprock, Chinle, Ganado, and Tuba City) soil conditions and assured water supply permit intensified farming, and livestock plays a secondary or insignificant role.

THE ROLE OF THE GOVERNMENT IN THE NAVAHO ECONOMY

SOIL CONSERVATION AND STOCK IMPROVEMENT

When The People returned from Fort Sumner, they had few livestock left. About 14,000 sheep and 1,000 goats were issued in small family lots. Perhaps eventually as many as 35,000 animals were given out, but the record on this point is not entirely clear. Most of the administrators from the time of Fort Sumner to the start of the New Deal were imbued with the current philosophy that quantity expansion and exploitation of nature is the way to prosperity, so they urged the Navahos to increase their flocks. The People complied with such enthusiasm that within a few years' time their livestock had outgrown the country's ability to feed the stock and at the same time maintain its plant cover—at least under the impact of the natural erosion cycle which apparently began in the 1880's.

As the range became overgrazed, the rainwater, which should have been caught and held by surface growth, swept down from the steep slopes and cut deep gullies that sometimes stretched for more than a hundred miles, eating the bottoms out of fertile valleys. The damage was accelerated by every fresh storm and by wind. In time these washes and gullies cutting down below the surface drained away subsurface waters. The loss of these waters and the lack of rain caused the perennial grasses to dry out while hardier but less useful weeds took their place. This process went on over thousands of square miles as The People moved their sheep, goats, and horses into the more remote reaches of the country set aside for them.

By 1933 erosion had reached a critical state. The new administration pointed out to the Navahos that it was imperative to bring about drastic reductions in the number of horses and unproductive livestock and considerable reductions in the number of useful sheep, and it undertook an energetic program to reduce the numbers of livestock. While this program undoubtedly caused much hardship and suffering, it seems evident that in the long run it will pay cash benefits in better wool and mutton as well as in preserving the grass cover of the soil. A careful study of the facts indicates that overstocking is one important reason why in recent years the wool has been poor and the lambs light. If the number of animals on the range is reduced, the same amount of feed can produce better sheep and thus actually raise the income.

Concomitant with the reduction in numbers, the Navajo Agency has tried to improve the breed and breeding practices. The tribe has spent considerable money for good rams, which are rented out to individual owners, and the government has established a laboratory at Fort Wingate to experiment with developing the best type of sheep for the range, which would produce the wool and meat of the type needed by Navahos and also be salable in the commercial market.

Moreover, a livestock disposition project has been established to make it possible for the Navahos to sell their poor-quality sheep, which are unsalable commercially and pull down the quality of the flock if kept and used for breeding. These sheep are bought for a reasonable price and sold as fresh meat locally or canned for use in Reservation schools and hospitals. While not profitable commercially, the meat is nevertheless perfectly good as food and has been of great help in improving the diet in government institutions, where meat was formerly too costly to be served frequently.

Actual results of the various efforts can be seen in the following figures assembled in 1944:

Navaho sheep *reduced* from 594,000 to 423,000.[4]
Navaho lambs *increased* from 317,000 to 326,000.
Average weight of lambs *increased* from 53 to 60 lbs.
Average weight of fleece *increased* from less than 4 to 6 lbs.
If wool is worth 30¢ and lambs are worth 10¢ a pound, the total value of these two products *increased* from $2,126,747 to $2,681,630.

In spite of this gain in value, the Navahos do not recognize very thoroughly the benefits of and the necessity for stock reduction, and the program has encountered strenuous opposition. Part of this hostility might have been avoided if communication had been less faulty and if the decisions made by highly competent technicians in the early stages of the program had taken into account the human problems of land use and the unreasoning sentiments which The People have for their sheep and horses. For example, range allotments followed the pattern for the U. S. Forest Service tradition—not the Navaho custom. Without adequate preparation along the lines of emotional reorientation and education, the government has tried to alter the whole technological basis of Navaho society in a few years' time.

Many Indians still feel that their means of livelihood is being stolen from them. Part of this opposition stems, no doubt, from the natural skepticism and resentment on the part of the dirt farmer toward the theories of the desk farmer, especially when these theories are backed up by fiat. In this reaction Navahos do not differ greatly from many white farmers who have opposed and still oppose conservation measures. As recently as May 1944, Vermont farmers armed themselves with rifles to "prevent a Federal invasion" in connection with a flood-control project.[5]

Yet opposition to the government land-use program is not universal among the Navahos, and some of them now request the services of the Soil and Moisture Conservation division of the agency. Besides the control of erosion and the conservation of water, this division coöperates with other parts of the agency staff to promote fertilization of farm lands, crop rotation, reforestation, conservation of wild life, fire control, revegetation of ranges and pastures, construction of livestock waters, and control of floods and silting.

The agency's farm program is mostly restricted to the irrigated areas, where Indians are supervised in their use of water and encouraged to improve their farming practices. No control is exercised over other farms beyond requiring a permit for breaking uncultivated ground.

TRIBAL ENTERPRISES

The Navajo Tribe and the government jointly have set up a number of projects known as "tribal enterprises." Two of these—the Livestock Disposition Project and the Livestock Improvement Project—have already been mentioned. The five coöperative trading stores will be referred to in a following section.

The largest and most important of the other tribal undertakings from the commercial point of view is the sawmill located on the plateau above Fort Defiance. Large ponderosa pines that are ripe or overripe are harvested scientifically so that the forest is not depleted. Many thousand board feet of lumber milled from these trees helped to supply building materials for the war effort and work opportunities for the Indians (of 170 mill and shipping employees, all but 15 are Navaho Indians). The mill is managed by white foremen, but profits revert to tribal funds.

The flour mill at Round Rock, near Many Farms, was established in the center of the wheat-growing area of the Reservation to give the Indians an opportunity to have their wheat processed near home. It also undertakes the marketing of Navaho wheat and flour.

Other enterprises within the Tribal Program, as it is now called, include the Arts and Crafts Guild, the Tribal Department of Water Development, Insect, Predator and Disease Control, Farm and Range Conservation, the Higher Education Scholarship Program, and the Tribal Legal Department. In short, The People are attempting to take care of their own needs.

OTHER ECONOMIC SERVICES

The Traders Relations Divisions of the Navajo Agency sees to licensing traders on the Reservation, investigates complaints against them, helps with the new Navaho coöperatives, and keeps record of the volume and types of business in the stores as an index of the economic state of the tribe. The Roads and Communications Division maintains highway and telephone systems.

Government contributions to Navaho income through wage employment and the provision of relief have already been mentioned. Wage totals have been greatly increased during recent years by large outlays for public works, including soil conservation, construction, wells, roads, hospitals, schools, etc. In the three fiscal years 1934–1936, for example, the government spent over ten million dollars on improvements within the Reservation and another million in areas immediately adjacent. Through these expenditures, The People gained not only the improvements themselves, but also many opportunities for employment during the construction period.

DISTRIBUTION OF GOODS

A great deal of gift-giving, barter, exchange, buying and selling, goes on among the Navahos. One family, for instance, was asked to keep an exact record for a few months. During one month the family received the front quarter of a sheep from a clan relative of the husband, a liver from the husband's nephew, half a goat from the husband's sister. They traded a pair of earrings to a clan brother of the husband for a ewe lamb. They received $2.25 in trade at the store for mending silver jewelry for another relative. The following month they received three pieces of mutton and two pieces of horse meat from various relatives. They again made a little cash by doing odd jobs.

A major proportion of livestock income is used to buy food, clothing, and household or productive equipment from traders or from merchants in the towns. Wages, rugs, jewelry, and pinyon nuts also move through the trading posts in exchange for items needed for home use. Agricultural products have only a local market, largely because there is no surplus production, but it should also be remarked that the types of corn ordinarily raised by Navahos cannot be sold commercially. In 1940 traders paid The People $1,865,150 for their various products, while the Navahos bought goods to the value of $2,640,450. Of this, 62 per cent went for flour, coffee, sugar, potatoes, and other foods; about 25 per cent was spent on clothing; and most of the rest purchased household and farm equipment. One estimate gives $37 spent by the average family in 1940 for food at the trading store as against $20 per year of home-grown foodstuffs.

The wants of The People used to be few. Today they purchase from commercial channels more than half of what they consume. The average expenditure of four families in the Ramah area at one of the four trading posts in 1936–37 was distributed as follows:

Food		*Clothing*	
Flour	$44.07	Blankets & Shawls	$33.37
Fruit	20.51	Cloth	19.08
Sugar	16.70	Shoes	13.95
Coffee	14.55	Overshoes	6.30
Cooking Fat	12.56	Shirts	5.27
Jams & Jellies	8.29	Blue Jeans	4.89
Bread	5.91	Trousers	3.65
Potatoes	5.79	Coats	3.41
Baking Powder	4.67	Stockings	2.00
Soda Pop	2.22	Hats	1.87
Candy	1.98	Gloves	1.33
Onions	.64	Total	$95.12
Tea	.55		
Total	$138.44		

THE TRADING POST

Charles Crary opened and operated the first trading post in the land of The People in 1871 or 1872. In 1943 there were 146 trading posts on and adjacent to the Reservation. Of these, 95 are licensed and bonded posts under Indian Service control. There are also now five coöperatives owned by the Navahos of the "communities" which they serve.

The trading post has been well characterized as "the best remaining example of frontier commerce." One can buy there anything from a bottle of pop to a farm wagon. The posts serve the same social functions as did the general store in rural white society a generation or so ago. Trading is prolonged as much as possible, since the store is also a center for the exchange of news and gossip, and for seeing one's relatives and friends. It is usually the post office, and mail received by the Navahos is discussed in great detail.

The storekeeper is banker as well as merchant. The seasonal nature of the livestock economy and the fluctuations in other sources of cash income mean that even well-off families need credit during most months of the year and sometimes advances in money as well. In 1940 outstanding accounts amounted to $370,500. Poor and rich alike get minor credit through pawning jewelry, saddles, guns, or any article which has a resale value. In 1940 traders advanced $190,670 on pawned articles. Jewelry, in particular, is a Navaho substitute for a bank. Reserve capital is invested in silver and turquoise which can always be pawned or sold if need arises.

Some traders, foolhardy or unscrupulous, have granted credit so liberally as to keep families in perpetual debt, have reduced them in fact to a state of peonage dependency. The trader also has a source of power in that he is able to advance silver and tools to silversmiths, dyes to weavers. The risks which he takes in advancing unsecured or inadequately secured credits justify him in charging higher prices than those of the cash stores in town. If Navahos were always able to pay cash, the whole price scale could come down at least 10 per cent. Further, since The People are exchanging raw materials or simple craft products for costly manufactured articles, they labor under the continual disadvantage of buying in a protected, and selling in an unprotected, market.

Recently, with the increase in cash income and closer acquaintance with white economy brought about by the war, more and more Navahos have opened bank accounts in nearby towns. They have also invested in war bonds, their first significant participation in the capital-investment system.

THE FUTURE OF NAVAHO ECONOMY

To some outside observers it seems that the resettlement sooner or later of large numbers of Navahos outside their present lands is indispensable to satisfactory solutions to the problems of the Navaho. However, plans definitely formulated at present center upon the re-creation of basic land and water resources within the Reservation and the improvement of methods of agriculture and animal husbandry. There is no doubt that much can be accomplished along these lines. Through irrigation developments, especially in the San Juan valley, between 110,000 and 160,000 acres of irrigated farm lands might be provided—if funds could be obtained and complicated legal and political questions solved.

If even 5,500 irrigated acres could be added to the lands now farmed, The People could produce annually all the unprocessed agricultural products which they now purchase. An additional 14,000 acres would produce the 35,000 tons of wheat flour that the Navahos buy each year. The wheat could be ground at tribal mills, thus providing employment for an appreciable number of men and women. In many ways these measures would effect a major readjustment in present Navaho economy. Experts disagree, however, as to whether this much land could be made available without exceedingly expensive dam and waterworks constructions. Furthermore, it should be realized that, even with this undertaking completed, the per capita agricultural acreage would be increased by only eight acres. Agricultural income can, however, be appreciably increased when The People learn to use better farming methods. At present, for example, they use almost no fertilizer, although quantities of sheep manure are readily available.

Livestock income can perhaps be doubled through stock improvement and sensible land and stock management. It has been shown that one animal of good breed is worth several of inferior quality. The Sheep Laboratory at Fort Wingate is making good progress in its efforts to develop a type of sheep that will be readily salable in the commercial markets and also meet Navaho needs for meat and wool.

Within the "demonstration areas" wool clippings have been increased from the Navaho average of 4 pounds per head to 8 pounds per head. The lamb crop has risen to an average of 76 per cent, even to 90 per cent in one such area. The total income from sheep has been increased from \$1.33 per breeding ewe to \$3.84 per breeding ewe, and from \$1.13 per forage acre to \$1.27 per forage acre. However, it is doubtful whether without close supervision The People will handle their flocks so efficiently. It should also be remembered that many Navahos own only very small flocks and cannot realize profits from large-scale enterprises. Perhaps the pooling of herds can be encouraged, with a saving in manpower and a gain in efficiency of herding practices.

Further development of present tribal industries and creation of new ones would add to wage income and also lower the cost of a few purchase items. Tanneries could produce leather locally. Pinyon nuts might be processed within the Reservation, at least for the western market. A small industry might be made of the pinyon post and firewood trade. Exploitation of nonmetallic minerals may perhaps provide employment for many.

However, the success of these and other objective plans can be realized only if the human factor is dealt with as skillfully as the technical factor. Means of communication must be enormously improved if Navahos are to be persuaded to abandon established routines of handling their sheep in favor of more efficient habits. Here is the great opportunity of the Education Division, especially the day schools, and of the Navajo Agency generally. Rich stockowners could be encouraged to lease land off the Reservation. But obviously neither encouragement nor simple persuasion will be enough. If measures are put through by force or threat of force, the rich men will rouse their relatives and the general population unless educational programs (in the broadest sense) make the majority see and feel that such an objective is unequivocally in their own interest. The People's present feeling about proposed changes is eloquently indicated by the following paraphrase of a recent speech at the tribal council:

> Give us our sheep, give us our mutton, let us have herds as our fathers and our grandfathers had. If you take away our sheep, you take away our food, and we have nothing. What then will become of our children? What will we say to our young men who have gone to war? What will they eat and how will they live when they come back to us? They are fighting now for our homes and our land, and these things will be useless if you take away our sheep. This is not right. You must let us keep our sheep or we die.

We have seen that Navahos are willing and able to adopt white technologies—that, unlike the Pueblos, they do not insist on preserving old ways merely because they are old. Yet, although The People have not always lived by sheep raising—it has come only within the past 400 years—they now feel that sheep have always been the basis of their economy. The emotional value and prestige value of their sheep has come to be so great that only the most skillful and patient explanation will convince them that other ways of making a living for at least some of the tribe will save their soil and make it possible to support their rapidly increasing numbers.

3. LIVING TOGETHER

Human beings always get their food and shelter by working with other human beings. These social interactions, of course, come to have significance far beyond making possible the physical survival of the group, but it is well to remind ourselves that, at bottom, the established patterns for human relationship represent adjustment to needs for subsistence. In what groups does most of the social participation of The People take place? How is it organized by the tradition of the tribe? First, however, let us see The People as they appear to the visitor.

WHAT THE PEOPLE LOOK LIKE

Most white visitors find The People interesting and attractive, both in physique and in costume.

PHYSIQUE

There is by no means a single Navaho physical type. The fact that about twenty of the Navaho clans are said to have been started by non-Navaho ancestresses is at least symbolic of historical truth. It is certain that during the last few centuries, and probably earlier also, The People have absorbed large numbers from other tribes. Not inconsequential amounts of white blood are also present, much of it dating back to the seventeenth and eighteenth centuries, when the children of Navaho women who had been captured and kept as slaves by the Spanish escaped and returned to the tribe. Some white blood has come indirectly through the Pueblos, and since the establishment of the Reservation, some white traders have left various progeny with and without benefit of wedlock. Even Navahos who are known to have a white father, however, think of and refer to themselves as Navahos.

Hence the range of physique is great. While, for example, Navahos tend to be taller than Pueblo Indians, some individual Navahos would be indistinguishable in various Pueblo villages, except for costume. It may be that certain western and northern Navaho types are more representative of the "original" Navaho population, but this is a complicated problem. Perhaps they represent rather a greater infusion of Ute, Walapai, or other strains, as opposed to the greater Pueblo admixture elsewhere.

The reader will probably find looking at the photographs of Navahos more helpful than any extended description of physique. A few facts, however, may be of use. Navahos are not among the tallest American Indian groups, but they fall in the second tallest category. About nine hundred men, measured at many different places on the Reservation, averaged 66½ inches in height, but single individuals ranged all the way from 60 to 72 inches. A smaller sample of women had a mean stature of 61 inches, with a variation from 56 to 65½ inches. Most Navahos are light in weight; the nine hundred men averaged 140 pounds but varied from 91 to 240. Almost all Navahos are broad headed, but the cradleboard flattens the natural head shape in infancy, and this influences the measurements. In a very general way, one may say that there are two principal Navaho types: the shorter, stockier "Puebloid" type and the taller, leaner, longer-faced, more frequently moustached, raw-boned "Tuba City" type. Body build is often best described as "medium."

The most typical Navaho woman may be described as having thin legs, small feet, hands, and arms, long face and nose, thick lips, and long chin. A less common type is distinguished by delicate lips, nose, and face and large eyes.

As with body structure, there is great variety in skin color, which is partly correlated with the amount of exposure to the sun and partly with the admixure of other Indian and white blood. Hence there are some fairly light faces on the Reservation, some very dark, and others markedly ruddy. The slanted oriental eye is fairly common among children and women.

There is a characteristic Navaho style of walking, typical gestures, and other motor habits which strike the eye but are difficult to describe briefly in words. Flora Bailey, who has made a special study of these typical movements, makes the following general characterization:

> One of the most striking differences first noted between Navaho movement and that of the white American is the smoothness and flowing quality of the action. Briefly, the Navaho gestures and moves with sustained, circular motions rather than with the angular, staccato movements characteristic of white culture.[1]

CLOTHING

By and large, the present dress of Navaho men and boys is a colorful variation of the cowboy costume: blue denim pants, bright shirts and scarves, and large felt hats. A few old men still wear the calico shirts and trousers which show Pueblo (and ultimately Spanish) influence. Fancy cowboy boots are prized possessions, but heavy work shoes are more common. Buckskin and cowhide moccasins are worn chiefly by older people and for ceremonial occasions. Breechcloths are worn under the trousers by most Navaho males after puberty.

Women's costumes are much more conservative. The long, fluted calico skirts and bright calico or velveteen blouses reflect the Spanish influence and also the fashions worn by the wives of American Army officers at Fort Sumner in the later 1860's.

In public, women wear Pendleton blankets draped over the shoulders except in very hot weather, when the blanket is usually carried folded over the arm. Men, on the other hand, usually wear these blankets only for warmth. In cold weather children and adults may wear several layers of clothing, but as a rule underclothing is not worn by either sex except where white influence is strong. Men sometimes wear heavy "union suits" in winter.

The hairdress of women and of conservative, long-haired men is adapted from that of the Pueblos. Both long-haired and short-haired men often wear a scarf tied across the forehead.

THE WORLD OF THE HOGANS

The word *hogan* has been taken over into English and designates two general types of the dwellings of The People. The more ancient variety has three forked poles for its chief support. This older style is today less popular than the more spacious six-sided hogan. For this type, some builders set a framework of four forked posts in the ground to form a square. Braces are laid in the forks of these posts to connect them rectangularly. Around this framework six walls, leaving a space for the door, are built of small logs that at times are slightly cut at the corners to hold them in position. The roof logs are gradually built in toward the center, forming a crib-work roof shaped like the top of a beehive, with a central opening left for a smoke hole. Some builders omit the framework inside, so as to obtain as much space as possible. Others round off the corners or even make the hogan eight-sided, and still others (where timber is scarce) build the walls of stone laid in mud mortar.

In summer families often live in rude brush shelters that afford shade. In a sheep camp, a hastily constructed brush

3a. A three-forked-poles hogan

3b. A "modern type" hogan

3c. An earth-covered hogan

windbreak usually suffices, but canvas tents are frequently seen.

Cabins of wood or stone which follow white prototypes are now common in the regions closest to the railroads, but native dwellings are still in the majority for a variety of reasons. In the first place, further imitation of European examples would be expensive in materials, and most Navahos lack carpentry skills. In addition, the hogan is an excellent simple adaptation to the climate: its thick walls keep out cold in winter and, to some extent, heat in summer; the centrally placed fire keeps all parts of the dwelling warm, and there is room for more occupants to sit or sleep around the fire. The writers have found hogans generally more comfortable than the thin-walled cabins of white homesteaders. Furthermore, the crevices in the walls and the "eaves" of the crib-work roof provide storage space. Finally, curing chants can be carried on only in a hogan. Since few of The People have abandoned their religion, even those who live in white-style cabins must also have hogans.

Every Navaho establishment includes more than a single structure. Even a sheep camp has a brush corral for the animals as well as a windbreak or tent. At permanent residences there are corrals, "shades," and usually one or more storage dugouts. Out of sight, in the timber or in a secluded hollow or rock cove, will be found at least one sweathouse, a small-scale replica of the old-style hogan without the smoke hole. It is exceptional to have only a single hogan as the nucleus of a Navaho establishment. Two or more related families often reside in close proximity, and there is at least one hogan or cabin for each biological family. More often than not, even an isolated family eventually builds two or more dwellings, one of which is used mainly for storage. The supplementary cabin is increasingly popular as a place where women can weave or sew when it is raining hard and whither they can withdraw for tasks requiring concentration when the weather is neither so hot nor so cold as to make the cabin uncomfortable.

The greater number of families have more than one permanent establishment. The need for these is dictated by such factors as the desirability of getting the herds some distance from crop lands, the fact that grazing lands may be desirable in summer but unusable in winter because of too much snowfall, seasonal variations in water supply, and availability of wood for winter fires. Some families who possess a thousand or more sheep have as many as five or six separate clusters of buildings. Usually, however, each family has one location which is its main residence. It should be emphasized again that no establishments, except sheep camps, are in any true sense transitory. If a previously dependable source of water for humans or animals disappears, then a radical shift of residence may occur. Otherwise, the new buildings which are built when death or lice infestation or some other event brings about abandonment of an old hogan will be located within a stone's throw (or at most a half-mile) from the previous dwelling.

To The People, their hogans are not just places to eat and sleep, mere parts of the workaday world, as homes have tended to become in the minds of white people, particularly in cities. The hogan occupies a central place in the sacred world also. The first hogans were built by the Holy People, of turquoise, white shell, jet, or abalone shell. Navaho myths prescribe the position of persons and objects within; they say why the door must always face the rising sun and why the dreaded bodies of the dead must be removed through a hole broken in the hogan wall to the north (always the direction of evil). A new hogan is often consecrated with a Blessing Way Rite or songs from it (see Chapter 6), and, at the very least, the head of the family will smear the sacred corn pollen or meal along the hogan poles with some such petition as *hózhóó łełgoo 'ót'é,* "let this be assurance that the place will be happy."

"A ROOM OF ONE'S OWN"

To the white visitor it is astonishing how many individuals can eat, sleep, and store many of their possessions within one room not more than twenty-five feet in diameter. As a matter of fact, livable order is attained only by adherence to a considerable degree of system with respect both to objects and to persons. Women always sit on the north side of the hogan, men on the south. Small children stay close to their mothers. The male head of the family and officiating "medicine men" (or other distinguished visitors) sit on the west side, facing the doorway. The places of other persons and the seating arrangements under special circumstances are prescribed in considerable detail.

Goods have a fixed disposal which utilizes all available space. Herbs and some types of dried foods, ceremonial equipment, guns and bows and arrows, hats and articles of clothing in current use, are stowed away in corners of the rafters or suspended from beams by thongs or nails. Reserve clothing and bedding, prized jewelry and ceremonial articles are stored in trunks or suitcases, which are stacked against the walls where the roof is lowest. Pots and pans are stacked near the central fire or placed with the spoons and supplies of flour, lard, coffee, and sugar in crude cupboards made of boxes nailed to the wall by the door. There may be a sack of salt from Zuni Salt Lake, which will be ground to the desired fineness as it is needed. Ordinarily there are no heavy or bulky pieces of furniture. Stoves and beds are very much on the increase but are much more apt to be placed in the supplementary cabins than in hogans. The same may be said for tables, but these are still quite unusual.

The area around the hogan is also used as living space

when weather permits. Sheepskins, blankets, and women's skirts are hung to air and sun on poles placed between branches of trees. In summer coffee pots, frying pans, and three-legged iron Dutch ovens stand under the trees or hang from their branches until time to cook the next meal. The loom is frequently set up outside. Smiths too sometimes work in the open near the hogan.

White persons who are told of the strong Navaho sensitivity with regard to bodily exposure wonder how privacy can possibly be maintained under hogan conditions. There are several answers. Navahos do not undress when they go to sleep. Sex relations take place during the hours of darkness. Excretion is done outside the hogan. It should not be forgotten that there are occasions when work or an excursion to the trading store or a ceremonial takes most of the family away for a considerable time, giving a lone remaining person a long interval of seclusion when a bath or a complete change of clothing in privacy is possible.

SLEEPING AND EATING

There is no set hour for the children to be put to bed, and the whole family usually retires rather early if there are no guests. Sheepskins and blankets are brought in from outdoors, if they have been airing, or unrolled and spread on the floor around the fire or stove. The baby lies in its cradle near the mother. Several small children will probably sleep together. If the family has a number of older children, there is apt to be a second hogan where the boys sleep. In summer some or all of the family will probably sleep outdoors. Indoors or out, everyone takes care not to step over a sleeping person, lest some evil befall him.

When the group to be served at a meal is large and two "settings" are necessary because of space considerations, the men and boys may eat first and the women who have been preparing the food may eat later. But usually the whole family eats together. A sheepskin wool-side down, blanket, or tarpaulin—among more prosperous families or on state occasions a piece of oilcloth—is spread on the ground and bowls of food placed on it. A few families now use tables and chairs. Since individual plates are not the rule, several persons will probably use a common bowl. Spoons are the usual eating implements, and bread may be used to hold pieces of meat or to dip up gravy. In summer the whole family is likely to eat outdoors.

Navaho diet has changed greatly since The People's contacts with whites. Except for some corn dishes, strictly native foods are infrequently seen on other than ceremonial occasions. The taste for coffee and tea was acquired during the Fort Sumner period, and one or the other is an indispensable part of every meal, even for small children. The use of milled flour also dates from that time and has gradually supplanted hand-ground corn flour. Despite the fact that salt can be bought at every trading store, many Navahos still make long journeys to various "sacred" salt deposits. Although this procedure is often more expensive, the ancient habit persists, partly because, as The People say, this salt is not so "bitter" as the commercial variety. Food preparation shows considerable non-Navaho influence, as in the ordinary form of bread, which resembles the Mexican wheat-flour tortilla. In all likelihood, however, mutton, goat, and beef are prepared in the fashion formerly used for venison.

Bread and meat—usually mutton or goat flesh—are the staples of the diet. A few families in some sections have pigs or keep chickens for their eggs. A prosperous family will slaughter a sheep or a goat nearly every week throughout the year, but poorer people get much less meat. Though meats, peaches, and melons are sometimes dried and most families store roasted corn in a pit, not much food is accumulated because of the size and type of dwellings and the movements to sheep and other camps.

The energy content of most Navaho foods runs between

4a. Shearing a sheep

4b. Woman husking corn

3.5 and 4.5 calories per gram of air-dry matter, but meats have a higher value. The habit of eating the internal organs and indeed all edible portions of the animal is a compensation for the deficiency of vegetable greens, and this food is probably the principal source of many needed vitamins and minerals. The rarity of decay in the teeth of Navaho adults as compared to whites suggests dietary adequacy from this point of view.

Most Navahos are accustomed to tightening their belts and going for days on nothing more than coffee and a little bread, but they will gorge when opportunity offers. They pride themselves on being able to go a long time without food. The whole pattern is that of alternation between eating a little and eating a lot.

CLEANLINESS

Cleanliness of clothing, bedding, and other furnishings varies a great deal from hogan to hogan. Some Navaho women—like some white women—tend to be "immaculate housekeepers" and, at the other extreme, some are slovenly. The number of lice differs in accord with the newness of the bedding and frequency of sunning it, but there are few hogans where no lice are ever to be found. Sometimes a family will move and build a new hogan primarily to escape these pests. Delousing, particularly of the hair, is usually a social activity, performed for the child by the mother or some older relative or by two children for each other.

There is likewise much individual variation as to personal cleanliness. Washing the hands and face one or more times daily is seldom neglected, but bathing is less frequent. This is partly, of course, because water is scarce and laborious to haul. Whites are easily shocked by Navaho habits in this regard, but the writers have observed that whites who for weeks are deprived of running water, privacy, and the comforts of bathing in evenly heated rooms rapidly abandon the daily bath. How often the Navahos wash their clothes depends on the season and the availability of the water. Except in very hot weather, changing the shirt or blouse tends to be a matter of putting the clean garment on top of the dirty one.

DIVISION OF LABOR

The husband takes the primary responsibility for building dwellings, corrals, and fences, although his wife and other women folk assist in plastering and chinking the hogan. The wife airs the bedding and keeps the dwelling and cooking utensils clean and orderly. She cooks, butchers mutton, gathers those crops from the field which are to be used for immediate consumption, and looks after the children, although the man will assist in all these tasks if the woman is ill, or under other special circumstances. The man is expected to cut most of the firewood, unless there are boys old enough to do this. All assist in bringing wood to the fire, although this is a special chore of children.

Men do most of the work in the fields, look after horses, wagons, saddles, and cattle, and haul wood and water. At times of heightened activity in the care of the sheep, as when the lambs are being born, every able-bodied family member assists. At other seasons responsibilities are distributed according to availability of personnel and to arrangements within the extended family, but herding tends to be the duty of youngsters and of the old. Women spend their spare time in weaving, and occasionally in making baskets or pots. Dressing skins and making moccasins are male occupations. Some men are silversmiths, and women are also beginning to participate in this craft.

Many activities are sex-typed to such a degree that many adults would find it embarrassing to perform a task associated with the other sex. A young married man, for example, refused to be photographed milking a goat, protesting that "it wouldn't look right." Nevertheless the distinctions are less rigidly drawn in some respects than in white society. Many Navaho men find it no disgrace to cook, even when their wives are present. They will publicly assume responsibilities for babies and children which white men commonly evade. There is also highly specialized coöperation in many activities such as housebuilding, farming, and various work connected with the flocks and herds. At the sheep dip, for example, the men conduct the full-grown animals through the vats, but the women usually superintend the lambs and kids. And so, in many ways, the line between the sphere of men and the sphere of women is less obvious than in white society.

Exactly who does what depends upon all sorts of accidents of the situation. The whole system of division of labor and assignment of tasks is—like all Navaho social organization—highly informal from the white point of view. There are endless discussions and disputes about it within the extended family.

Occupational specialization is slight, on the whole. Almost all women who have good eyesight and general health are weavers. A few spend some proportion of their time as midwives, ceremonial practitioners, or herbalists, and in making baskets or pots, and some assist their husbands in making silver jewelry. A few men weave, make moccasins for persons beyond the circle of their immediate families, or gather plants for sale; others assist silversmiths part of the year. Half of the smiths themselves, according to Adair, work only intermittently at their craft. In some areas a returned schoolboy or two makes all or most of his living through a white craft such as blacksmithing or carpentry. Some figures for the Dennehotso Valley in 1935 will put these generalizations into the concrete for one "community." Out of 669 persons covered in the census, there were 177 weavers, 27 "medicine men," 6 silversmiths, 12 stone masons, 4 interpreters, 2 blacksmiths, 1 basketmaker, 1 carpenter.

RECREATION

Navahos love to have a good time. In and around the hogan, they make cats-cradles or play the moccasin game, stick dice, or the arrow game. In some areas "American" card games are played. During the winter evenings around the fire, myths and folk tales are repeated, often for the edification of the children. Men and boys hunt in groups of two or three, and they have small informal foot or horse races and cowboy sports.

The People enjoy singing and they believe that it is important in keeping their peace with the Holy People. They sing as they make fire in the morning, as they let the sheep out of the corral, as they work silver, and as they ride.

But—as is natural for isolated people—the greatest pleasure lies in an occasion which brings crowds together. This may be a ceremonial, held at home or at that of a nearby neighbor. Or it may be a distant "squaw dance" in summer or a Night Way or one of the other great chants held in the autumn. At most ceremonials there are talk, feasting, games, and races. Or the occasion for getting together may be a meeting or a communal rabbit hunt. Trips to "chicken pulls" or rodeos near trading stores are times of excitement.

Singing and watching or participating in races and in cowboy sports are felt to be delights in themselves. But in all the major recreational activities there are common threads: the exchange of news and gossip, seeing and being seen in one's best finery, laughing and joking with old friends, opportunities for sexual adventures. Drinking must be mentioned as another diversion for an increasing number of Navahos on these occasions. There is also an opportunity at public gatherings for some serious business, for jewelry and other articles are bought and sold, trades

5. Recreation: an impromptu horse race

6. A Navaho family

of animals or equipment are arranged, and parents can look over prospective mates for their children.

Less frequent are visits to the Gallup Inter-Tribal Indian Ceremonial, the Flagstaff "Powwow," or various Pueblo fiestas. A shopping expedition to Gallup or Farmington or Winslow is a major diversion. Movies are much enjoyed, even by Navahos who know not a word of English.

NAVAHO HUMOR

As W. W. Hill has written:

> A popular fallacy has long existed that the American Indian is a stolid, unemotional individual incapable of expression or appreciation of humor or wit. Nothing is farther from the truth. Examples taken from the Navaho show that in his own social sphere the Indian can and does scintillate in conversation and in action in a manner comparable to that of peoples of European cultures. His humor runs the gamut of puns, practical jokes, and obscenities. In addition, he is an excellent mimic and pantomimist with a superb sense of timing and climax.[2]

All observers agree that The People have a keen sense of humor. They appreciate ridiculous or incongruous situations, either accidental or prepared, at least as much as do whites. However, their practical jokes are seldom cruel, and individuals are not often satirized in their presence. All types of humor are about equally indulged in and reacted to by all classes of persons. There is much less difference due to age, sex, and social position than there is in white society. A respected older man who is usually quite dignified does not feel that there is anything out of the way in acting the buffoon for a few minutes.

Wit and repartee are highly valued in conversation. Many Navaho jokes have a whimsical quality. For instance, kinship terms may be applied to dogs and other animals. The nature of the language permits some quite subtle digs: if a fat person is seated in a hogan, someone may use the verb form which means "the round object is in position" instead of the correct form, meaning "the living object is in position."

Much Navaho humor is expressed in a patterned kind of teasing that is supposed to be carried on between different classes of relatives, as illustrated by the following incidents related by a middle-aged Navaho:

> My brother is riding a good horse. It is his best one and I say how much will you sell that horse. He says $10 or $20 and I say you're not so good-looking on that horse. And he says your wife won't like you to ride that horse, you're not so good-looking as he is. Afterwards I say you don't look very good on top of that horse. We say that if a man has a new hat or shoes or shirt. My brother comes to visit and early in the morning before the sun is up we would have some very cold water. Then I would pull his blanket off and pour water on him. He won't say anything but he'll remember it for a year or two years and when you visit him he'll do anything. You ask to use a gentle horse, and he gives you a bucking one. He says this horse is a gentle one, you don't need to hold him. Then in a little while he bucks.
>
> The last time my brother and I teased he was mean. We were rounding up some horses and we couldn't catch one. We used to rope one- and two-year-old colts in a sandy arroyo and then ride them bareback. He was older than I was and he could ride better. But we used to bet and then if he fell off I could double up the rope and hit him on the back. And if I fell off he did the same to me. Well, we were trying to rope his horse and every time the horse ran by me and I tried to rope him my brother would hit me with that heavy buckskin rope. I cried and after a while I picked up a rope and ran after him. He was scared and ran as fast as

he could. [How old were you?] Seven or eight years old. After that we never teased.

But the only one you can tease about girls is your sister's son. He would come and joke with me about girls. He would say I can still hear the noise we made together. Then I would give him that name "hears the noise." And he would give me a name like it.

My half-brother [actually, father's brother's son] and his grandson were taking a sweatbath together. They came out and they were joking. The old man said, I've got to get some wood, I have to go home. The boy went back into the sweathouse. Then the old man took the boy's clothes and took them away and hid them. The boy came out and he couldn't find his clothes and some boys helped him. It was getting dark and then they found them. When he got home he and his grandfather laughed very hard. But the boy remembered. And some day they had another sweatbath together and when the old man went in the sweathouse the boy put a piece of cactus in the toe of his shoe. Then afterwards they put on their clothes and the boy was watching. The old man put on his trousers and his shirt and his moccasin and when he pulled the other one it went on fast and he jumped up and let out a holler and he was hollering all over the place. The boy ran away. Everyone laughed and yelled what's the matter. The grandfather stopped then and he doesn't tease the boy any more. [Did you see this?] No—but the old man tells this story when Navahos get together.

My half-brother lived over there with my grandmother. She used to tease him by hitting him on the shins and she'd say go get some wood. Sometimes he cried. He had a .44 pistol and one day she went to the store and bought a lot of things. She put the things on her back and started home. He followed her. She couldn't look back with that big bundle behind her and he made no noise. When he got close he fired the gun and the woman fell right down and hollered. The boy rolled on the ground laughing and from that time on she wouldn't tease him any more.

PERSONAL RELATIONS IN THE WORLD OF THE HOGANS

The importance of his relatives to the Navaho can scarcely be exaggerated. The worst that one may say of another person is, "He acts as if he didn't have any relatives." Conversely, the ideal of behavior often enunciated by headmen is, "Act as if everybody were related to you."

THE BIOLOGICAL FAMILY

The basic unit of economic and social coöperation is the biological family, consisting of husband, wife, and unmarried children. Descent is traced through the mother.

Where the husband has more than one wife, each wife with her children usually occupies a separate dwelling. Joint wives are most often sisters. If a man has married a woman who has a daughter from another marriage, he may also marry the daughter when she becomes mature. Marrying an older woman and her niece was another old Navaho form but is not very frequent today. When the two or more wives are relatives, the dwellings are ordinarily side by side or, at any rate, within sight of one another; when a man marries unrelated women (which is much less frequent), they usually maintain quite separate establishments some distance apart. It is very seldom that a man has more than two wives, but a few cases of as many as four are known.

Since missionaries and formerly the government have combatted plural marriages, an attempt is made to conceal them from whites. Hence it is difficult to estimate their frequency. In one area where the facts are definitely established, seven out of about 100 married men have more than one wife. In general, plural marriages are associated with higher economic status. There is also some correlation with the type of basic economy. Where livestock is the main source of income, men have more than one wife much more frequently than in the farming areas, where monogamy is characteristic, possibly because the extended livestock operations make large families very useful. Matrilocal residence is more uniformly prevalent in livestock than in farming areas. Probably 85 per cent of the families in the western livestock region follow matrilocal practices.

Formally, from the Navaho angle, the "head of the family" is the husband. Whether he is in fact varies with his personality, intelligence, and prestige. Navaho women are often energetic and shrewish. By vigorous use of their tongues they frequently reverse or nullify decisions made by their men. The Indian Service has made the mistake of dealing too exclusively with men (just as social welfare agencies in white society tend to deal too exclusively with women) only to wonder or be annoyed when agreements reached with them were not carried out.

It is understandable that the superficial white observer concludes that the Navaho woman is little better than a chattel of her husband. She may be seen walking when her husband is on horseback; the casual white visitor does not realize that the reverse is also true, depending on which of them has a horse available, for horses are individually owned and there is no conception of joint property between husband and wife. The white man sees the men of the Navaho family riding in comfort in the front of a pickup, with women exposed to cold winds in the open truck behind. He notices a Navaho wife trailing with apparent meekness behind her husband as the pair walk the streets of Gallup. He marks the absence of small courtesies and deferences that white men normally show to their wives. A Navaho husband never, for example, assists his wife in alighting from a wagon or automobile.

Despite the absence of the symbols which whites associate with high status of women, however, there can be no doubt that the position of women among The People is very good. Their ownership of property, the system of tracing lineage through the female, the prevailing pattern of residence with the wife's people, the fact that more women than men have a ready and continual source of extra income (through their weaving), all give women a strategic advantage. Such situational circumstances are reinforced by mythology and folklore. The oft-repeated songs of Blessing Way drum in the conception that woman is supreme in the hogan. The east pole is that of Earth Woman, the south that of Mountain Woman, the west that of Water Woman, and the north that of Corn Woman. The fact that some of the most powerful and important divinities (Changing Woman, Spider Woman, Salt Woman) are female speaks volumes for the high place of women in the traditional conceptions of The People.

THE EXTENDED FAMILY

Some tasks, especially animal husbandry and agriculture, are carried out more often than not by a wider group of relatives than the simple biological family. Commonly this "extended family" consists of an older woman with her husband and unmarried children, together with her married daughters and their husbands and unmarried children.

Not all groupings, however, conform to this picture in every detail. In the first place, a considerable number of biological families live apart as independent units. In the second place, there are usually one or more unattached collateral relatives on the scene: the aged father of the older woman, or her widowed, childless sister, or a crippled niece who has never married. Such isolated individuals usually occupy separate quarters if they are able to care for themselves. If not, they may eat and sleep in the dwelling of one of the biological families, or they may have their separate hogan with some youngster assigned to cut their firewood and otherwise assist them. One study of one hundred biological families showed the following composition: 184 parents, 369 children of these unions, 182 other dependents.

In the third place, not all married daughters invariably live in or even near this group. One daughter and her husband may live alone and at a distance, or they may have associated themselves with the husband's people. Whether a young married couple goes to live with the girl's or the boy's parents depends upon a variety of factors: the relative economic status of the two groups, the need for workers in one or the other, various prestige elements, the congeniality of the persons involved, and indeed all the considerations of interpersonal relations. The influence of white customs and especially of white interpretations of inheritance laws has increased residence with the husband's people in recent years, but there is evidence that this was not unheard of as long as two generations ago. Some couples regularly divide their time and their services between the two groups. In some sections it is the custom for bride and groom to live and work for some years after marriage with one of the parental families, and later, after they have established their ability to care for themselves, to move some distance away into a state of almost complete independence.

Economic and other individuality is not lost in the extended family. But for many purposes there is economic coöperation. While every adult may have his separate account at the trading store, the older or more prosperous members of the extended family will see to it that credit is extended to the more dependent if food or clothing is really needed. Labor is pooled in herding and other productive activities.

Under the system of residing with the wife's people, men commonly participate in the activities of two extended families; for, even though their residences are with the extended families of their wives, they continue to visit frequently at the homes of their own mothers or sisters. There they often leave their sheep or other property. They are expected to attend ceremonials at their old homes and to share the expenses of these. Not infrequently the demands of a man's family of orientation (his mother's) and family of procreation (his wife's) are conflicting, and this is a deep source of strain in Navaho social organization. Perhaps the husband becomes resentful of the criticism of his father-in-law, or one brother-in-law feels that another shirks his share of the work. Some part of these tensions may be released by the patterned kind of joking that has been described previously. However, the struggle for subsistence survival is so intense that continued quarreling is too great a threat to all concerned. Either the antagonisms are repressed or suppressed most of the time, or one or more of the marriages is dissolved. These frictions within the extended family have probably been accentuated in recent years because white example and practice give no support to the native patterns.

DEALING WITH KINFOLK

The lines of contact in Navaho society are primarily those of kinship. The Navaho language differentiates many categories of relatives, making distinctions which are unfamiliar to white people: relatives on the mother's side are normally called by different terms from the corresponding relatives on the father's side; younger and older brothers and sisters are always distinguished; some relationships are foreshortened, so that the children of the mother's sisters, for example, are addressed with the same word as actual biological brothers and sisters, just as the mother's sisters are also called "mother."

Toward relatives of different classes there are, of course, prescribed ways of behaving. Some must be treated with varying degrees of respect or avoidance. Thus the relation between adult brothers and sisters, while one of deep affection, is marked by great reserve in physical contact and by certain restrictions in speech. Conservative Navahos are still careful in addressing some relatives by marriage to employ the same special linguistic forms as brothers and sisters use. These "polite" forms give a rather stiff or stilted effect to a conversation. Mothers-in-law are never supposed to look upon their sons-in-law. With some relatives one is not supposed to joke at all, with others one may not "joke bad," while with certain relatives one is expected to make jokes of sexual or obscene connotation.

Traditionally, the relationship of maternal uncles to their nephews and nieces was of great importance. These uncles assumed many of the disciplinary and instructional functions which fall to the lot of the father in white society. They had great influence in arranging, encouraging, or vetoing the marriages of their sisters' sons and daughters (particularly the latter). Moreover, there were various economic reciprocities and inheritance rights involved. A niece, in particular, could expect to inherit at least a small amount of property from each of her maternal uncles.

OWNERSHIP AND INHERITANCE

One of the difficulties in understanding an alien culture lies in concepts of ownership and inheritance. The kinds of things that are owned by persons and may be transmitted by them to their heirs, and the kinds of things which belong only to larger or smaller groups vary greatly between societies.

Among the Navahos certain things are "communal property," in which no individual or family has vested or exclusive rights. Water resources, timber areas, and patches of salt bush (which serve livestock in lieu of mineral salt) belong to all The People, and certain conventions are observed in regard to this type of property. It is not good form to cut wood within a mile or so of someone else's dwelling. One uses no other than his accustomed water hole except when that source fails or he goes on a journey. Attempts of some Navahos to emulate white practices with respect to wood and water rights are among the most bitterly resisted of all innovations.

Farm and range land "belongs" to a family. The dominant Navaho idea of ownership of such land has been well called "inherited use-ownership"; that is, the man who "owns" farm or range land can only control it for a limited period, and no "owner" can give away or otherwise alienate land from his family. Furthermore, in this matrilineal society, the real "owners" are the wife and children, and the husband is hardly more than a trustee for them.

In recent times a few wealthy Navahos who are heads of "outfits" (see p. 109) have acquired virtual control over extensive ranges. In regions off the Reservation, the prevalence of allotments and recent fencing under the Taylor Grazing Act have brought Navaho range practices closer to that for farm land and to the white pattern in general.

The concept of inherited use-ownership applies to some degree to livestock. Every animal in a flock is assigned to some member of the family, but he is not altogether free to sell his animals in quantity in order to buy a car or satisfy some other personal whim. Persons who do so are severely criticized.

Even young children have their own animals with private earmarks. In well-off families a child is given new animals each year, and this undoubtedly adds to his sense of security. Yet there is subtly implanted in him the notion that the family—not the giver, but the family as a whole—retains the right of "eminent domain." The child must take his turn in supplying meat for family meals and contribute his share when animals are being slaughtered to feed participants and guests at a ceremonial. Always it is emphasized that the produce of animals (wool, lambs or kids, milk) is in part for the general use; when necessary it is entirely for the general use.

Peach and other fruit trees are owned by a family or

an individual. If they are located on land not now in the possession of the family or individual, the owner may come only at harvest to claim the fruit.

The only property which is indisputably that of the individual consists of clothing, ornaments, saddles, ceremonial equipment, and intangibles such as songs and prayers. These the individual may dispose of exactly as he likes.

In former days Navaho inheritance was largely through the mother and her relatives, to whose clan every individual belonged, as he does today. In some areas today the usual practice is for daughters to inherit from the mother and sons from the father. In other localities, the bulk of all except "personal property" of both father and mother is divided before their death equally among sons and daughters, but land and livestock undivided at death remain within the extended family where the deceased was resident. In still other places, white inheritance customs are becoming more prevalent; wills are made and the surviving spouse shares in the estate. But in almost every area there is doubt and dispute.

There is no formal transmission of rights to grazing land. Every person, as a member of his family, inherits the right to graze livestock within a fairly well-defined area. Unused lands, so long as there were any, belonged to the first comers.

The inheritance of farm land, livestock, and fruit trees is confused at present. Much of such property is transmitted to children during the lifetime of the "trustee-owners." By the time the children are adult, each may have most of the livestock he can expect to receive from his parents. The herd which is still earmarked for elders is probably small, and will often be largely used up in connection with the ceremonials which can be expected during the illnesses of old age.

Sons who have become permanent residents with the families of their wives often ask for and receive their full share from their own parents so that they may care for their own growing children. There is usually strong pressure on them to leave the animals in the parental herd, however, and there follows the difficulty and friction which usually attend absentee ownership. A woman who "owns" farm land gradually turns it over to her daughters and their husbands, and a son may receive a piece of the farm if there are no daughters, or only one or two. As indicated previously, the man who "owns" farm land is under conflicting pressures. His wife and daughters urge him to surrender his rights, while he is still living, to his daughters or sons-in-law acting as trustees for his grandchildren. At the same time his own mother or aunts or sisters remind him that his land belongs to their (and his) clan and that he should give it to one or more of his nieces and nephews.

The inheritance of personal property is also not without doubt and dispute. Much personal property is buried with the dead. This property is usually selected by the owner before his death, and he often specifies which survivor shall receive this or that saddle or piece of jewelry which is not to be buried with him.

Items that have not been thus disposed of before the burial are parceled out at a meeting of relatives, where the older and closer family connections take the lead in the discussion. When a prosperous man or woman dies the gathering is ordinarily quite large, and includes many who, according to white standards, are very distant kin but who will expect to receive at least some token gift, however small. It is of great importance to be on hand when the division occurs, even if one is a member of the immediate family. Such a remark as this is frequently heard: "I was at school when my father died, so his relatives didn't give me a thing."

There is usually an informal understanding that ceremonial equipment goes to sons or sororal nephews who know how to carry out the appropriate rite. Failing this, the property will be claimed by the nearest relative (including clan members) who can qualify. Some ceremonial equipment, however, especially that connected with Blessing Way, is retained by the immediate family, even in default of practitioners, because it is believed to afford protection to the dwelling and its occupants.

It is obvious that differing patterns of inheritance are likely to be sources of conflict within the tribe. Furthermore, the incompatibility of persisting Navaho usages and white inheritance laws and court interpretations is the source of serious friction between Navahos and whites.

RELATIVES BEYOND THE HOGAN GROUP

A Navaho's "relatives" include more than the members of his biological and extended families and affinal kin. "Outfit," clan, and linked clan are important extensions of the circle of relations.

THE "OUTFIT"

This Western term is used to designate a group of relatives (larger than the extended family) who regularly coöperate for certain purposes. Two or more extended families, or one or more extended families linked with one or more independent biological families, may habitually pool their resources on some occasions—say, planting and harvesting, or the giving of any major ceremonial for an individual member. The differentiae of "outfit" and extended family are twofold: the members of the true Navaho extended family always live at least within shouting distance of each other, whereas the various families in an "outfit" may be scattered over a good many square miles; an extended family has its focus in the families of sisters or of brothers and/or parents and their married children, whereas the families in an "outfit," while always related, include a wider circle of kin. Participation in coöperative work is not absolutely regular, and indeed membership in an "outfit" is somewhat fluid. But the solidarity of an "outfit" will always be recognized, however vaguely, by the white trader who knows the region; he will take this unit into account in extending credit and the like.

The variations in the size and composition of "outfits" are infinite. Commonly, one biological or extended family is a kind of nucleus for the whole group, and the "outfit" will be referred to colloquially by using the name of the principal man in the nuclear family. Careful analysis shows, however, that when the traders or Navahos speak of "So-and-so's folks," this does *not* include *all* his relatives within certain degrees. Geographical distance and other factors may have the effect of excluding some relatives actually closer by blood than others embraced within the "outfit." The test is always the intensity and regularity of the economic and other reciprocities involved. The size of an "outfit" tends to depend on the wealth of its leader or, more exactly, of the leader and/or his wife or wives. Wealthy Navahos who control thousands of sheep are often the focal points of "outfits" which include a hundred or more individuals in a ramified system of dependence. Sometimes the members of an "outfit" live on lands that have unbroken geographical contiguity. In this case the "outfit" constitutes a "land-use community" which may occupy from 12,000 to 80,000 acres and include from fifty to two hundred persons.

One can usually see best who actually belongs to an "outfit" when communal ploughing is taking place in the spring or sheep dipping in the summer. Some data from the Dennehotso area in the north and from the Klagetoh area in the south give a specific picture of how individuals split up into these various units. In the Dennehotso Valley in 1934 the 669 people lived in 131 hogans. Eighteen of these were isolated; the remainder made up 37 distinct extended family groups, each of which had from two to six hogans. Nine different "outfits" could be recognized, but 108 persons could not be said to belong to any "outfit." At Klagetoh in 1939 there were 233 people living in 29 hogans. All but four of these families combined in various ways to make up eight or nine extended families. There was some coöperative work between any two or more of these extended family groups at the busy seasons.

THE CLAN

Like white people, the Navahos use relationship terms toward all "blood kin." However, The People do not limit their "relatives" along strictly biological lines. They also designate as "sisters," "fathers," etc., all members of their own clan and, in theory, all members of the clans linked with their own. The term used depends upon the sex and the relative ages of the two speakers. Members of one's father's clan are also considered relatives, but they are grouped in a smaller number of categories.

There are, or have been, sixty or more Navaho clans. The names are predominantly those of localities, suggesting that the clan was at one time a local group. Even today the clans, though having a wide geographical spread in individual membership, tend to be concentrated in certain sections. There is, for example, no area of a few hundred square miles within which members of every clan can be found, but 888 persons in the Chaco Canyon in 1938 did include one or more representatives of thirty-one different clans. It is seldom, however, that any "community" goes beyond twenty. There were members of twenty-one different clans in the Dennehotso Valley, but three of these were represented only by single individuals. The people at Klagetoh belonged to fourteen clans, and the majority represented only a few of the clans. In Chaco Canyon the Poles-Strung-Out, Under-His-Cover, Mud, Zuni, Red-Forehead, Standing-House, Parallel-Stream, Bitter-Water, and Trail-to-the-Garden clans included 595 out of the 888 persons, while the other 293 were scattered among twenty-two other clans. At Dennehotso, the Shore, Red-Forehead, Bitter-Water, Under-His-Cover, and Red-House clans accounted for 315 out of 665. Similarly, five of the fourteen clans at Klagetoh had a much larger representation than the others. The clans represented by not more than four or five persons have usually been brought in by those who enter the region through marriage.

Each Navaho belongs to the clan of his mother, but it must not be forgotten that he is equally spoken of as "born for" the clan of his father. The father's clansmen are all considered to be relatives. Thus a girl might identify herself in Navaho by saying, "I am Bitter-Water, born for Salt."

In the contemporary life of The People the principal importance of clan is that of limiting marriage choices: one may never marry within one's own clan or one's father's. There are still exceedingly few violations of these prohibitions. The Navahos treat incest of this sort and witchcraft as the most repulsive of crimes. Incestuous persons are inevitably suspected of witchcraft and are thought to be, or to be doomed to become, insane. On the other hand, at certain periods and in certain sections there have also been positive marriage preferences connected with clan. For example, to marry into the clan of paternal or maternal grandfather is still highly approved in some areas.

Clan is also important in establishing the larger circle of one's relatives. Clans may be thought of as threads of sentimental linkage which bind together Navahos who are not biologically related, who have not grown up in the same locality, who may indeed never see each other, or may do so but once in a lifetime. This sentimental bond gives rise to occasional economic and other reciprocities. Sometimes clansmen who discover each other accidentally at a large gathering will exchange gifts. A Navaho will always go out of his way to do a favor or show preference for a clan relative, even if the individual in question has been previously unknown.

In the past the clan was, with little doubt, an important agency of social control. All clansmen were responsible for the crimes and debts of other members of their clan, hence it was in their own interest to prevent murder, rape, and theft on the part of any and all clan relatives. Since any person, moreover, was dependent for emotional and economic support upon the good will of his relatives, he was usually responsive to their pressures. Government imposition of a law-and-order organization based on white patterns has tended to destroy this aspect of the native social system. The great increase in population has probably also played a part in breaking down the old pattern. Certain it is that the two systems do not mesh well together. Under the present setup native judges, policemen, and other officials are constantly accused of favoring their clan relatives. Enough of the old sentiments remain so that Navaho officials probably do feel pressure toward this sort of favoritism. But a judge, for example, is not disqualified according to the new law because he is a clansman of a plaintiff or defendant, for government officials have not recognized clan relationships.

LINKED CLANS

Every clan is associated with from one to five or six others. Thus, the Poles-Strung-Out, Mountain-Rincon, Who-Encircles-One, Close-to-Water, Grey-Earth-Place, and Yucca-Blossom-Patch clans "go together," as The People say. It is usually stated that originally the linked clans were but a single unit. They doubtless represent in most cases a splitting up under the stimulus of geographical dispersion or intra-clan quarrels, although in some instances the association is probably imaginary or accidental or the result of the affiliation of new clans derived from other tribes, rather than the product of actual historical splitting.

All of the prohibitions and obligations which apply to clansmen apply, in strict theory, to all members of linked clans, but, today at least, these must be thought of as binding only in a very mild form. Marriages into linked clans, especially those of the father, are not very infrequent. There are disagreements even among older Navahos as to whether or not certain clans should be considered linked, while many younger Navahos are almost completely ignorant of any such associations.

THE WIDER CIRCLE OF PERSONAL RELATIONS

Among The People relatives are all-important, but as in all other societies there are patterns for interaction with persons unrelated by blood or marriage.

NAMES AND NAMING

So long as the child's world is bounded by the family circle there is very little need for names. Kinship terms are enough for him to address or refer to everybody, and they in turn can designate him adequately. In case of possible confusion, a qualifier can be added to the kin term: "my oldest maternal nephew," "my maternal nephew who is the middle son of my youngest sister."

However, when the child goes outside his family group he must have a designation. Navahos do have names. The trouble is that they always have more than one "name," and this whole system is to the white man one of the most baffling aspects of the Navaho way of life. There are, first of all, the "secret" or "war" names. Names are powers to The People. To use a name very often would wear it out, whereas if the name is kept fresh and full of strength, uttering it may get its owner out of a tight hole sometime. Although "war" names are still called "secret" names by English-speaking Navahos, they are disclosed rather freely today, at any rate by girls and women. An adult woman may generally be referred to as "Tall Woman" or "Big Woman," but she will give a white census taker her "war" name with little or no reluctance. In an increasing number of families, parents will refer to their little girls or older unmarried daughters by such names. In the case of boys the "war" name is used or revealed much less often. Sometimes the name is still protected with much caution and spoken only in songs and proclamations at Enemy Way. (See Chapter 6.) It is a sign that a family has gone a long distance toward giving up the old way of life when the parents cease to give their children these "war" names, but this is not an uncommon happening among younger and more "modern" parents.

Besides these "war" names, during the course of his life every Navaho is dubbed with one or more nicknames. If a baby is tiny, the family is likely to refer to it as "Little One"; if it is unusually light-skinned they may call it "Clean Girl." These nicknames sometimes last throughout life, but more often people outside the family will coin a designation that refers to some personal characteristic or some event or occupation. Thus we get such names as "Bent Man," "Little Schoolboy," "Son of the Late Silversmith."

These nicknames are terms of reference, not of address. If a person is present, he will be spoken of by a kinship term or as "this one" and will be addressed as "my friend" or simply "thou." It is considered very impolite to use someone's name in his presence, and only Navahos who have spent much time with whites get accustomed to this. Many older Navahos will manifest embarrassment or resentment if they are called by their names to their faces. However, the white practice of summoning children by name is rapidly gaining in popularity. Usually the English or Spanish names are called out, but Navaho nicknames and even "war" names for girls are heard more and more.

Finally, school children and adults have one or more (usually more!) European names. When a child enters a school, it is asked its name. Today many are prepared for this contingency and can give both a first and a last name, or produce them on a paper written by some literate member of the family. However, the acquisition of these names hardly conforms to white practices. The youngster is as likely to use the family name of the mother as that of the father. Often the first name will be placed before the first and last name of the father. Thus we get Lilly John Pino, Frank Sam Pino, and the like. There is a tendency in some regions to use the name of one's clan for a last name. Sometimes a teen-age youth will take a name which is not that of any relative just because it happens to strike his fancy. It is quite common for a family or an individual to alter a first name which has been carried for a number of years. Someone known for ten years as Charles suddenly becomes Ben.

The European names come directly or indirectly from school names or from names assigned by traders or government officials for convenience. Some of the earlier teachers either were hard pressed to avoid duplicates or had a perverted sense of humor. Such names as Algernon Schuyler and Mumbo Jumbo do not ease the adjustment of Indians into a white world. This was amply demonstrated in recent Selective Service activities, when candidates for the Marine Corps had to answer to such names as Shadowing Lady, Popsicle, Fish Sombrero, and Angel Whiskers.

What really confuses white people is the fact that many Navahos have two or more different European names, each of which is or has been in use and appears in one or more different records. A Navaho living among or near Spanish Americans may have been assigned a Spanish name by a Spanish-speaking rancher, trader, or priest. But a government representative finds this difficult to pronounce and spell, so he provides an English substitute. Or an English-speaking trader tells an old Navaho he will put his account under "Shoemaker," but when the Navaho renders this for the trader's successor it sounds so improbable that the new trader invents a fresh designation. Hence, a single Navaho will have as many as seven or eight different names which are current in a region. In white society only authors, actors, and criminals use aliases. If one goes into a new community and hears about Percival Q. Bloggins and also about Archibald L. Smythe, one is justified in assuming that two different people are being spoken of. Not so among the Navahos. But because census takers work on an assumption which is correct enough among whites, one and the same person appears upon the census rolls as several individuals.

THE "LOCAL GROUP" OR "COMMUNITY"

These terms are used in quotation marks to warn the reader that they are not intended to convey the meaning and connotations which apply to a close group like a village. But groups which are determined by locality and cut across the lines of kinship are important today in the workings of Navaho society. It is probable that in the old days the band was the significant large social grouping, and today certain local groups—especially those isolated from the rest of the Navahos, like Ramah, Puertocito, and Canyoncito—tend still to have the character of a band. They are referred to by other Navahos by words designating the locality, and they have, or in the recent past have had, a single headman each.

The extent to which The People who live in areas set apart either by topography or by tradition have developed definite rules for working together varies greatly. In some sections the local group simply lives in the same area. In others there is regular coöperation in such activities as building or caring for a day school, the annual sheep dipping, "meetings," and "courts." Any mention of "chapters" established by the Indian Service in the 1920's, cf. Chapter 4.

LEADERSHIP AND AUTHORITY

When The People work together in groupings other than those of kinship it is exceedingly difficult to define the integrating forces or the basis of leadership. At a ceremonial it is, of course, the "medicine men" who give directions. Otherwise, one can only say that older men and women are generally deferred to and that there are local "headmen." But both of these statements need qualification and explanation. In some areas at present leadership appears to be less in the hands of older people than of the middle-aged or even the young, largely because they have the great advantage of speaking English during a period when effective communication with governmental authorities is the principal means by which leaders justify their position or fail to do so.

Headmen have no powers of coercion, save possibly that the people sometimes fear them as potential witches, but they do have responsibilities. They are often expected, for example, to look after the interests of the needy who are without close relatives or whose relatives neglect them, but all they can do with the neglectful ones is to talk to them. Decisions as to "community" policy can be reached only by the consensus of a local meeting. The People themselves are the real authority. No program put forward by a headman is practicable unless it wins public endorsement or has the tacit backing of a high proportion of the influential men and women of the area. Rich men often exert great power through economic pressure, but they work mostly behind the scenes and are seldom invested with the authority of formal leadership. This avoidance of choosing the wealthy for public office is seen in Ramah, where most headmen and delegates to the tribal council have come from the lower economic half of the group.

Headmen were formerly appointed by the Indian Service, but in many cases this constituted only official recognition of *de facto* leadership. In some areas today the chapter presidents or delegates to the tribal council perform the functions formerly exercised by the headmen, but in other localities a headman exists in addition to the chapter officers. Elections are held each year at meetings in which all adults in the locality, both men and women, may participate and vote for the delegate to the tribal council and the president, vice-president, and secretary of the chapter. Sometimes the same individuals are reëlected year after year, but more often there is quite a turnover in these offices. The headman, on the other hand, normally holds office for life unless he so completely loses the confidence of his group that a forced, formal abdication or a gradual, informal abdication takes place, or unless he feels that he no longer has the energy to carry out his duties. In the latter case he usually recommends a successor, ordinarily a nephew or some other clan relative or his son, but possibly a non-relative. Such a recommendation is more often than not accepted by the meeting.

When a headman dies suddenly, his successor is selected after discussion in a meeting. In case the succession is not so clear-cut there is a long talk in a meeting. It is not expected that a man will openly seek the office, but rival candidates will often make speeches at the invitation of others. In the old days, after group approval had been expressed at a meeting, the final warrant of authority was the performance of a special form of Blessing Way (Chief Blessing Way) over the new incumbent. Today this rite is often omitted, but there appears to be a strong bias in favor of selecting as headman someone who is himself a practitioner of Blessing Way.

Selection of headmen and of chapter officers and all formal choices of policy are arrived at by group decision in assemblages convoked by the headman or by a chapter officer. Meetings are also often held on the occasion of a "court," when Indian judges visit the community. Once the meeting occurs, anyone present may introduce new business of any sort. Excessive drinking or the sexual conduct of individuals may be discussed. Complaints of injury to property or person may be made, and the offender instructed to make payment by way of restitution. Meetings are almost invariably long drawn out. Talking goes on interminably with great respect for conventions of oratory which prescribe various courteous references to preceding speakers, endless repetitions of matters previously covered, extended circumstantial accounts of events which are—from a white point of view—utterly irrelevant. When a Navaho family go to a meeting, they go for all day. Discussion continues for many hours without a break, but individuals walk in and out of the building or the outdoor circle where the speakers are holding forth. The gathering provides an occasion for the exchange of gossip, for trading, and for negotiations between families over a projected marriage, as well as for the announced business. The present practice of actually voting for candidates or on policy decisions is a white innovation and still makes most older and middle-aged Navahos uncomfortable, since the Navaho pattern was for discussion to be continued until unanimity was reached, or at least until those in opposition felt it was useless or impolitic to express further disagreement.

While meetings are interesting and of great importance as providing an occasion for free voicing of sentiments and for public thrashing out of disagreements, their significance is considerably less than the decisions informally arrived at between the heads of "outfits" and other leaders behind the scenes. Indeed, informality is the keynote to the whole system.

The contrast here with Pueblo Indians is instructive. Although Navahos and Pueblos have much in culture and in situation which is very similar, Pueblo social organization is mainly formal, whereas Navaho social organization is mainly informal. This makes inevitable different ways of attaining ends and different types of social change.

Other leaders, as well as headmen, exert their influence in an informal way. Age and experience, ceremonial knowledge, oratorical skill, wealth, and any combination of these factors can bring prestige and influence which may extend beyond the blood and affinal kin within an "outfit." To such leaders, quarrels between husband and wife, between relatives, between extended families or different "outfits" are brought for mediation. These leaders will be called upon to give general advice and moral exhortation to all assembled at a curing ceremonial or a wedding. At the larger gatherings for a "squaw dance" or a Night Way (Yeibichai) or Mountain Top Way Chant several leaders may speak more formally, deploring the amount of drinking carried on by the young, condemning an outbreak of petty thievery, exhorting coöperation with (or resistance to) a government program of the moment.

An important part of the difficulty in describing the Navaho patterns to outsiders is that The People have a set of categories altogether different from that of white Western culture. The category "government," something fixed and powerful to white people, is foreign to Navaho thinking. Authority, to their minds, extends only indefinitely and transitorily beyond the established rules of behavior between sex groups, age groups, and, especially, classes of relatives. There are headmen, but the sphere of their influence widens and narrows with the passage of time, the emergence of a new leader, the rise of a new faction. The prestige of some headmen often spreads beyond their own local region. Through channels excessively informal they can sometimes "swing" most of the population of a number of local groups to a given course of action. By and large, however, control of individual action rests in The People as a group and not in any authoritative individual or body.

The whole mechanism of Navaho social control is too fluid, too informal, too vague to be readily understood by white people who think of authority in terms of courts, police, and legislative assemblies. But Navaho social controls are extremely effective for those who remain within their own group. Never to be lost sight of is the fact that the basis of the system was and still is the family. To live at all in this barren region the individual must have the economic coöperation of others, and such coöperation is hardly likely to come to those who deviate from the "right way of doing things," as The People see it. Thus the major threat which restrains the potential offender is the withdrawal of the support and the good will of his neighbors, most of whom are "family" to the Navaho. Gossip and criticism were and are major means of social control throughout Navaho society. These diffuse sanctions are less effective today than in former times because, by taking up wage work for whites, the offender can escape both the need for economic coöperation by the group and the criticism which the group aims at deviants.

Still significant are a variety of diffuse and organized sanctions involving the supernatural. Navaho ideology, in effect, defines disease as a social sanction. If a man or a woman gets ill, the question is asked: What has he or she done which is socially disapproved? Likewise, those who engage in certain forms of antisocial behavior are liable to suspicion, accusation, and, in extreme cases, execution as witches.

THE PEOPLE AS A TRIBE

At times in the last century there tended to be a major headman for the northern, eastern, southern, and western Navahos respectively—though such a simple schematization is misleading. "Twelve peace chiefs" or "the twelve peace chiefs and twelve war chiefs" are mentioned in old descriptions of the Navahos, but it seems likely that these are ideal patterns with a strong element of retrospective falsification. Whether they ever existed or not, it has not been established that there ever was a "Navaho Tribe" in the sense of an organized, centralized "political" entity.

Just as there is no complete cultural or "racial" unity, so also The People are only beginning to have what may accurately be designated as a "tribal" or "national" consciousness. Previous to 1868, the largest unit of effective social coöperation seems to have been a band of Indians who occupied a defined territory and acknowledged the leadership of a single headman. These local bands acted without much reference to other such units. Interior groups, for example, habitually raided Mexican settlements, knowing full well that they themselves were protected by distance and inaccessibility and that bands whom the troops could reach more easily would bear the brunt of the reprisal. When The People were all treated as a unit by the United States Government and were assigned a common Reservation, this doubtless had the effect of promoting tribal cohesiveness. This tendency was counteracted, however, by the later division into six administrative districts, which existed until 1933. Moreover, the original separatist tendencies were reinforced by the establishment of trading posts, missions, and schools in localities which often corresponded to the centers of the earlier bands.

Whatever tribal feeling The People have today rests upon the following factors: a common language; a common designation for themselves as The People as distinct from all others; a cultural heritage which is, *in general*, the same; a territory with a certain topographical unity, where the occupants are mostly Navahos and where many mountains and other natural features are enshrined in a common mythology; the fact that almost all The People constitute a single governmental administrative unit with a single elected council for the whole tribe. The system of clans and linked clans also makes for unity, to the extent that they have cross-regional representation and make legion the number of individuals whom any given Navaho addresses as "my relative." To some degree, all of these factors point to a general tendency: The People are becoming increasingly conscious of common background, common problems, a common need to unite to protect their interests against the encroachment of whites.*

* Considerable additional material, both factual and psychological, on interpersonal relations is to be found in Leighton and Kluckhohn, *Children of The People* (Cambridge: Harvard University Press, 1947).

4. THE PEOPLE AND THE WORLD AROUND THEM

For 300 years some Navahos have had some contacts with white people, and their contacts with other Indian tribes of course go back beyond the dawn of history. But in the last century The People's contacts with their neighbors have been greatly intensified and have been far-reaching in their results, and of this period the last twenty-five years have perhaps had the greatest total effect upon The People in terms of their relationships with the world around them.

The relations of The People to non-Navahos in recent times have been principally, of course, a matter of their relations with whites, for all The People have been directly or indirectly affected by the white world, whereas many Navahos have never seen even those other Navahos who live on the opposite side of the Reservation from themselves. In some of the more remote parts of the Reservation, face-to-face contacts with whites are limited to a few white persons, none of whom (except perhaps the trader) is seen very often. But, even where actual penetration of whites into the tribe is so limited, no Navaho is immune today to the conflicts engendered by the dissemination of white ideas through missionaries, traders, government employees, and other white persons. Furthermore, during the war years at least 20,000 Navahos left the Reservation to join one of the armed services or to engage in other work related to the highly increased labor market during the war years. The very large majority of these people has returned either to the Reservation or to its borderland. In the years following the war, this process of departure and return has continued. The reasons are many and varied, and although the intensity is less than during the war years, it nonetheless continues with great regularity. This has accelerated the dissemination of white ideas almost beyond belief.

OTHER INDIANS

The relationships of Navahos with other Indians are conditioned by geography. The People of the Navaho Mountain region trade and intermarry with a small remnant band of Piutes. Navahos of the Shiprock region have all seen Utes, and a number of them have attended Ute ceremonials. Navahos of the southwestern part of the Navaho country see Havasupai and Walapai Indians, if only at the white-sponsored Fourth of July celebrations in Flagstaff, and many have had some dealings with White Mountain or San Carlos Apaches. Those on the extreme east meet the Jicarilla Apaches, those of the southeast meet the Mescalero and Chiricahua Apaches occasionally. Contacts with the various Apache groups tend to be more intimate than those with other Indians (except possibly the Pueblos) because of the similarities in language and the sense of a common ancestry and background. Certain Navaho and certain Apache families have a "guest-friend" relationship. That is, they visit back and forth every year or so, exchanging hospitality and gifts. This same pattern prevails between many Navaho and Pueblo families. Almost all Navahos except those in the northwest Navaho country have had fairly frequent dealings with Pueblo Indians—Hopi, Zuni, Jemez, or Laguna-Acoma—depending upon where the Navaho family lives.

With all these Indian groups there are more or less systematic exchanges of goods. The Navahos trade rugs and silver to the Utes for the baskets used in the Navaho ceremonies like that of marriage. They get beef from Apaches, corn and fruit from the Hopi, gourds, reeds, and other things used ceremonially from Rio Grande Pueblo Indians. Certain items of ceremonial equipment are regularly obtained from as far off as Taos. Enterprising Laguna and Hopi Indians peddle peaches, melons, and other fruit in trucks over wide stretches of the Navaho country in late summer and autumn.

In recent years, the Gallup Inter-Tribal Indian Ceremonial has become a magnet to Navahos from all parts of the Reservation—but in like manner, it has attracted numbers of all of these other neighboring groups, and indeed, has even brought members of tribes from as far away as Florida, North Carolina, and the Plains states. The annual Ceremonial, which occurs in midsummer has for the Indian a twofold purpose. It provides a major outlet for the display and sale of craft and art work from all participating Indian groups. The range of materials brought to the Ceremonial is wide indeed: one may find many of the best examples of the traditional weaving, silverwork, pottery and basketry. Other fine examples, however, are not traditional, but designed with the needs and desires of the outside world in mind. A traditional silver conch belt is exhibited only a few steps from a table service for twelve; a sand painting may be equally close to a watercolor or oil painting. In spite of the variety in type, quality of the works brought to the Ceremonial is consistently high. Ceremonial prizes are an added incentive for preserving traditional crafts and maintaining high standards of workmanship.

The social activities conducted during the Gallup Ceremonial are probably the greater attraction. Far more Indians come for this reason than come to display and sell their wares. Indeed, it may be said that for many of The People, the Ceremonial is the highest social event in the year. At various times during the day, traditional dances are performed before a large public audience. For many, however, the contacts made during "non-working" hours are far more important. Navaho squaw dances are held throughout most of the day and night, and are quite freely attended by Indians of all the other groups, and not infrequently by whites. Most other Indian groups hold similar gatherings at some point during the festivities. In its entirety, the Gallup Inter-Tribal Indian Ceremonial offers The People the widest range of face-to-face contact with both Indian and white peoples.

At the local level also, there is a good deal of mutual interest in each other's ceremonies and attendance back and forth, though Pueblo Indians (especially those of the Rio Grande valley) exclude The People from certain rites. Some Pueblos have dances that are called "Navaho" or in which Navahos are impersonated; others have borrowed Navaho songs; sometimes Pueblo clowns mimic or burlesque Navahos at public out-of-door ceremonials. Conversely, there is no doubt that, in both ancient and recent times, Navahos have borrowed myths and rituals from Pueblo Indians.

In all contacts—ceremonial, social, and economic—exchanges of ideas and information occur. In past years this has also taken place in off-Reservation boarding schools where some of the students have come from Indian tribes whose territory is distant from the land of The People. Recently this has also occurred in some mixed day schools, and occasionally in colleges. Thus many young Navahos have had personal contact with the thoughts and ways of Indian groups that older Navahos seldom or never knew.

More adequate generalizations about the relationships of Navahos with their Indian neighbors would entail lengthy and complicated discussion, but the most interesting fact for our purposes would seem to be the growth during recent years of some sense of solidarity with all other Indians, in spite of historical particularism and animosities. A few words should, however, be said about the more clear-cut stereotypes. In many contexts the Navahos classify all Pueblo Indians by a single word which means "town-dwellers." The feeling-tone is an intricate mixture of the old contempt (for Pueblos as poor fighters and as a trifle effete generally) and fearful respect (for Pueblos as skillful magicians and as sophisticates in rational techniques), together with "realistic" hostility in those cases (Hopi, Zuni, etc.) where there are disputes over land rights.[1] The Pueblos return the contempt with interest, looking down on Navahos as ignorant, barbaric, and untrustworthy. The Navaho attitude toward the Apaches is sometimes patronizing—the Navahos seem to feel that the Apache way of life is ruder than theirs—but there is also a strong note of respect based upon the war prowess of the Apaches and their general toughness. Piutes, Utes, Havasupais, and Walapais are usually spoken of (and sometimes treated) with a slight superciliousness tinged with mockery.

DIVISIONS AMONG WHITES AS SEEN BY THE PEOPLE

Over and above the distinctions made among whites on the basis of their occupational roles as traders, missionaries, Indian Service employees, and the like, the Navahos tend to have a picture of groupings in white society which differs from the one that would usually be given by the white resident.

Navahos almost invariably make the distinction between "Americans" and "Mexicans" (Spanish Americans), most of whom are the descendants of Spanish colonials whose settlement of New Mexico long antedated the founding of the present Mexican nation. The differentiation has a historical foundation but also reflects present-day variations in behavior. The relationships between Indians and Spanish Americans in towns like Gallup, Grants, and Flagstaff show many instructive nuances. On the one hand, there are many subtle recognitions of the fact that both are "depressed groups." A common front is implied in frequently reiterated verbalizations, and is expressed in action as well. For example, Spanish Americans will not only sell Indians liquor for profit but also obtain it for them as a favor. They will shelter drunken Indians and otherwise protect them against the law of the "Anglos" as non-Spanish-speaking whites are called in the Southwest. A "Mexican" who thinks he has been "witched" will sometimes go to a Navaho "medicine man" to be "treated." It is most exceptional for Indians to receive hospitality in white homes in the towns, but many Indian and Spanish-American families in rural areas maintain a connection of reciprocal guest-friendship. On the other hand, gangs of adolescent or young adult Spanish Americans often waylay, beat up, and rob Indians (especially intoxicated ones) by night, as they would not dare to treat Anglo-Americans. Bitter and bloody knife fights between small groups of Indians and Spanish Americans are common—but not between either group and Anglos.

While in many contexts Navahos lump all Anglos together, they frequently refer to Mormons, and occasionally (fairly consistently in some regions) to Texans, by separate words. The complete story behind these practices would be interesting but long. One comment, however, should be added. During the past forty years, more and more trading stores on and near the Reservation have come into the hands of Mormons. This trend is partly a function of geography, of intra-Mormon solidarity, and of economic practices characteristic of Mormons. But other evidence could be adduced to show that in the early days Mormons got along a little better with Indians than did most pioneers who entered the region. The writers are inclined to connect this fact with Mormon teachings that Indians are descendants of the lost tribes of Israel. Hence, Mormons tended to show more respect for and interest in Indian customs; more than other whites perhaps, they gave Indians a sense of being a part (and a worthy part) of the world as a whole. Today the picture is not so clear; nevertheless, Navahos continue to apply a different word to Mormons from that used for other Anglos.

We see, then, how a thoughtful Navaho who was asked about the relations of the various groups of people in his country would not differentiate them merely as "Indian" and "white." Each of these groups would be clearly subdivided in his mind and his attitudes toward them would be quite distinct. Unfortunately many white people do not grasp this fact. It is not a priori inference but mere reporting of firsthand observation to declare that the intelligent white administrator who visits the area fleetingly sees the problem solely in terms of the Indian non-Indian dichotomy or, at best, in terms of whites and different Indian tribes. Most resident administrators (whose understanding of other aspects of the situation is often far from superficial) grasp only the latent or active hostilities between various Indian tribes and the fact that these tribes differentiate, somehow, between Anglos and Spanish Americans. The strong feeling attached to the various terms used by The People in their own language colors their reactions to the white individuals who play various occupational roles in the Navaho country.

TRADERS TO THE PEOPLE

As noted in Chapter 2, the place of traders in the Navaho economy is a highly important one, but perhaps even more significant is their role as white individuals who have spread white ideas and practices among The People. During decades when most Navahos saw government employees only rarely and felt the government chiefly as a remote limiting agency, they had weekly or even daily contacts with the nearest trader. He and his family constituted, for all practical purposes, the white world.

Today, when most parts of the Reservation are not so completely isolated from the larger white world, traders are still thought of as important exemplars of white ways of doing things. Storekeepers perform a variety of social services for The People: the trader's wife often dispenses simple medicines and gives first aid; the trader sometimes buries Navaho dead, mediates in quarrels, assists in settling estates, and translates and writes letters. This latter service became doubly important during the war years. In many ways the trader acts as a buffer against white society: he may help a Navaho get an automobile license or intercede with the police in his behalf. Navahos seek the opinions of trusted traders on governmental policies and programs and have acquired from them much useful information on animal husbandry, agriculture, and weaving.

It is hard to make fair generalizations about the character of the traders. Some of the finest men and women the writers have ever known have been traders to The People. There have also been a few who have mercilessly and shamelessly exploited the Indians' ignorance of markets and of simple arithmetic. The old situation is rapidly altering with the great increase in the number of stores, with more frequent opportunities for Navahos to trade in the towns, and with the increase of their school knowledge. But traders are still significant in helping the Navahos market their goods, in encouraging native handicrafts, and in otherwise promoting the economic development of the tribe.

As always in the field of relations with whites, there is a great deal of pure misunderstanding. In past times, because The People objected to any change in the prices of such staples as coffee, flour, and sugar, some traders instituted the practice of selling these items at a constant figure, which was sometimes below cost; naturally they compensated by markups on other articles. These devices were not necessarily dishonest, but those who have left the Reservation and returned noticed the discrepancy. In a general atmosphere of suspicion, they interpreted these practices as further evidence of the victimizing of Indians by whites. On the other hand, the advent of several Navaho community-owned stores has been felt by many white traders as a threat.

THE WORD OF AN ALIEN GOD

The Franciscan Fathers and the Christian Reformed, Presbyterian, Episcopal, Methodist, Baptist, and Latter Day Saints (Mormon) churches carry on missionary activities in the Navaho country. There are also a number of non-denominational Christian groups working among The People. Each group has one or more mission stations on the Reservation which serve as centers for religious activities, and staff members visit government schools to give religious instruction to pupils whose parents request or accept it. By 1942 for example, there were at least 300 workers among the Navaho; by 1945 the number of missionaries increased considerably, due in large part to the cessation of missionary activities in various war areas. Many of the missionaries represent aggressively "fundamentalist" denominations. Today many of these workers are Navahos. Although in the past they served almost exclusively as interpreters or in other subordinate capacities, Navaho preachers have recently been conducting Sunday services in Navaho built churches.

In addition to teaching and preaching the Christian religion, the missionaries operate schools and hospitals and offer various other social services. Their curriculum resembles that of the traditional public school of the area rather than the work in the government schools, where the objectives are to prepare children for life on the Reservation as well as in white society. Mission vocational work is mostly the traditional shopwork, homemaking, and typing taught in white schools. All of the mission schools place great emphasis on learning English, and some of them have had marked success, though this has been accomplished in certain instances at the price of forbidding children to speak their native tongue in or out of the classroom.

Both on and off the Reservation, hospitals, clinics, and other medical facilities are provided for the Navahos by the missions. In connection with the hospital at Ganado, for instance, there is a school of nursing whose special objective is to train Indian nurses of various tribes.

Missionaries offer other social services, such as reading and writing letters and giving advice on business and legal matters. They also distribute clothing and other forms of assistance.

It is difficult indeed to evaluate the influence of these religious groups in the past and at present. The number of nominal Christians among the Navahos is fairly large in some localities, but most of them continue their adherence to native beliefs and practices. Perhaps one factor to account for this is the sheer number of missionaries, and the divergent tenets of their religions. Of those who practice the Christian religion exclusively, it is merely factual to point out that a higher proportion are directly or indirectly dependent on the missions for their livelihood.

The smallness of the number of practicing converts is not too difficult to account for. Christianity speaks of far-off lands and places which the Navahos cannot visualize; their own stories tell of the four sacred mountains, at least one of which is visible almost everywhere in the Navaho country. The Bible speaks only of a male God and of a society where authority and responsibility centers chiefly in men. Navahos miss Changing Woman, perhaps the principal Navaho divinity, and the whole feeling for the position of women embodied alike in their own social organization and religious lore. The picture of a god who is entirely good is hard for The People to understand, for their whole outlook insists that all beings have an evil as well as a good side.

Navahos do make wide use of the social services provided by the missionaries, and the advice of some of them is frequently sought. Some of the medical facilities are good, and Navahos utilize them freely.

The difficulties that have arisen from missionary activities appear to have stemmed largely from their efforts to suppress native custom or to urge strenuously the substitution of white customs, oftentimes in spheres which seem to the Navahos outside the province of the missionaries. This policy has engendered resistance among The People, and even ridicule. The comment of one young mission-school graduate is representative.

> That missionary came here today and tried to make my husband buy a marriage license, but my husband said he didn't have a dollar. He has been trying to get my brother to buy a license for a year. The other missionary tried for two years and got tired of it. His wife said, "We're married all right. We don't need any paper. You tell him you don't know, you'll have to ask your wife—then he won't talk so long to you."

Certain Protestant schools, in particular, have consistently followed a policy of exterminating the native culture. Students who want to attend Navaho ceremonials are forbidden to do so, and thus are caught between the expectations of their parents and the demands of the missionaries. This sort of activity results in the confusion of those young Navahos who belong to both worlds—white and Indian.

Much of this policy comes from the failure of many missionaries to understand the native point of view and their apparent lack of interest in doing so. For example, a young Navaho woman was asked in 1933 what she remembered about her school experience. Her account, which is given below, refers to the period between 1918 and 1926, but its high points can be paralleled from accounts by recent students in mission schools, though physical punishment seems to be rare today.

> My sister got sick and they brought her home. I wanted to take her place so bad that they let me, so my father and mother took me to the Mission School

and the matron wanted to take our pictures, but I didn't want to and I ran away but the matron caught me and dragged me back by my blanket. I put my blanket over my head and that is the way they took my picture. The matron wanted to give me a bath but I cried so hard my mother had to come. They took me into the bathroom and the matron tried to take my clothes off but I didn't want her to and I screamed so hard my mother spanked me and that made me cry harder. Then they put me into the tub and I jumped out and tried to run away but they caught me and my mother told me to shut up. I stayed at — through the eighth grade . . .

[Do you remember sometimes when you were scared, or had a good time?] Once, I ran away. The teacher wanted us to sing songs and some of us didn't sing. She said if we didn't sing we would have to stand up and sing alone. She made some of the boys do this, but I wouldn't. The song was "My Country 'Tis of Thee." She took me into her room and strapped me. Then she looked at me, she wanted me to cry but I wouldn't. She said, "Have you had enough?" I didn't say anything so she strapped me again. [Did you sing?] Yes, I sang a little bit. She said, "If you haven't had enough I'll send you to Mr. X. He is the head missionary and he has a long heavy strap." Then I ran away but my family sent me back again. [Were some of the teachers nice?] Yes, some were, but that lady was always that way . . . Then once in the sixth grade, we had a man who brought the food to the dining room. He was always strapping the boys and when we worked in the kitchen the cooks always strapped us. Once I was hit very hard and my nose bled because I peeled the potatoes too thick. But when this man came around he strapped a boy and the boy jumped up. He was going to fight. [Was the man an Indian?] No, he was a white man. [Was he a missionary?] No, he was just a Christian. He knocked that boy down and he sat on his stomach and then he kept hitting him in the face and one of the cooks ran in and she was crying but she couldn't stop the man. That boy's face was all red and swollen, and his sister swore at that man and he came over to our table and said to me, "Did you say that?" I said I didn't say anything but he made me come in the kitchen and he took some thin pieces of wood from a box and he hit my hands until he broke the wood but I wouldn't cry, so he got a piece of pinyon from the woodbox. It was that kind they use in the stove. He kept on beating my hands. They got cut and swollen and I couldn't close them. That night he took me over to his room where he lived. He said, "Why did you say those things?" but we said, "We didn't, we told you so." We got after him and he said, "Well, I want you to be good girls. I am leaving here." I think of that man lots of times. I hate him. Sometimes I see him even now and get so mad I want to get even with him.

[But you were there eight years and you only got punished twice.] Oh, no, lots of times we had to hold out our hands so they could hit it with a ruler. Generally they did this twelve times. Then we got demerits. Most of us got them for talking Navaho. We were not allowed to talk Navaho. When I got a few they made me eat standing up. Sometimes they made us stand on a stool while everyone ate supper. [Did everyone laugh at you?] Yes, that's what they did. And after supper when we could sometimes play they made us stand in a corner. But if you had more demerits the worst thing was on Sunday afternoon they made us stand in the sun all afternoon out by those posts. [You mean for half an hour?] No, from one o'clock to five.

It should be stated here that this sort of senseless brutality to Indian children was not peculiar to the mission schools, for similar treatment of children in government boarding schools for Indians at that period is a matter of record. It may be suspected that in the mission schools (at least in the past) it arose in part out of the frustrations experienced by missionaries and their assistants. Most of them were unquestionably sincere people. They worked hard at their self-imposed task, but—with reason—they despaired of attaining their objectives. For six or eight or more years before the children came to the missionaries, they had heard the myths and seen and participated in the small rites of daily life. They had been patients in the curing chants. They had gone with their families to all-night public exhibitions, where dancers, masked to imitate the Navaho divinities, sang, danced, and shouted in the light of large fires. This imagery and the excitements and fears accompanying it were stored away in the unconscious long before the youngsters could reason or objectify what they saw. All this conditioned them fundamentally, so that subsequent Christian imagery could not supplant or alter it. Anything which affected them from white culture in later years was a veneer which readily cracked when they had occasion to reëxperience their own tribal religious emotions.

The very woman whose story appears above, after eight years at a missionary school where every possible effort was expended to erase the influence of her culture, and after she herself thought she was a Christian, went through the Navaho initiation ceremony at her very first opportunity. She was already twenty-one years old at this time, but white influence dating back thirteen years had not quieted the emotional values of her tribal imagery. This is how she described her initiation a few years later:

> They say you must do this four times and if you don't your eyes will be bad when you are old because you have looked at the Yeibichai's masks. I was so scared when the men came. [You mean when they yelled at you?] Yes, I thought my heart would stop and I was shaking all over.

Another woman of about the same age who is a graduate of the same school was also a "backslider." She said:

> I went to the Mission School when I was a little over five and I went away when I was fourteen. Later I was married. I was a Christian. I told everyone they had better be Christians or they would be lost when they died. When I think how I talked to my people I am ashamed. My father said I had better stop that talk, why did I want to go with white people after I died and leave my people? Then my baby about two years old got sick. I took her to the hospital at that Mission and they couldn't make her well. She got worse so I brought her home and they had a four-night sing. In two days she was well. Then my sister died when she was having a child and a couple of days later I was walking to a hogan in the moonlight and I saw her. She was on horseback and she rode right by me. She was just two yards away. I was so scared I didn't know anything . . . After that I don't believe all that stuff the Christians talk about. They say after you die you go to heaven or you go down and get punished. I don't believe that. I believe after we die we live right here. We go around just the same. Some Navahos believe we go back to the world we came from.

Apart from the results of their medical and social service aids to the Navaho and certain aspects of mission schooling, the influence of the missionaries would seem to be restricted to rather small clique groups. The effectiveness of their purely religious activity has been limited in part by the fact that so few of them have had any command of the language of The People. There are some exceptions to this generalization. Some of the Franciscan Fathers, for example, have learned the language, lived long among the Navahos, and won their confidence. In general, it can be said that the effect of any given missionary is chiefly dependent upon his personal qualities. On the whole, however, the attitude today of most missionary groups is more tolerant and understanding than was the case thirty and more years ago.

THE PEOPLE AND THE GOVERNMENT: THE NAVAJO AGENCY

Most of the contacts of The People with the government for the past three generations have been with the Bureau of Indian Affairs in the Department of the Interior, referred to subsequently as the Indian Service, through its local agency, now called the Navajo Agency. Prior to 1934 there were six separate agencies for the Navahos. The Navajo Agency, which is responsible for the economic and social welfare and the health of seventy-five thousand Reservation Navahos, performs functions which are probably more varied, multiform, and complex than those of any other governmental unit in the country. They include services rendered in white communities by local, county, state, and federal agencies in the fields of natural resources, engineering, administration, and community services such as health, education, social service, and law and order. Thus the Navajo Agency carries on many of the activities of county supervisors and farm agents,[2] boards of education, departments of public welfare, public health departments, and the general administrative machinery of city governments. In addition it has functions which elsewhere are commonly performed by insurance companies, banks, and other private agencies. All of these tasks must be carried out in the face of linguistic difficulties and old and deep-seated antagonisms and misunderstandings, in a vast area where travel and communication are uncertain at best. It is small wonder that such duties require for even curtailed services an immense staff (nearly 1,200 persons in 1945), many of them technicians. The prewar annual budget ran to almost $3,000,000, but was cut during the war years to $1,800,000 (1944). Since the war, the budgetary appropriation of the Federal Government to the Navahos has increased somewhat—in 1957, $4,604,545. But, during this period, and especially in the last decade, the income of the Navajo Tribe derived from natural resources has greatly increased—$50,000 in 1940 as compared with almost $30,000,000 in 1958. With these increased funds, The People, through the Tribal Council, have undertaken many services formerly provided by the Federal Government.

THE ADMINISTRATIVE SETUP

In 1934 the six independent Navajo agencies were unified and centralized into the Navajo Agency with headquarters at Window Rock. The Resources Branch of the Agency has divisions responsible for land use and management, soil conservation, farm extension work, livestock management, grazing, and forestry. The Engineering Branch directs irrigation, construction, roads, and communications activities. Community Services includes all work in health, education, and social service. In the Administrative Branch are centered the fiscal, personnel, and other "housekeeping" functions of the Agency. Traders relations and the maintenance of law and order are functions of two other sections of the Agency. The work of the Resources and the Engineering Branches, traders relations, and the furnishing of relief have been indicated in Chapter 2. Other community services and the maintenance of law and order will be discussed in following sections of the present chapter.

All the work of the Navajo Agency is carried on under the direction of the general superintendent at Window Rock. For purposes of local administration, the Reservation and nearby areas are now divided into nine districts, which range in size from 185,000 to 1,750,000 acres and in population from about 1,800 to 8,500. Each district is in the charge of a district supervisor, who is responsible for carrying out in his district all programs of the Agency except education, health, and construction. His duties therefore include administrative relations with Navahos in the work programs of farm, range, and livestock, the maintenance of law and order, distribution of relief, and selective service. One of his principal responsibilities is increasing Indian participation in the programs of the Navajo Agency. The job of the district supervisor calls for almost superhuman ability if it is to be carried out with real success, but some district supervisors have excellent relations with the Navahos and real understanding of them and their problems.

EDUCATION FOR NAVAHOS

It is not certain when the first schools for Navaho children were established. The first recorded institution, a day school, dates from about 1870, but there may have been earlier establishments. The first boarding school was built at Fort Defiance in 1883.

The guiding principle of early Indian education was that the children must be fitted to enter white society when they left school, and hence it was thought wise to remove them from home influences and often to take them as far away as California or even Pennsylvania in order to "civilize" them faster. The policy was really to go behind the existing social organization in order to dissolve it. No effort was made to prepare them for dealing effectively with Reservation conditions. Yet more than 95 per cent of the Navaho children went home, rather than to white communities, after leaving school, only to find themselves handicapped for taking part in Navaho life because they did not know the techniques and customs of their own people. Moreover, many of the government boarding schools did not differ greatly from the mission school previously described. The children were forbidden to speak their own languages, and military discipline prevailed. Pupils thus spent their childhood years under a mercilessly rigid system which could not offer the psychological ad-

7. Council meeting in a schoolhouse

8. Early morning at a ceremonial

vantages of family life in even the poorest Indian home. Small wonder that many students of that era are today bitter critics of the government.

Eight of the old boarding schools still exist on or near the Reservation, and most of these have been expanded or rebuilt. The plants consist of boys' and girls' dormitories, dining hall, classroom building, farm and shop buildings, and teachers' and other employees' quarters. None of these plants could be called modern and few major improvements have been made since 1912. Since about 1933 the curriculum and philosophy employed have differed radically from the earlier program. The present attempt is to provide the pupil with the necessary educational tools to enable him to take his place in either the white or the Navaho world. Only three of the boarding schools maintain a high-school department at present, and there are approximately eight hundred high-school pupils. The other boarding schools carry instruction through the sixth grade. However, the whole picture of Navaho education is at present undergoing rapid expansion; for example, during the years 1951–1958, the Federal Government appropriated over $32,000,000 for Navaho school construction.

In addition to the boarding schools, community day schools were built at nearly fifty locations, in order to bring schooling to the Navahos instead of taking Navahos away to the school. It was felt that the children's adjustment would be easier if they had been in touch with home life throughout their elementary education. Moreover, it was desired to give unschooled adults a chance to have some contacts with the program.

Most of these day schools were (and some still are) two- or three-room buildings, although a few are much larger. Some are hogan-shaped structures, and others are more in the Spanish architectural tradition, usually built of locally quarried rock. The plant includes a kitchen and dining room where the children get their noon meals, and shower rooms which are available to adults as well as to the children. Most schools also have sewing and laundry facilities and some shop or blacksmith equipment. In the last decade, trailers have been utilized as additional day schools at the elementary level.

Originally it was planned to have the children brought from their homes daily by bus, but bad weather, poor roads, shifting of family residences, morning darkness during the winter months, and other factors have made this plan nearly impracticable. Hence, wherever possible, simple dormitories have been put up near the school, so that children can sleep there during the week and return to their families over the weekend.

Some schools might be even smaller and simpler than the present style and be located within walking distance of the pupils' homes, where there are enough children within walking distance and where water, roads, and other such facilities can be provided economically. Such schools would be sponsored by local leadership and intimately related to the structure of nearby "outfits." This plan was tried experimentally before the present program was inaugurated; but before a year had passed, white missionaries, traders, and government employees had persuaded the Navahos that they were being offered inferior education and should demand better, which they did. (One evidence of the alleged inferiority was the fact that the desks were freely movable instead of being screwed down to the floor!) It must be admitted that the difficulties of supervising hundreds of little schools would be very great.

In 1958, the following schools were in operation: 49 boarding schools, 37 trailer day schools, 17 off-Reservation boarding schools, and approximately 25 mission schools. The total school enrollment (all grades) has increased from 6,375 in 1939 to 28,055 in 1958. Estimated additional facilities for the period 1958–1963 are for an additional 1,200 elementary students, 500 additional junior high, and 600 high-school students. Higher education is also advancing, and the majority of funds for this have been provided by The People themselves, through the Tribal Councils Scholarship Committee. In the academic year 1957–1958, almost 300 young Navahos were attending colleges, universities, and nurses' training schools, most of them within the Southwest, but some as far afield as New York City.

The present program is designed along "progressive" lines rather than in the more traditional pattern. Teachers are provided with materials and information about Navaho life-ways, which they are expected to use in teaching the children to speak English and to read, write, and number. At the same time the children learn about soil erosion, what to do in a trading post, how to improve their health, etc. The specific studies or "projects" are not the same year after year but vary with the assortment of pupils and the interests they show. Some of the boarding schools have programs a little more traditional in tone than that of the day schools. On the other hand, there are considerable efforts to inculcate many white values. Indeed the observer familiar with a variety of cultures may suspect that there is so much in the curriculum (e.g., strong emphasis on routines and time-mindedness, a perhaps exaggerated preoccupation with vitamins, nutrition, daily bowel movements, and the like) that later historians will judge even these progressive educators to have been pretty thoroughly imbued with the fashionable mythologies of white society in the mid-twentieth century.

It can easily be seen that guiding such a program is much more difficult than taking pupils through one textbook after another. It requires real ingenuity and resourcefulness on the part of the teacher, particularly since she may have students of widely differing ages and school experience in the same group. Thus one of the problems of Navaho education lies in the securing of adequate personnel. The solitude of the day-school teachers adds to the difficulties of recruitment. Although fairly satisfactory living quarters are provided in or near the day-school building, most of the schools are so far away from towns and white communities that the trader and his family may be the only other white persons within miles. In past years, this disadvantage was not compensated for by high salaries. As of 1944, 90 per cent of the teachers received $1,620 per year; only 10 per cent received $1,800 or $2,000. Recently, however, salaries have increased to a point where they are competitive with those offered in most white areas. For example, a position open in 1960 at the Shiprock school included a salary of over $4,000 and rent-free accommodations.

Up to 1933, most of the Navahos employed in the school system were custodial or other unskilled workers. Since that time, more and more native teachers have been utilized. Even twenty years ago, for example, five of the day schools had entirely Navaho staffs. Other schools had Navaho teachers of weaving and silver work, matrons, boys' and girls' advisers, and housekeepers. It is hoped that many of the Navaho men and women who return from experiences off the Reservation will help to increase education of Navahos by Navahos. But salaries of workers without college training are still often ridiculously low.

If teachers were Navahos from the community it would eliminate the shifting around of teachers which is one of the evils of the present system. The use of Navaho teachers would also solve the problem of cultural isolation to which so many of the white teachers object. The very fact that most of the returnees are not college graduates is an advantage in many respects. The Navaho who has gone through college has almost inevitably broken the most intimate ties with his own people. But the returnees will have had national and international experience which may make them more useful as teachers of the Navaho than would any amount of college training.

The principal conscious educational goal expressed by Navahos today seems to be the ability to use English. They realize that without it they are at a disadvantage, and they have discovered the usefulness of communications and records in writing. At the same time, English is so different from their own language that it is very difficult for Navahos to learn. (See Chapter 8.) Selective Service records, during World War II, classified 88 per cent out of a total of 4,000 male Navahos between the ages of 18 and 35 as illiterate. English remains a problem, but, with 93 per cent of the children between the ages of 6 and 18 attending schools, this is becoming less so. The children work hard at it and are much more likely to practice it among themselves—on the playground, for example—than are Pueblo pupils.

One promising project in the language field was the attempt by the Navajo Agency to teach reading and writing in Navaho to both children and adults. A number of readers on Navaho subjects, with texts in both Navaho and English, were prepared for use in the schools, together with a dictionary-grammar and a number of translations of literary, scientific, and historical works. A monthly newspaper published in Navaho had a paid subscription list of over 100 at the time during the war years when it had to be discontinued. It has since been reinstated. If this teaching were carried over into the entire school system, or even only into the early grades, the results might prove well worth the effort. Children might learn English much more rapidly if they were first literate in their own language. Children coming to school for the first time should be able to learn more quickly in all subjects if they were taught in their native tongue instead of having to acquire all information through an alien language. The greatest single problem faced by the government has been that of communication. And in considerable part this boils down to the problem of communicating with a people who as yet are not wholly literate.

The figures shown in Table II indicate the general trend of Navaho enrollment in the various types of schools.

In addition to teaching the children of The People, Nav-

TABLE II

NAVAHO SCHOOL ENROLLMENT BY TYPE OF SCHOOL, 1939–1958*

Type of school	1958	1957	1956	1955	1954	1953	1952	1939
Reservation Boarding	7,921	6,935	7,012	6,414	4,609	4,183	4,081	3,244
Community Boarding	1,201	1,416	1,511	1,575	1,338	1,272	1,259	1,206[1]
Peripheral Dormitory	1,636[2]	2,003[3]	1,581	1,030	0	0	0	0
Trailer Day Schools	711	981	934	1,119	179	117	0	0
Reservation Day Schools	495	349	326	622	625	425	352	245
Off-Reservation Boarding	7,195	6,849	6,949	6,882	4,969	4,934	4,709	648
Public	6,900	6,000	5,000	3,900	2,847	2,393	1,846	234
Mission	1,553	1,483	1,483	1,408	1,219	1,175	1,168	650
State Deaf-Blind	40	43	33	33	30	26	18	7
All other	403	728	448	688	294	240	47	141
Total	28,055	27,013	25,287	23,671	16,110	14,765	13,480	6,375

1 These were day schools in 1939, since converted to boarding school basis.
2 Includes 543 children housed in Bureau Dormitories and attending Reservation Public Schools.
3 Excludes children attending public school but residing in the bordertown Reservation dormitories.

* The Navajo Yearbook, Report No. VII, ed. by Robert W. Young. Window Rock, Arizona, 1958, p. 355.

ajo Agency schools—particularly the day schools—have an important function as community centers where various types of visual education for adults as well as children are carried out. As noted above, the day schools also have shower rooms which are available to all the people of the community; this is indeed a service to inhabitants of a region where water is so hard to come by. Navaho women use the sewing and laundry facilities in most schools to make, repair, and wash clothing and bedding, and men can repair implements and make other use of the shops and blacksmith equipment. The adult literacy classes in Navaho were formerly held here, and there are or have been projects for making mattresses, learning agricultural methods, and the like. The schools also furnish a place where doctors, extension agents, and other specialists of the Agency can meet with The People. Although the potentialities of the schools have by no means been fully realized, they offer a great opportunity for reaching the whole Navaho tribe.

The People have had varied and mingled reactions to the present school program on the Reservation. In the past, some children objected to going to school, and parents have respected their wishes. Many parents have opposed any schooling because it takes away the young herders and the other helpers they need in the business of wringing a living from the barren soil. Others have feared that in the present as in the past their children would be unfitted for Navaho life or that girls might be led astray. Mainly, however, objection has been to the type of schooling. Those adult Navahos who have been in the old boarding schools and others who know something of the different methods of mission and public schools in the region have felt (and some still feel) that they had a second-rate brand of education foisted upon them. They interpreted the progressive method as useless play and demanded that their children be made to work harder and be disciplined as they themselves were disciplined or see their neighbors' children disciplined in other schools. The project to teach reading and writing of the Navaho language was held by some Indians to be an attempt to hold back the wheels of progress.

The day schools once were the prime target of the resentment Navahos felt for all sorts of government programs. They expressed their disapproval toward other government activities by withdrawing their children from school. Until recently, when a crisis arrived in the sheep reduction program, or in relief, or in any other sphere, the attendance at the day schools dropped either locally or generally. Such withdrawal served an important function as a safety valve for the large number of not openly aggressive Navahos who had no other ready means of protest against the white administration.

At present, 1961, however, one hears little criticism from Navahos of the program in the government schools. More children than can be accommodated wish to enter. The tribe has sent a delegation to Washington to ask Congress and the Bureau of the Budget for adequate funds to repair buildings and pay salaries. Many Navaho parents are clamoring for compulsory education. This would, of course, require readjustments in Navaho economic practices, for the young shepherds would all be in school and elders would have to assume entire responsibility for the care of the flocks during most of the year. With sheep permits rigidly limited, however, there is now less need for herders. In fact, one of the reasons some parents are at present eager to find place in school for their children is because children are around the hogans with time on their hands.

To the observer who knows something of modern educational techniques and of the history of Indian schools, the administration of Navaho schools seems uncommonly enlightened and progressive. True, there was too much haste at first and too much unfettered experimentation. Some of the day schools were hurriedly built and badly located. The sympathies of many Navahos were alienated because, through lack of proper interpretation, they got the impression that this was a back-to-the-blanket movement. When Navahos who are to compete with whites find themselves judged by the standard of more conventional education, it does not matter to them which standard is *better;* what does matter is that the standard by which they are judged is *different.* A small but vocal Navaho group who take civil service examinations or try to enter college feel bitterly that their education is unrealistic, just as graduates of white "progressive" schools did at one time.

All minority groups fear differentiation, especially educational differentiation. On practical grounds they may be right in doing so, no matter how enlightened the educational system is from the broad point of view.

On the other hand, it must be admitted that for Indian Service educators to follow outworn and inefficient methods just because they continue to be followed to a large degree by the public school systems of surrounding areas is hardly a justifiable procedure. Moreover, the state of New Mexico is itself now officially urging a statewide "progressive" school program. In such a program as that of the Navajo Agency schools, much depends upon the effectiveness and temperance of the administrative leadership, upon the quality of the individual teachers, and upon the skill with which the Navajo Agency handles the public relations problems involved. Adoption of "progressive" methods is certainly an invaluable check upon the inevitable tendency of the teacher to urge his pupils to strive for what the teacher wants most in life. Obviously, this tendency is particularly dangerous and disruptive when teachers and pupils come from such different backgrounds and have such varying expectations and needs as must be the case between Navaho pupils and their instructors. One of the urgent needs is for a systematic study of the habitual assumptions, ways of life, and value systems of the teachers.

Another need is for more effective communication to the Navahos of the reasons for various practices. Navaho parents do not always understand why their children do not learn to read their first year in school. It can be explained in simple and convincing terms why it is necessary to teach oral English first and postpone reading until later. Parents can be made to see that their children after starting to school must acquire a vocabulary that English-speaking children have taken five or six years to learn at home before starting to school. Similarly, Navahos have very little comprehension of the role of the specialist in white culture. If this were explained with some graphic examples within the framework of their experiences, they would be more likely both to seek the advice of trained technicians when needed and to realize the limitations of the specialist in affairs outside his own field.

Perhaps the most hopeful sign is the extent to which adult Navahos have coöperated during the past twenty years in building new dormitories. Part of the trouble in the past has been that too much has been given without their request or participation. Naturally The People have not felt that the schools were theirs as much as would be desirable. If schools are built on their initiative and with their coöperation, much better understanding and more constructive attitudes will grow. If respected elders were occasionally invited to give oral instruction in Navaho on Navaho ethics and values, the older generation would have less reason to feel that schools create a gulf between the young and the old.

Perhaps, if the teachers were mostly Navahos, and if nurses, physicians, local sub-agents, judges, road and irrigation men coöperated in educational activities centered in the small community boarding schools, they might become what present teachers seldom have time to make them: community centers as well as effective instruments of education for The People of every age.

Some things need more thought and action. The system (for all its "progressiveness") is still amusingly culture bound. For example, the school terms are set in accord with white tradition rather than to fit the special circumstances of Navaho life and seasonal weather conditions in the Navaho country. But time and patience are required, for the complications are many and great. Indian education is not a simple situation in which the Indian Service merely deals directly with Indians. There are all sorts of interferences: from missionaries, from traders, from congressmen, from associations of white people organized to protect Indians. It is hard to get money from Congress for adult education, because the fact that with Navahos the problem is that of "educating" not just 30,000 children but virtually the whole tribe has not been sufficiently dramatized. Congress has assumed that adults are already "educated" and that such things as agricultural extension work are just fancy touches—not absolute essentials.

MEDICAL SERVICES AND NAVAHO HEALTH

A large and important branch of the Navajo Agency is that which deals with health, and in it lies one of the best means of establishing better collaboration between The People and white society. Illness is a matter of much concern to the Navaho, and he is perhaps more willing to try new methods of healing than new methods of raising sheep.

This attitude toward illness is not without foundation, for the incidence and severity of some diseases are thought to be higher among The People than among whites.[3] World War II physical examinations by Selective Service physicians disclosed tuberculosis in one out of every eleven Navaho men examined. The estimated death rate for this disease is very high: 52.5 per 100,000 Navahos as against a rate for the United States as a whole of only 8.4. In the past two decades there has been a marked drop in the incidence of tuberculosis, but the ratio remained virtually constant: 386 for Navahos versus an overall rate of 43.

Other respiratory diseases—chiefly pneumonia (25 times

the national incidence) and upper respiratory ailments—make up the majority of cases in government hospitals in all seasons except summer. From August through October, when flies abound, infant diarrheas are common. Contagious diseases appear in cycles among both adults and children, often in severe form; most prominent is measles, but chickenpox, whooping cough, mumps, and diphtheria occur frequently. Trachoma was formerly noted in about 40 per cent of all Navaho children examined at government institutions, but since the development of antibiotics and treatment by Indian Service doctors this figure has dropped to around 3 per cent (still much higher than the national average). The casual observer will still notice many cases of blindness and bad eyesight among older Navahos, however, of which a large proportion is due to trachoma.

Another point which immediately strikes the visitor is the high frequency of persons who walk with a limp. Some of these instances are due to unset fractures sustained in horseback accidents. Others may be traced to tubercular lesions or to birth injuries.

There are many deaths among young children (three times the national average) and maternal mortality is high. Miscarriages may be more frequent because women are subject to being thrown from the saddle or out of wagons by refractory horses. One might expect that Navaho women would be more likely to die during pregnancy or childbirth than white women because the later occurrence of "change of life" among Indian women provides more opportunities for pregnancy. If they survive childbearing and the menopause, however, their chances for attaining a ripe old age are excellent.

Certain diseases do not claim so many victims among Navahos as among whites. Some degenerative diseases—cancer, circulatory diseases, and some neurological conditions—appear to be less frequent.

Average life expectancy is apparently shorter for Navahos than for whites. Peaks in the mortality curve occur in the age periods 19–24 and 30–38 for men and at 13–18, 29–44, and 49–62 for women. However, if a Navaho is tough enough to survive the many hazards to health until he nears 65, he is likely to be exceedingly tenacious of life. The proportion of the very old is quite striking, and there may well be a greater number of octogenarians and nonagenarians per 1,000 population in Navaho than in white society.

Given these health problems and expectancies to deal with, how does the Navajo Agency discharge its responsibilities for the health of The People? Hospital facilities on the Reservation are good and are being used increasingly. The largest hospital is at Fort Defiance, where there are 115 beds. Other smaller hospitals, each with an outpatient clinic, are located at Shiprock, Crownpoint, Fort Wingate, Winslow, and Tuba City. During the year 1957–1958, these hospitals admitted a total of 9,625 patients. In addition, Health Centers have been set up (for outpatient treatment only) at Chinle, Gallup, Tohatchi, and Many Farms. Hospitals and Health Centers combined received visits by The People totaling approximately 150,000 (1957–1958). In 1958, the total medical staff was comprised of the following: 37 doctors, 12 dentists, 76 hospital nurses, 28 Public Health nurses, 14 Sanitarians, and 360 other personnel—a total of 527 trained medical personnel.

While relationships between Navahos and white physicians (both missionary and government) have been much improved in recent years, there is still a long way to go.[4] Physicians have been often too openly contemptuous of all Navaho "medical" practices, too fierce in their condemnations of Navaho lack of cleanliness and sanitation, generally too little able or willing to see things from the Indians' point of view. It is useless and only provocative of irritation to harp continually on certain health practices that in the nature of things cannot be achieved at present. How can people wash their hands before eating each meal when water is so precious? Indian Service stress upon medical propaganda has more than once affected Navahos as it did a headman who said at a meeting, "We shall all be very healthy and die of starvation." Whites look at "health" as much more a separable category of experience than do The People. The Navaho attitude is expressed in the folk saying: "When the land is sick, The People are sick."

Recently, however, there has developed an interesting departure from this white attitude toward Navaho health problems. The Navajo-Cornell Field Health Project, opening in 1956 at Many Farms, Arizona, has understood that Navaho "medicine" may have a real place in treatment. The staff of this partially research-oriented institution has developed a "working arrangement" with many of the local Singers. The Clinic realized that Navaho "medicine" could serve two important functions for the general improvement of health conditions in the area. The first, and most obvious, is the general reassurance given to a patient by providing him with the best assistance from both worlds. The second function of the Singer is to provide quasi-psychiatric assistance in what are essentially psychosomatic illnesses. All those who have a reasonable knowledge of The People have observed cases in which an apparently quite sick individual was cured by the appropriate ceremony. (Indeed, this phenomenon and its related forms, is quite familiar to the practitioner of physical medicine within the white world.) The Cornell group has understood this and capitalized on it. In consequence, Singers within the area have become much less reticent about suggesting "white medicine" to their patients. The results of this system have proved remarkable, and it is to be hoped that similar arrangements will come into being at other medical centers.

In the general course of medicine, however, the irritation of the physicians is also understandable from their point of view. They are exasperated by the fact that Indians sometimes refuse to be operated upon even when operation is probably the only remedy. They are frequently frustrated by Navahos' coming to them as a last resort, when the disease is so advanced that the chances of cure are slight. They likewise resent Navahos' leaving the hospital in the midst of treatment in order to have a ceremonial. All sorts of Navaho attitudes and behaviors are incomprehensible to them. For example, a Navaho was taken to a hospital and given a pillow. He put it under his feet. Nothing could induce him to put it under his head. He said: "Feathers under my head would make feathers grow on my neck and shoulders." The reactions of one Navaho to white medicine, as indicated in the following passage, are typical of unacculturated Navahos:

> You go to a hospital and maybe once a day the doctor comes around and he stays three, maybe five minutes. He talks a little bit but he asks you questions. Once in a while they give you a little medicine, just a little of it. About the only thing they do is to put something in your mouth and see how hot you are. The rest of the time you just lie there. But the medicine men help you all the time—they give you lots of medicine and they sing all night. They do lots of things all over your body. Every bit of your body is treated.

LAW AND ORDER

Navahos on the Reservation are under federal and tribal law. In the past, enforcement of the law and maintenance of order were in the hands of the Law and Order Division of the Navajo Agency. However, the Navajo Tribal Council has assumed more and more of this responsibility. The tribal appropriation for the maintenance of law and order began in 1953 at $32,669 to equip and support an initial force of six officers. This appropriation has increased to (1958–1959) $768,766, which pays the salaries of 93 law enforcement officers and 15 administrative personnel. This has also provided, among other things, for the operation of four enforcement centers, all radio equipped, and for fifty similarly equipped radio units. In addition to these officers, the Navajo Agency has kept a small force of federal agents responsible for the enforcement of those laws and ordinances which must remain within the federal jurisdiction. In point of fact, however, there is a high degree of coöperation on all crimes by both forces. However, the Federal Government is finally responsible for trial and punishment in the following cases (by Act of Congress, 1952): murder, manslaughter, rape, assault with intent to kill, arson, burglary, larceny, robbery, incest, assault with a deadly weapon, and embezzlement of tribal funds.

THE PEOPLE PARTICIPATE IN GOVERNMENT

The People have a large measure of self-government in the Navajo Tribal Council, and they are largely responsible for the administration of the tribal code of law, and, through the years, of the tribe's accumulating funds.

THE NAVAJO COUNCIL

The history of tribal "self-government" among the Navahos has been marked with zigzags of official policy, misunderstandings, and confusion that have stemmed from ignorance on the part of white administrators of the original patterns of Navaho authority, and from their attempts to superimpose white patterns only partially understood by the Navahos.

Army officers and the first civilian agents tried to work through the supposed "chiefs" and headmen. When these men failed to obtain the desired coöperation, new heads were created by governmental fiat. Of course, such ersatz leaders had little or no control over their people. Their prestige declined after 1900, and neither the Navahos nor the white administrators had much faith left in them.

For some time there were no really effective channels of communication. The Indian Service depended largely upon local policemen, while Navahos who were disturbed enough would make a trip to their agency for a personal interview with the superintendent. But there were a good deal of dissatisfaction and a few serious disorders. As recently as 1914 the military had to be called into the Beautiful Mountain area to deal with threatened uprisings over government attempts to suppress plural marriages.

In 1925, "chapters" were established for various local areas, and it was hoped that these could be made into responsible local units. But such groupings corresponded to nothing in Navaho experience, and the techniques of operation which were laid down were still more foreign. The cultural provincialism of the Indian Service was shown in the fact that each chapter was told to elect a president, vice-president, and secretary and to carry on according to parliamentary procedure. These conditions alone made it inevitable that "educated" Navahos took the leading role, while the participation of the older and probably wiser "medicine men" and wealthy livestock owners was very limited. The whole system was entirely artificial, and once again the government made the mistake of insisting that "headmen" either agree with its program or be forced out. As a result, many chapters became centers of antigovernment gossip and agitation. The Indian Service then timidly withdrew its backing and financial support, and most of the chapters collapsed.

The discovery of oil on Navaho lands near Shiprock in 1923 made urgent the creation of some body which should speak, at least in form, for the tribe as a whole, and this led to the organization of a Navaho council. The members of this first council were largely hand-picked "yes-men" who were not the effective leaders of the working social organization.

The present Indian Service administration early offered

The People full self-government under the provisions of the Indian Reorganization Act. But in an election in 1934, in which the issues were distorted or but little comprehended, the tribe voted by a narrow margin not to accept the Act. Nevertheless, the Indian Service proceeded administratively, and under the legal principle of inherent and unextinguished tribal authority, to extend to the elected council some control over tribal affairs. In 1936, a team of men headed by Father Berard Haile undertook the task of combing the Reservation for men of proven ability and leadership. Two hundred and fifty names were submitted for consideration to the Navajo Agency. Seventy of the men whose names were submitted were arbitrarily chosen to compose a constitutional assembly. The old council was disbanded, and the new assembly appointed a provisional Executive Committee to conduct routine tribal business until such time as a constitution could be completed and another Tribal Council duly elected. This assembly was never able to agree on an acceptable constitution, but they were able to finally agree upon, and obtain Indian Service approval for, a series of rules providing for the election of a new Council. The first election under these new rules was held in 1938.

The new Council was to be composed of seventy-four members, and a Chairman and Vice-Chairman, and each member was to be elected on the basis of population with 400–500 constituents per member. The new rules also provided for an eighteen-member Executive Committee to be composed of one person from each administrative district, chosen by other members to be the Chief Delegate of that area. There was, however, great general suspicion of an Executive Committee in that the prior one had attempted to enforce the unpopular livestock reduction plan and grazing regulations. The pressure was sufficiently strong that the Council did not reëstablish an Executive Committee to handle routine tribal business until 1947, and then only in the form of an advisory committee to the Council. This new group however was soon delegated more and more authority by the Council, until it took over the function of an executive committee. It was (and is) composed of nine members of the Council, and nine alternate members; at present (as of 1958) the first order of business of a newly elected Tribal Council is to vote on membership on the Advisory Committee, as this group is now known. In addition to this group there have been recently established other Council committees on Health and Welfare, Education, Law and Order, Administration, Budget, Trading, Loans, and Engineering and Resources. The Tribal Council has also developed its own legal department, primarily to represent The People as a whole in litigation with the Federal Government or with other Indian peoples.

Until the end of World War II, most action taken by the Council was initiated by the government, and its functions were mainly to approve or disapprove governmental proposals or to advise with administrators, rather than to initiate policy or pass laws. Since that time, however, this has rapidly been changing and The People, through the Council, have taken over much more of their own complete self-determination. It still works closely with the Navajo Agency, but now as often as not the representatives of The People are the initiators of action, though the programs of each group are quite closely coördinated. The end in mind is, of course, the eventual self-extinction of the Navajo Agency and its full replacement by the Council.

A major problem in the past, and still present to a degree, has been the lack of tribal feeling of unity and solidarity. Navahos understand responsibility to relatives and even to a local group, but they are only commencing to grasp the need for thinking in tribal terms. Further, they have no notion of representative government. They are accustomed to deciding all issues by face-to-face meetings of all individuals involved—including, most decidedly, the women. The native way of deciding an issue is to discuss it until there is unanimity of opinion or until the opposition feels it no longer worthwhile to urge its point of view. Moreover, because they are not familiar with the representative principle, The People (like many other groups) by no means always send to the Council the men who really count in local affairs. This fact, and the comparatively small number of women in responsible positions, tend to make Council meetings more a sounding board for ambitious politicians than a true expression of tribal sentiment. In addition, it is not yet a Navaho practice to plan far ahead or even to think much beyond the present. The result is that, although the delegate now knows that he is expected to speak for his own people back home, neither he nor they thoroughly realize that he might by his vote bind their future actions.

These conditions still pertain to a certain extent, particularly involving the more remote districts of the Reservation. Nonetheless, the return of others from wage work outside the Reservation, the great increase in school facilities and attendance, and the added communication, through the building of many new roads within the Reservation; all these are sharply increasing The People's knowledge of the outside world and their own feeling of unity. Coupled with this has been the sharp increase during the last decade of the income to The People from natural resources; this increase has almost automatically given the Tribal Council more real power than ever before. This change has been further enhanced by the government's decision to allow the Indian to vote. So far this right has by no means been fully exercised, but a large part of the reason for this is the still quite low over-all literacy rate among The People. Still, in the U.S. general election of 1956 some 4,600 actually did exercise their franchise. It is very much to be expected that the next decade (1960–1970) will bring to The People a much greater political awareness, in terms of their active participation both in their own self-government and development and in their role as U.S.

citizens; indeed the system of tribal self-government within the framework of the state and federal governments might well be likened to that of an incredibly large (in area) township or county in other areas.

TRIBAL COURTS

Navahos, like other Indians, are subject to state criminal laws when they are off the Reservation, but when they are within the Reservation they are answerable only to federal or tribal courts. As noted above, the Federal District Court has jurisdiction in cases involving eleven major crimes as well as over offenses which are ordinarily under federal jurisdiction throughout the country. All other offenses committed by Navahos on the Reservation are tried in the Tribal Court on the basis of a tribal code of law adopted in 1937, which takes Navaho custom into account. However, the total number of offenses tried under the tribal courts is immensely larger than that tried by the federal courts. In 1958, for instance, only 88 cases were presented for federal prosecution, and of these, 73 were remanded to the Court of Indian Offenses. On the other hand, during that same year, there were 8,351 convictions in the Tribal Court—the majority of these for disorderly conduct (4,980) and liquor violation (1,585). The types of offense handled by the Tribal Court in 1958 include seven out of the eleven offenses which may be tried under federal jurisdiction (10 cases of manslaughter, 6 of rape, 1 of incest, 35 of assault with a deadly weapon, 11 of burglary, 9 of larceny, and 1 of embezzlement). In addition, the following offenses are normally handled only by the Tribal Court system: assault, assault and battery, theft, disorderly conduct, reckless driving, liquor violation, adultery, illicit cohabitation, failure to support dependent persons, resisting arrest, disobedience to Court Order, use of peyote, and tribal divorces.

The judges of the Tribal Court are all Navahos and are

recommended by the Navajo Council. Thus the field of law and order is the one in which The People themselves have a large share. Ironically, it is one in which they have little positive interest and much strong resentment. If judges and policemen do not speak both English and Navaho fairly well, misunderstanding arises because the instructions of their white superiors are not completely clear to them or because they fail to translate well the accusations or the sentences to those brought before the court. The strong family loyalties of The People subject judges to powerful pressures. The very best of judges and policemen are constantly placed in most difficult positions because they must serve as intermediaries between two different worlds, so they are often made the scapegoats for the piled-up resentment of The People against the government and white men in general.

THE GOVERNMENT AND THE PEOPLE: PRESENT PROBLEMS

To speak of problems in this area now is very different than to do so twenty years ago; they have become far, far fewer. At that time the rather paternalistic efforts on the part of the government, and its major symbol, the Navajo Agency, were widely mistrusted by The People. Much of this distrust also rubbed off on the Tribal Council, as they too were regarded as acting on the basis of a strange and foreign set of premises—the white man's ways. However, since the vast increase in education among The People and their much greater experience with the outside world, these attitudes have changed remarkably. This is not to say that problems do not exist for The People. Land reclamation, development of resources, raising of the per capita Navaho income, health and welfare, education, all of these and more remain problems, but they are problems which are being jointly faced by The People and the Navajo Agency. This has been one of the most remarkable changes; now

The People and the government stand almost as equals, working toward the same ends, and, more remarkable still, using primarily the same means—the white man's ways.

In 1950 the Federal Government appropriated over eighty million dollars to support a long-range program of development for the Navaho and Hopi Reservations—this to be over and above the usual operation expenses for the Navajo Agency. At approximately the same time, the tribal income began to increase vastly. Shortly after this, the Navaho became a full-fledged citizen. The various factors have come together to produce a Tribal Council and a Navajo Agency which work fairly much together toward solving the practical problems still faced by The People. Gone are the days when the Council's function was that of a poor relation, there to give advice (only when asked) and without any real power. The two stand today almost equal in stature, with bargaining between equals the rule of the day, and coöperation the result.

It is still true that neither agency is fully understood by all of The People, all of the time. Mistrust and misunderstandings still occur, but they are so much rarer now than at the beginning of the war that the infrequent visitor is amazed at the immense change occurring every few years. This does not mean that The People are changing suddenly to white ways; they still live between two worlds, but at least they have gained a far greater understanding of the "other" world, and have found its ways to be best in dealing with many kinds of problems, and particularly in dealing with its representatives, official and otherwise. Just as the Chinese in Hong Kong has been able to deal with Western businessmen and their methods, with a British administration, etc., but still keep in his personal and family life the ancient traditions of China, so the Navaho now has two sets of rules and customs. They usually apply to different situations, and so do not too often come into direct conflict. He has not given up his language, but he has come to know the value of learning the other language.

He has come to understand that the white man knows far more about how to improve land and livestock than he, but he still honors the Navaho rules of inheritance of that land and livestock.

This change in attitude (and behavior) has not only meant that The People understand more and appreciate more the intents and services of the Navajo Agency—it has also brought about a change in attitude on the part of the Agency personnel. They have come to place far more reliance upon the judgment and ability of the Navaho, especially on those who serve as representatives and officials of The People. Thus, through a long and gradual approach, and with the help of some fortuitous circumstances (such as the discovery of uranium and other minerals on tribal lands), The People and the government stand together, using common means to gain a common end: the development of The People as a whole, the improvement of their land, and their eventual, complete self-support and local autonomy.

Yet The People are still not always at one with the government, nor with neighboring tribes. Under the provisions of the Indian Claims Act passed by Congress in 1946, the Navaho (and many of the neighboring tribes) have brought suit against the United States for lands taken in the westward expansion of the mid-nineteenth century. A boundary dispute between the Navaho and the Hopi has been heard by the Indian Claims Commission, but the matter has not been decided. Arguments in this dispute, and in the pending Navajo Land Claims Case have tried to take into account the conditions of the mid-nineteenth century. The determination of the life and location of The People at this, however, has proved difficult at best. Before the Navajo Claims Case can be settled, arguments from the neighboring tribes (some against the Federal Government, some against each other)—the overlapping claims—will have to be heard. The ultimate solution of the claims cases may be a long time in coming. In this,

The People are taking an active part; but they are turning to the white man's ways.

NAVAHOS WORKING IN THE WHITE WORLD

Population growth is forcing an increasing number of Navahos into direct economic competition with white people off the Reservation, chiefly as unskilled workers. The general pattern of interrelations between these Navaho laborers and their white employers is not very different from that which prevails between other "depressed" ethnic groups and white employers elsewhere in the country. The Navaho is conditioned to subordination. Almost all action is initiated by whites; Navahos merely respond.

On their own ground, the Indians will sometimes express hostility by truculent behavior. But when the situation is "white" and whites are clearly in control, Navahos usually manifest their discomfort and resistance passively. They withdraw; they scatter like a covey of quail; as a psychologist would put it, "they leave the field." White employers frequently comment, "Navahos are good workers but not steady. They work hard on the job, but you can't count on them. They disappear for days at a time to attend a Sing or to help their families out."

In the prewar and early postwar period, it was the writers' impression that many Navahos who sought wage work with whites tended to be those who, for one reason or another, did not get along in their own society. Such maladjusted persons were of course likely to be unstable. Almost all Navahos used to feel so out of place, so uneasy, in a white environment that they could stand it for just so long. They grew desperately homesick. They felt lost without the support of their families. With a few days or weeks at home, attending ceremonials and renewing the sense of participation in the coöperative activities of their familial society, they feel sufficiently relieved and restored to go back to their jobs. But the job to them was a way of earning necessary money, not a way of life.

To a limited extent this is still true. But this set of attitudes is now held only by those of The People who remain relatively isolated on the mesas, and in the canyon bottoms of the interior of the Reservation. For the rest, it has become quite acceptable—indeed almost usual—for members of the family group to take jobs in the white man's world, and even to go far away from the Reservation in order to work, or to go to school. This is particularly true for the southern and eastern parts of the Navaho Reservation, and even more so for those living in settlements off the Reservation.

Those who argue that the solution of the "Navaho problem" is immediate absorption into the white world overlook the tremendous adjustments which The People must make, and the time required for such adjustments, before any considerable number can take their places as permanent members of the white economic system. The linguistic difficulty will be decisive for a time, but more important is the fact that Navahos simply do not understand the rules for competing in the white world. These rules cannot be learned by rote in school—in fact, the white man's way of "getting ahead" in some situations is the reverse of what he teaches in his schools. White competitive methods can be learned only by experience and over a period of time. Otherwise, 85,000 people will sink to the level of "poor whites" and alternate between wage labor in good times and relief in bad. The Indian Service can help, however, by the creation of better placement agencies and by facilitating normal representation of Navahos in state-wide groups (e.g., livestock associations). In this way the isolation of Navahos from other citizens of the state and of other citizens from Navahos may be diminished. To the extent that manpower (the major resource of the tribe) is employed with a minimum of segregation and that mingling of Navahos and whites in public schools, hospitals, etc., is encouraged, the dividing lines between The People and the white world will gradually become less distinct.

BETWEEN TWO WORLDS

Most of The People today who have not left the Navaho country permanently live in a world which is neither white nor Navaho in the traditional sense, a world where values are shifting and where rules of conduct are in a state of flux. Most of the heavy stresses and pressures for readjustment to white ways have come to the bilingual generation of Navahos, particularly the school children; yet even those who speak no English cannot escape all the frustration and conflict introduced by the impact with white society. At the very least, they are disturbed to see their children adopting non-Navaho ways, and indeed they see their whole world dissolving around them. But so long as they do not speak or understand English, they have an important measure of insulation against many psychological insecurities.

Those few Navahos who speak no Navaho at all, or very little, are also protected in some degree. They have largely lost contact with the Navaho world except in a very superficial way. However unsatisfactory their position in the white world, they are at any rate freed from the necessity for constant choosing between the white and the Navaho ways of living.

It is the English-speaking generation which must make relentless choices. The Navaho girl who has been at boarding school for many years usually has no desire to live in a hogan when she marries. But to have a house with a wooden floor, running water, and other conveniences to which she has become accustomed, she and her husband must move to a white town or an agency settlement, where they are cut off from their kindred and generally isolated. Whichever alternative they choose, they are exposed to criticism from either Navahos or whites. Their middle position is extremely difficult. One must therefore take with some reserve the statement so frequently made by whites of the Reservation country, "Give me an uneducated Indian every time." In part this eternal slogan does reflect the fact that many "educated" Navahos are maladjusted and hence difficult to deal with. But it must be remembered that in part also this view reflects the fact that schooled Navahos know their rights better and cannot be coerced by white misstatements or cheated because they are ignorant of writing and of arithmetic.

Different sets of Navahos (depending partly upon age, schooling, location of residence with respect to intensity of non-Navaho contacts, and other factors) have shown different major responses to the insecurities, deprivations, and frustrations of the immediate past and especially to the "between two worlds" problem. The same individuals, of course, manifest different responses on different occasions, but most age, age-sex, areal and other groups tend eventually to settle down to one or more preferred reaction patterns. Some focus their energies upon trying to be as like whites as possible. Some find relief in becoming followers of vocal leaders. Others dissipate much hostility in factional quarrels or scatter their aggression in family fights, in phantasies about witchcraft or in attacking "witches," in verbal and other indirect hostilities toward whites, or they turn their aggression inward with resultant fits of depression. The culturally patterned releases in humor and in "joking relationships" with certain relatives continue to play some part. The central response of certain individuals is in flight—either in actual physical withdrawal or in the escape of narcotics, alcohol, and sex. Still others turn to intensified participation in rites of the native religion and to new cults (e.g., peyote). Partial solutions are achieved by a few individuals by rigid compartmentalization of their lives and feelings and by various rationalizations.

Those who have set themselves to follow the white man's trail find themselves—as have representatives of other minority groups—in a (rationally) odd dilemma. While as youngsters they are rewarded by school teachers and others for behaving like whites, as adults they are punished for having acquired skills that make them competitors of their white contemporaries. The more intelligent ones had, by early maturity, realized that their education would bring them into conflict with or isolation from their own unschooled relatives. But the experience of being turned on by their white mentors comes as a painful surprise. They find they are seldom received on terms of social equality, even by those whose standards of living, dress, and manners they have succeeded in copying almost perfectly. They learn that they must always (save within the Indian Service) expect to work for a salary at least one grade lower than that which a white person of comparable training and experience receives. They overhear remarks by those same groups of whites who had goaded them to give up "those ignorant Indian ways": "You can never trust these school boys." "Give me a 'long hair' every time. They may be dumb but they are honest and they work hard." "Educated Indians are neither fish nor fowl. They give me the creeps." Rejected by the white world they have made so many emotional sacrifices to enter, some attempt a bitter retreat to the Navaho world. Others, in sour disillusionment, abandon all moral codes. Still others achieve a working (but flat and empty) adjustment.

NAVAHO ATTITUDES TOWARD WHITES

Navahos are well aware of the difficulty of their situation. Surrounded by powerful pressures to change, they know that indifference and withdrawal can no longer serve as effective responses. They are conscious of the need to develop some compromise with white civilization. But doubt as to the best form of compromise makes them angry and anxious. Until recently suspicion and hostility were a major emotional tone of their relationships with whites. On the other hand, as the number of trained and educated Navahos has increased, there has been a change in attitude on the part of the whites; with the influx of skilled and unskilled laborers in many areas, whites have become less patronizing and more openly hostile than was true in the past—due to the threat of open competition on an almost equal basis.

This is not, of course, the whole picture, for it is nearly impossible to describe such a complicated set of interactions without distortion. It should go without saying that the relationships of some whites with some Navahos have been marked with understanding and cordiality on both sides. Since the early days of the Indian Service, some government representatives have been kind and even devoted to the Navahos. Some of the missionaries, particularly the Franciscans and the Presbyterians at Ganado, have won the affection of many of The People. Many of the white traders have been persons of unusual character who earned abiding trust and loyalty from the Indians.

The picture also requires correction from other angles. While there have been anti-white movements during the last twenty-five years, while there are Navahos who can but will not speak English, while a large number of Navahos are reserved and suspicious in all dealings with whites, still the generalized Navaho pattern is not like that of the Pueblo Indians—to encapsulate themselves and their culture in an almost impenetrable hard shell of resistance. On the contrary, the Navahos are distinguished among American Indians by the alacrity, if not the ease, with which they have adjusted to the impact of white culture while still retaining many native traits and preserving the framework of their own cultural organization. It is almost true to say that in some areas the culture of the Navahos has altered more in the past generation than has the culture of their Pueblo neighbors in the whole four hundred years during which these town-dwelling Indians have been in contact with European civilization.

Yet this very rapidity of change makes for uneasiness, and uneasiness makes distrust or active hatred of whites the prevalent attitudes. With each new generation that goes to school, a larger proportion of The People must face the difficult problem of compromising between the demands of the two cultures.

The hardship is increased by the treatment meted out to Indians in getting jobs off the Reservation, in day-to-day social contacts, and even in state laws governing the fundamental rights of citizens.

A further cause for distrust and hostility is the fact that Navahos are dependent upon a distant and mysterious white institution called "the market." In the old days of bartering raw materials, a sheep or a sack of wool maintained a rather constant value. When both are sold to the trader, The People never know in advance whether lamb will bring ten cents a pound or only five cents, and they see no sense in these variations. They share the common distrust of farmer folk for those who buy and resell the products of their hard labors, but they are at a greater disadvantage than the white farmer because they are unfamiliar with white marketing customs and have no means of understanding the reasons for the apparently senseless fluctuations in price and demand. Moreover, since they feel that they usually are underpaid for their sheep and wool and that the price they will get varies with no rhyme or reason, they feel uncertain about improving their products. Education, the efforts of the Tribal Council and of the Navajo Agency have begun to produce a marked change in this attitude. Many of The People now understand the white man's way of investment now for future return.

While many of these problems and conflicts would arise in some degree if the Navahos had been surrounded by greater numbers of any other group, still it is certain that it would have been easier for them if the surrounding society had been one of a more homogeneous and consistent sort. The fact that white American culture has itself been changing at such a dizzy rate for the past three generations has added enormously to their difficulties. Much of what the early teachers and missionaries taught as "the way white people do things" is now only a memory to even the most conservative whites. Moreover, with the breaking down of the former rules, white society has split into groups that look at life differently, have different interests and ideals. The Indians are exposed to not one but a variety of these groups. It is no wonder that they conclude that white people and their ways are past understanding.

All these feelings and the conflict between old ways and new ways, between the school generation and the non-school generation, come out vividly in the following excerpt from the report turned in by a Navaho government employee who had been sent to a Navaho ceremonial to show motion pictures as part of the prewar educational program in connection with soil conservation and livestock management.[5]

Original

We get to dance late in the evening and we went to call of that dance to talk to him instead he pointed to the Navaho policemen of that dance and we told them right from begin to end of our work and what we are trying to do to the people. He said there no just such thing the land sick or die we leaving just found we leave on our sheep and goats what do we about show we no

Translation

We got to the dance late in the evening. We went to call on the leader of that dance to talk to him. Instead he pointed to the Navaho policemen of that section. We told them everything about our work, from the beginning to the end, and what we were trying to do for the people.

They said, "There is just no such thing as that the land can get sick or die. We white men. The white told us lie so many time now and we don't care to believe now. I said him what the lie about. He told us he was going to have Navaho the work and money if they only reduce the sheep and goats now then the goats has gone and no work no money don't you think we will try again and then if we let white man work around our reservation and on they say it they land because they worked on and soon they will try to ran the land all over so we don't want anything now we living good rite now.

are living just fine. We live on our sheep and goats. What do we know about a show? We are no white men. The whites have told us lies so many times that we don't care to believe them now."

I said to them, "What lie are you talking about?" They said, "They told us Navahos would have work and money if they would only reduce the sheep and goats. Now then the goats have gone, but no work, no money. Don't think we will try it again. If we let white men work around our Reservation and on it, they will say it is their land because they worked on it, and soon they will run all over the land. So we don't want anything now. We are living well right now."

I told them we were not a white man but one and we not asking to save land for somebody else or for the money this is to tell you save by you own hand and head and that it will be your land and to tell you that you could have a better wool and sheep in peace

I told them we were not white men, except one of us, and we were not asking them to save the land for somebody else or for money. We wanted to show them how to save it by their own hands and heads, and it would be their own land. We wanted to tell them and all way as it is they is many sheep and goats right now and that the land is about to go to pieces now if we don't care make we lose our land some day.

Well they said if you going to tell us we will hear you at big dance tonight but we don't want the show. They were four big head men there and three men wanted show and one not.

The head medicine man of that dance came up after we get the show wagon was set up. He ask what's all the things was have and what's all about we going to do there.

I told him we going to give a picture shout if they can let us. He said to go on and show to white men and not come around to their ceremonial place and try to take picture and make money on it.

I told him this was the Soil Conservation Service

how they could have better wool and sheep, in peace and for always. As it is now there are too many sheep and goats, and the land is about to go to pieces. If we don't take care of it, we won't have any land someday.

"Well," they said, "if you are going to talk to us, you can do it at the big dance tonight, but we don't want any show." There were four big headmen there. Three men wanted the show and one did not.

The head medicine man of the dance came up after we got the show wagon all set up. He asked about all the things we had there and what we were going to do.

I told him we were going to give a picture show if they would let us. He said to go on and show it to the white men, but not to come around the Navahos' ceremonial place and try to take pictures and make money on it.

I told him this was Soil Conservation Service work,

work with Indian to understand just what it mean to save the land from Erosion and over grazing land by too many goats and sheep that just running around over the land.

Why your coming back again with the white man idea trying to do away the goats and sheep from our poor people as you might think your helping your people but you not for you helping the white or the people of Erosion are trying to run the Navaho land and when they do we the poor one are going to be the end and you young men that are trying to be like a white man are going to get what you wanted and not the poor one.

I tell him that I was Navaho myself that we were working for Navaho not against them and that if we can show let our old man Police talk to them.

He told me if we was going to have show and teach-

trying to make the Indians understand just what it means to save the land from erosion, and how the land was being overgrazed by too many goats and sheep that were just running around over it.

"Why are you coming back again with the white man's idea of trying to do away with the sheep and goats of our poor people? You might think you are helping your people, but you are not. You are helping the whites, or the Soil Erosion people. They are trying to run the Navaho land, and when they do it is going to be the end for us poor ones. You young men that are trying to be like white men are going to get what you want, but not the poor ones."

I told him I was a Navaho myself, and that we were all working for the Navahos, not against them and to let our old policeman ask the people if we can have the show.

He said to me, "If you are going to have a show

ing why don't we go to school and not come around or ceremonial place for that was no place for it.

and some teaching, why don't you go to a school instead of coming around our ceremonial, which is no place for it?"

One woman beside us objected but I didn't ask the reason but soon learned that it was for the fox pictures we show at first dance and she was afraid we show again but we didn't for it was strong up against religious ceremonial.

One woman beside us objected. I didn't ask her the reason, but I soon learned that it was because of the coyote pictures we showed at the first dance. She was afraid we were going to show that one again, but we didn't because it is a very bad thing to have around a religious ceremonial.

Finally some Indian want to see and they all started talking about it and it was OK. After the show we heard nothing bad about the talk but just a little about the picture. That was a picture about snake which part of the great ceremonial and they didn't want to see in first place but they like the show and talk.

Finally some Indians said they wanted to see the picture, and they all started talking about it and decided it was OK. After the show we heard nothing bad about the talk, just a little they didn't like about the picture. There was a picture of a snake, which is a part of the great ceremonial, and they didn't want to see it. But they liked the show and the talk.

NOTE: Much additional data on attitudes and behavior toward whites appears in Leighton and Kluckhohn, *Children of The People* (Cambridge: Harvard University Press, 1947).

5. THE SUPERNATURAL: POWER AND DANGER

The arrangement of the materials in this book follows a pattern which is a white abstraction—not Navaho. Earlier chapters have described the "economic life" and the "social life" of The People. We are now beginning several chapters about "religious life." This grouping is convenient because it fits the way in which white people are accustomed to think. But it is very important to remember that the grouping really does violence to the intricate interconnections between these aspects of the Navaho's daily life. From one point of view, all Navaho "rituals" are socio-economic techniques; that is, they are techniques for securing food, restoring health, and ensuring survival. Yet this statement is also one-sided. It would be equally true to say that much "economic" activity is motivated by the desire to obtain the wherewithal for giving costly ceremonials—many of which are great social occasions—and to acquire ceremonial property, tangible and intangible.

In white society too, religion has its social and economic aspects. Marriage rites of the church are commonly used to set up a new social and economic unit, the family. Prayers often begin sessions of legislative bodies, and the oath on the Bible usually establishes the integrity of witnesses in courts. Many other instances from daily life could be cited to demonstrate that the divisions between religious, social, and economic life in white society are not nearly so clear-cut as people often unthinkingly assume. Because Western thought is so much influenced by the supposedly watertight categories into which Aristotle and the scholastic philosophers believed they could separate all reality, white persons tend to forget that abstractions are just a convenience and that really everything in human life blends into everything else. They talk as if "a thing is *either* black *or* white," forgetting that it may be both or neither. Pure black and pure white are both rare; what we have mostly is an infinite variety of shades of grey, separated from each other by almost imperceptible gradations.

Still, it makes a little more sense to speak of religion as one separable part of life in white society than it does in the Navaho case. The white world is now mainly a secular world. As clerics so often complain, white people "turn religion on and off." They may go to church on Sundays and a few other occasions. Birth, marriages, and deaths are usually solemnized, but most whites do not feel that religion has anything to do with large sectors of life. With the Navaho it is quite different. Their world is still a whole. Every daily act is colored by their conceptions of supernatural forces, ever present and ever threatening.

In another sense, speaking of "Navaho religion" does violence to the viewpoint of The People. There is no word or phrase in their language which could possibly be translated as "religion." It is not that they too do not have their categories. The outstanding feature of their language is the fineness of its distinctions. But Navaho categories are much more concrete. And their categories cut across those of whites. Precisely because the Navaho world is still a whole, we should not expect to find some separate entity denoted by a word equivalent to "religion."

A famous anthropologist has defined religion as "man's confession of impotence in certain matters." In these chapters we shall be talking about all that The People do and say with respect to those areas of experience which they feel are beyond the control of ordinary techniques and beyond the rational understanding which works well enough in ordinary affairs. We shall be speaking of the *super* natural.

BEINGS AND POWERS

The universe of The People contains two classes of personal forces. There are the Earth Surface People, living and dead; these are ordinary human beings. Then there are the Holy People. They are not "holy" in the sense of possessing moral sanctity, for often their deeds have a very different odor. They are "holy" in the meaning of "powerful and mysterious," of belonging to the sacred as opposed to the profane world. They travel about on sunbeams, on the rainbow, on the lightnings. They have great powers to aid or to harm Earth Surface People. But it is better not to call them gods because the word "god" has so many connotations which are inappropriate. The Holy People are not portrayed as all-knowing or even as all-powerful. They certainly are not depicted as wholly good. While they are supplicated and propitiated, they may also be coerced. Probably coercion is indeed the dominant note. In general, the relationship between them and the Earth Surface People is very different from what Christians think of as the connection between God and man.

As described in the Navaho origin myth, the Holy People lived first below the surface of the earth. They moved from one lower world to another because of witchcraft practiced by one of them. In the last of the twelve lower worlds the sexes were separated because of a quarrel, and monsters were born from the female Holy People. Finally a great flood drove the Holy People to ascend to the present world through a reed. Natural objects were created. Then came the first death among the Holy People. About this time too, Changing Woman, the principal figure among them, was created. After she reached puberty, she was magically impregnated by the rays of the Sun and by water from a waterfall, and bore twin sons. These Hero

Twins journeyed to the house of their father, the Sun, encountering many adventures and slaying most of the monsters.

In the course of all these events, the Holy People developed ways of doing things which were partly practical and partly magical. When they decided to leave for permanent homes at the east, south, west, north, the zenith, and the nadir, they had a great meeting at which they created the Earth Surface People, the ancestors of the Navahos, and taught them all the methods they had developed, so that The People could build houses, obtain food, marry, travel, and trade and could also protect themselves against disease, hunger, and war. After the Holy People had departed, the various clans of the Navahos wandered in the east and the west, and at last there was a great meeting of all of them in the region where they now live.

Changing Woman is the favored figure among the Holy People. She had much to do with the creation of the Earth Surface People and with the meeting at which they were taught how to control the wind, lightning, storms, and animals, and how to keep all these forces in harmony with each other. This meeting was a ceremonial of the Holy People and has become Blessing Way, a ritual which occupies a key position in the Navaho "religious system." Changing Woman, ever young and ever radiant in beauty, lives in a marvelous dwelling on western waters.

Some Navahos say that Changing Woman had a younger sister, White Shell Woman, who was the mother of one of the Hero Twins, Child of the Water. Others claim that Changing Woman and White Shell Woman are one and the same being. Turquoise Woman and Salt Woman also seem almost to be variants of Changing Woman, different names for different aspects of her story and her activities.

Next to Changing Woman in importance is her husband, the Sun. Sun symbolism is all-pervasive in Navaho religion. Indeed, as Gladys Reichard observes, "the evidence is quite convincing that all of these master symbols represent the same thing, Sun's Weapons which aid man in controlling the recalcitrant elements in the universe."[1]

The Hero Twins—Monster Slayer and Child of the Water (sometimes called Reared-within-the-Earth and Changing Grandchild)—are invoked in almost every Navaho ceremonial. Their adventures establish many of the Navaho ideals for young manhood. They serve especially as models of conduct in war and can almost be called the Navaho war gods. The Hero Twins slew most of the monsters, but they did not kill all of these potential enemies of mankind. Hunger, Poverty, Old Age, and Dirt survived, for they proved to have a place in human life. The exploits of the Twins, as well as those of other Holy People, define many features of the Navaho landscape as holy places. The lava fields, which are so conspicuous in the Navaho country, are the dried blood of the slain monsters.

Changing Woman, the Sun, and the Hero Twins are the four supernatural beings who seem to bulk largest in the religious thought and lore of The People. In the background are First Man and First Woman, who were transformed from two ears of white and yellow corn, and others prominent in the stories of life in the lower worlds. Most of The People believe that First Man created the universe, but another version of the incident, possibly due to Christian influence, pictures a being called *be'gochídí* as the creator of the world.

Another group of Holy People are the Failed-To-Speak People, such as Water Sprinkler, Fringed Mouth, Hunchback, and others who are impersonated by masked dancers in the public exhibitions of the great chants. Still another type are the animals and personalized natural forces like Coyote, Big Snake Man, Crooked Snake People, Thunder People, and Wind People. Finally, there are various helpers of the supernaturals and intermediaries between them and man. Big Fly is "the messenger of gods and of men."

He and Corn Beetle whisper omens and advice to Earth Surface People who are in trouble.

The origin myth is told with variations by different narrators, but it shows a good deal of consistency in most of its central elements, and defines for the Navahos many of their basic conceptions of life. It tells The People that, from time immemorial, the universe has been a very dangerous place, inhabited by people who were untrustworthy, if not completely evil. True, not all of the Holy People are unfriendly to Earth Surface People. Changing Woman gave corn and other valuable gifts to them. Spider Woman and Spider Man taught them how to weave. Two of the Holy People helped Woman Speaker's husband, Bent Man, to escape from the place of ghosts. Spider Man established four warnings of death or disaster: noise in the windpipe, ringing in the ear, twitching in the nose, and pricking of the skin on the body. If these warnings are heeded—and The People take them very seriously—something may be done to avert the danger, or at least to postpone or lessen it.

But of these beings and powers, of whom we have mentioned only a few, Changing Woman alone is consistently well-wishing to the Earth Surface People. The other beings are undependable, even though they may have given mankind many of their prized possessions. The Sun and the Moon demand a human life each day; the Hero Twins are often pitiless; First Man is a witch; Coyote is a trickster. When Woman Speaker died and was buried by First Boy and First Girl, she gave them ghost sickness because they did not put her left moccasin on her right foot and her right moccasin on her left foot, as they should have done. All of these beings except Changing Woman—and many others as well—are forever present to Navaho consciousness as threats to prosperity.

GHOSTS

Not all the powerful beings who are always present as potential threats to the well-being of the Navaho are Holy People. Perhaps the most fearful of all to them are the ghosts of Earth Surface People.

The Navahos seem to have no belief in a glorious immortality. Existence in the hereafter appears to be only a shadowy and uninviting thing. The afterworld is a place like this earth, located to the north and below the earth's surface. It is approached by a trail down a hill or cliff, and there is a sandpile at the bottom. Deceased kinfolk, who look as they did when last seen alive, come to guide the dying to the afterworld during a journey that takes four days. At the entrance to the afterworld, old guardians apply tests to see if death has really occurred.

Death and everything connected with it are horrible to The People. Even to look upon the bodies of dead animals, except those killed for food, is a peril. Dead humans are buried as soon as possible, and with such elaborate precautions that one of the greatest favors which a white person can do for Navahos is to undertake this abhorrent responsibility.

This intense and morbid avoidance of the dead and of everything connected with them rests upon the fear of ghosts. The other Earth Surface People who have fearful powers—witches—are also very terrible, but they are, after all, living beings who can be controlled in some measure and, if necessary, killed. Ghosts are, as it were, the witches of the world of the dead, a shadowy impalpable world altogether beyond the control of the living.

Most of the dead may return as ghosts to plague the living. Only those who die of old age, the stillborn, and infants who do not live long enough to utter a cry or sound do not produce ghosts, and for them the four days of mourning after burial need not be observed, since they will not be injurious to the living. Otherwise, any dead person, no matter how friendly or affectionate his attitude while he was living, is a potential danger.

A ghost is the malignant part of a dead person. It returns to avenge some neglect or offense. If a corpse has not been buried properly, if some of his belongings which he wished interred with him have been held out, if not enough animals have been killed at his grave, or if the grave has been disturbed in any way, the ghost will return to the burial place or to the former dwelling.

Ghosts appear after dark or just before the death of some family member, in human form or as coyotes, owls, mice, whirlwinds, spots of fire, or indefinite dark objects. They are usually dark or black. They may change form or size before one's eyes or make recognizable sounds (as of familiar birds or animals) and noises of movement. Whistling in the dark is always evidence that a ghost is near. Since ghosts appear only at night, adult Navahos are afraid to go about in the dark alone, and all sorts of night shapes and sounds are fearful.

Ghosts may chase people, jump upon them, tug their clothes, or throw dirt upon them. Not only are their actions frightening in themselves but they are omens of disaster to come. When a Navaho thinks he has seen a ghost or one appears in his dreams, he is sure that he or a relative will die unless the proper ceremonial treatment is successfully applied.

Both the type of experience with ghosts which is commonly related among Navahos and the way in which children at boarding school interpret events there in terms of the old beliefs are illustrated in this passage from an autobiography.

> One time I was sure scared. I was at school in California and two men were doing the shot put. And one man got hit behind the ear and they took him to the hospital. I sprained my ankle and every day I went to

the hospital and the next day I asked for him and they said he is dead. And I said I want to see him so they took me up. And I was surprised—he was lying there with his eyes open and he didn't look dead. Everyone was sorry he was dead. He was our best football player. He played quarter back. So we dressed him in his football clothes and took his picture and then we put him in his citizen clothes and took his picture. We had a funeral and we all marched and the band played slow music. His bed was next to mine. We slept on a porch. And I went to bed and pretty soon I heard someone coming and then he opened the screen door. I didn't see his face. He came in and sat on the foot of that boy's bed. I reached for a flashlight under my pillow and I turned it on and he had disappeared. Boy, I sure was scared. I didn't believe in those things before that but I got out of bed and ran into the house where the other boys were. And I told them. And then we heard somebody coming another night. I was scared all right. So they gave me a bed upstairs and I was looking out the window and I saw somebody coming a long ways off. It was like something black and it came nearer. And I turned my flashlight on him and there was nobody there. The disciplinarian didn't believe it and I said well you go and sleep down there on the porch, so he did. And that night he heard somebody coming and he sure ran.

When I came home from school my father rode toward Perea one night and I was with my sister in the hogan. Pretty soon we heard my father galloping toward us and when he got to the door he fell off his horse onto the ground and he lay there and didn't know anything. So I got on the horse and I rode as fast as I could to a medicine man over there [pointing] by the mesa. And he didn't stop to get a horse. He just took his bundle and got on my horse and I rode behind him. He had a hard time with my father. He sang most of the night before he got him conscious. The next day my father said he was riding home and two black things came after him. They were on each side of him. And they rode down on him and one of them tried to get his reins. He rode around dodging them and finally he got away from them.

WITCHES

The Navahos believe that by witchcraft evil men and women, acting separately or in a group, can obtain property and produce the illness or death of those whom they hate. Like ghosts, these malevolent people are active mainly at night. They often wear the hide of a coyote, a wolf, or some other animal. English-speaking Navahos talk about them as "human wolves" or "Navaho wolves." They are ghouls, and they practice incest.

A witch may use four principal techniques against his victims. He may feed them "corpse poison," a preparation made of powdered human flesh, or blow it in their faces. He may utter spells, particularly over something closely associated with the victims—nail parings or hair or a fragment of clothing—which the witch secretes in a grave. Or he may magically shoot into the victims small objects, especially something connected with corpses, like a bone or a bit of ash from a hogan in which someone has died. (This is commonly "diagnosed" by the presence of a small bump on the head.) The fourth technique involves the use of a narcotic plant and is said to be employed primarily in seducing women, in gambling, and in trading. The principal symptoms manifested by the supposed victims are fainting, "epileptic" seizures, sudden onset of pain, emaciation, or a sharp pain in a localized area with a lump or other evidence of a foreign object there.

Witchcraft is a subject which most Navahos are unwilling to discuss, sometimes even to mention, before whites. This is in part because they anticipate ridicule or violent disapproval if they confess such a belief, in part because of their own intrinsic fear and dislike of talking about such an unpleasant subject. Consequently, some whites live for years in the Navaho country with only a vague awareness that Navahos suspect others as witches, gossip about them, hold trials, and occasionally carry out "executions." Occasionally accounts of witch killings get into the papers, like that near Fruitland, New Mexico, in 1942 when a man who thought witchcraft had caused the death of his children killed four "witches" and then committed suicide. Witchcraft belief is extraordinarily persistent. Navahos who seem to be completely "emancipated" from other aspects of their religion will still show tremendous fear of witches, once a situation takes on a certain coloring.

Various plants and other substances are believed to afford protection against witches. Still stronger protection is held to be afforded by possessing ceremonial knowledge and power and by having frequent ceremonies held over one. Curing is possible through certain ceremonials, when the witchcraft has not gone too far. Special features may also be added to help out victims of witchcraft. For example, if a person is convinced that he knows who the witch-aggressor is, he may have performed over him the Enemy Way ceremonial popularly called the "squaw dance." (See Chapter 7.) After the first night of chanting over the patient in the ceremonial hogan, a group of mounted Navahos ride off to another hogan some miles distant. The Indian mounted on the fastest horse carries a small bundle tied to a pole. If the patient thinks he has been bewitched, this bundle contains something belonging to the supposed witch (one of his hairs or a piece of his hat which has absorbed his sweat, for example). Upon reaching the second hogan this party is met by other mounted Indians, and a mock battle takes place. The net result of all this procedure is thought to be that the evil will be turned away from the patient and back upon the witch. The Navaho theory under all circumstances is that if the intended victim is too strong or too well protected the witch's evil backfires upon himself.

All ceremonial cures, if successful, are believed to cause the death of the witch before long, and various deaths are accounted for in this way. Some Navahos also believe that witches are commonly struck down by lightning. When public feeling is sufficiently aroused, the supposed witch is made to confess, which ensures his "magical" death within a year, or he is actually put to death, sometimes by bloody and brutal means.

The following stories, told (in 1944) by a fifteen-year-old school boy to the boys' adviser in his school, are typical of the tales about witches which are constantly circulating around the Navaho country.

> There is one of them down there towards those hills. They cover themselves with a skin of a dog, or a bear. They dig up the dead men, then they make them small so that they can fit in the hand and take it home. Then they sing and make the small dead man get big again. Then they put something on that dries them up, and they grind it up. Then they put the powder in a deerskin bag and carry it with them even if they don't have their skin on. When they put this powder on you, you die.
>
> Last summer when I was herding sheep, I was by myself and it was midnight. I saw a big dog standing in the middle of the sheep so I took out the 440 [410 gauge shotgun, no doubt] and shot at him. I missed him and hit a sheep on the other side. Then my sister came and I went to the other side. I shot at him and hit him this time right here [indicating his upper arm]. I saw him on top of one of the sheep, but when I hit him he jumped up and ran away. . . . When I saw the sheep, he had a cut on his neck this long [two inches], but the sheep was still alive when I saw it in

the morning. Then the next morning, one man told me that he was going to the sing and wanted me to go with him. I didn't go with him, but after he was gone I went to the place he said the sing was. When I got there, it was dark. I went into the hogan and sat in a corner that was dark. I saw a man with some bandages on his arm right here [indicating his upper arm]. I asked his sister what was wrong with the man and she said that he got his arm in the wheel of the wagon and got it hurt. I knew that that was the man that I shot.

Another man told me last summer that he watched where the Navaho Wolfs hold their meetings. They dig a big hole, about this size [3 feet diameter] and dig it for a long ways, almost over to that building there [30 yards] on the side of the mountain. He went inside and found a curtain; when he crawled about five feet more, there was another curtain. He went farther and passed about five more curtains. Then the last curtain, he could see through because it was thin. He saw about fourteen men sitting in a circle, and five women, with no clothes on. They were all singing, and there was a feather standing up and moving like this [indicating an up and down motion]. When the feather stands up like that, the Navaho Wolf who is out is all right but when the feather falls down, then it means that the Navaho Wolf is dead. When this man saw that, he went out and went about one hundred feet and climbed a tree and waited for the Wolf to come back. About five o'clock he came back, and this man went back and told all of the Navahos about it. They came back on horses, and made a big circle. They waited for a long time, and when these Navaho Wolfs came out, they got them and took them to Shiprock and got $1,000 for them. They took them with their skins.

Jack told us about a Navaho Wolf that he chased when he was looking for his horse. He chased him down about five miles, and then this wolf ran under a bridge.

When Jack saw him he took his skin down to his pants, and there was lines on the man. He told Jack to look that way, but Jack did not look that way because when a man looks that way, the Navaho Wolf takes out a gun and shoots him. Then the Navaho Wolf told Jack to come down to near Tohatchi where he lived, and he would give him two hundred dollars, if he did not tell anybody. Jack said that he wouldn't tell nobody, but he didn't go. When you go far away, you get tired and hungry, this Navaho Wolf will give you something to eat; but you will die if you eat that because he puts some powder on it. At the squaw dances you see some Navahos with long hair in a knot in the back. These are the ones that you have to be scared of.

The other night, like I told you, William see a man come to the dormitory. He was about this small [4 feet], and then he gets real big, then he gets small again. He couldn't hear his tracks. Then two nights passed and another man came in, but he could hear his tracks. He could hear when he shut the door.

If the Navaho Wolf catches you at the meeting, they bring you inside and ask you if you want to learn or die. If you want to learn, they bring you inside and say, "Who do you want, your sister or brudder?" If you say "brudder," two days after that he will die. Then they will send you after him, like they show you, and you bring him back. It is like paying to learn, only you don't pay in money. You have to pay with your brudder or sister.

The Navaho Wolf travels fast. Fast like the automobile or horse. They live over near Chinle, but they can come to Shiprock and go back in one night. Last year there was a boy here at school whose name was Albert. He died just about this time. His father was caught, and he named Albert too. They took him to Shiprock and he died there. [This boy died at the Shiprock Hospital on January 17, 1943, from complications of a mastoid operation.] They brought him over here and let everybody see him, but his brudders and sister and father didn't cry. Now the father is a Navaho Wolf.

The Navaho Wolfs are rich. The other day a teacher asked how a man can get rich, and William or James wrote on the blackboard, "Be a Navaho Wolf." When a Navaho Wolf unburies a dead man, he takes away his silver belt and sells it at Farmington, or away over at Phoenix. They don't sell it to the traders near where they dig up the man because the people know about it. They sell it far away.

THE NAVAHO THEORY OF DISEASE

We have seen that the possible sources of fear are very numerous. But what do all these dreaded things do to The People? Although Navahos worry about property loss or damage, their fears are primarily focused upon illness and death. Either disease or an accidental injury may be due to an attack by the Holy People, brought on by taboo transgressions which are described in the following chapter. Or the symptoms may be evidence of "ghost sickness," caused by either native or foreign ghosts. When there does not seem to be sufficient background for either of these explanations—as when an illness is persistent and stubbornly refuses to yield to the usual Navaho treatment, or when it is in any way mysterious from the Navaho point of view—then witchcraft is apt to be assigned as the cause.

Although The People distinguish between *naałniih,* "disease" (mostly contagious infections like measles, small pox, diphtheria, syphilis, gonorrhea) and the more generalized *tah honeesgai,* "body fever" or "body ache" (often translated by English-speaking Navahos as "sick all over"), still all ailments, mental or physical, are of supernatural origin. The notion of locating the cause of a disease in physiological processes is foreign to Navaho thought. The cause of disease, of injury to the body or to one's property, of continued misfortune of any kind, must be traced back to some accidental or deliberate violation of one of the thou-shalt-nots (see Chapter 6), or to contact with a ghost, or to witch activity. It follows logically that treatment consists in dealing with these causative factors and not with the illness or injury as such. The supernaturals must be appeased. If a visible sign of attack is present, it must be removed, or the patient must be treated on the general principle that he has been attacked by supernaturals or by supernatural means and that his supernatural relationships need to be restored to normal condition again. The ultimate aim of every curing ceremonial is this restoration. As Gladys Reichard has recently written:

> The Navajo wants to be natural, to be good, to be safe, well, and young . . . but he attains this ideal quite practically. Any deviation from it represents disease, which in turn makes the body abnormal.
>
> The Navajo can take things as they come and often tightens his belt but he also values possessions. If ritual can give him a body which can enjoy wealth, it can also give him wealth to enjoy.[2]

FOLK TALES AND MYTHS

The total body of The People's oral literature is extremely large. Many of the plots are familiar from other North American Indian tribes, but the style, the phrasing, the embroidery of incidents have their own local color and special Navaho quality. The organization of stories tends to be much looser and freer than is the case with the corresponding stories among the Pueblo Indians. Throughout there is humor, a delight in puns, a tremendous interest in places and place names, and great imaginative power.

FOLK TALES

Folk tales are secular in that, although things happen in them which could never occur in ordinary life and are hence part of the supernatural order of events, they are told primarily for amusement and entertainment. The most famous cycles are those of Trotting Coyote and of Tooth-Gum Woman. They are full of levity and indeed of bawdiness. Except for this last element, the nearest equivalent in English would be the Br'er Rabbit stories. They do often point a moral, but the moral is taken rather lightly. Folk tales have none of the high seriousness of the myths which explain the world and life, supply authority for all sorts of everyday behavior, give the rationale of the ceremonials.

ORIGIN MYTH

The content of the origin myth or emergence story has already been indicated in the section entitled "Beings and Powers." This myth is The People's nearest analogue to the Christian Bible. Just as the Bible is traditionally *the* book, so also for The People this is *the* story.

Mythology is the response of man's imagination to the uncharted areas of human experience. Since the Navahos have not rationalized their mythology into theology, there are some inconsistencies among various versions of the origin myth and between the origin myth and other myths. Whatever the discrepancies, the origin myth still gives definite form to many Navaho notions of things. It is also the final warrant of authority for carrying out many acts, ritual and secular, in prescribed ways.

RITE MYTHS

All ceremonial practice is based upon an accompanying myth which tells how the rite started and how it should be carried out. The separate myths which justify each of the many rites are usually connected in some way with the origin myth. They are, as it were, separable episodes which are primarily the private business of Singers who learn the rite.

Knowing the full myth by heart is not an indispensable prerequisite to practice, but such knowledge does give the practitioner prestige and the right to expect higher fees. Otherwise disparaging remarks are often heard: "Oh, he doesn't know the story," or "He doesn't know the story very well yet." Nevertheless treatment by a practitioner ignorant of the myth is regarded as efficacious. Navahos are often a little cynical about the variation in the myths. If someone observes that one Singer did not carry out a procedure exactly as did another (of perhaps greater repute), it will often be said, "Well, he says *his* story is different." Different forms of a rite myth do tend to prevail in different sections of the Navaho country and in different localities of the various sections.

Myths of the various rites are different, yet tend to share a good deal. As Leland Wyman has recently written:

> "As more Navaho myths are recorded the more apparent it becomes that the total mythology possesses a somewhat limited number of episodes and incidents or types thereof which recur over and again in the origin legends of different chants. It is almost as in the construction of the chants themselves, where a limited number of types of ceremony are combined in various ways and with various individual minutiae."[3]

There is much fine ritual poetry in the rite myths, and even the prose passages are often suffused with deep emotional feeling. Take this passage from the myth of the Mountain Top Way chant:

> But instead of looking south in the direction in which he was going he looked to the north, the country in

which dwelt his people. Before him were the beautiful peaks of *dibenca* with their forested slopes. The clouds hung over the mountain, the showers of rain fell down its sides, and all the country looked beautiful. And he said to the land "*ahalani*" Greeting! and a feeling of loneliness and homesickness came over him, and he wept and sang this song:

> That flowing water! That flowing water!
> My mind wanders across it.
> That broad water! That flowing water!
> My mind wanders across it.
> That old age water! That flowing water!
> My mind wanders across it.[4]

MYTHS AND TALES IN DAILY LIFE

Parts of the origin myth are widely known. The episode in which the Hero Twins slay the monsters, whose dried blood forms the lava fields in the Navaho country, is known to all The People. Other parts of this myth and some folk tales are known, if only in outline, by practically all adult Navahos. Men tend perhaps to know them in greater detail than women, but there are exceptions to this. Certain tales or episodes are more current in some regions than in others. In addition, there are special variants which are handed down in family or clan lines. Indeed, each clan has its own story which is attached to the end of the tribal origin myth.

Both the origin myth and folk tales are commonly told around family firesides in winter. Some individuals gain great reputations as narrators, so that they attract audiences beyond the circle of their immediate families. Such recitals serve the function of books in this society where the printed word is only beginning to be of importance to some of the younger tribesmen.

THE FAMILY IN MYTH AND FOLKLORE

The picture of Navaho family relations presented above in Chapter 3, which was based on observation of many individuals, is confirmed at some points by standard features of Navaho myths and tales. At other points, however, myths give a picture of social relations that diverges from what is seen in contemporary life. For example, the origin myth places very little emphasis upon the determination of residence and inheritance by the mother's line. These discrepancies may be due to the fact that the myth, at least in part, has been borrowed from Pueblo tribes. Or possibly Navaho culture has changed without a corresponding change in the mythology.

From the psychological point of view, however, the interpretations previously advanced receive considerable support from the myths. Folklore must be presumed to originate in the dreams and phantasies of individuals. But when the product of one person's imagination (as mingled with and modified by the phantasy of other persons over a long period) is taken over as a part of the mythology of a whole group, the themes may confidently be assumed to correspond to widely current psychological situations.

The largely suppressed and repressed tensions between brother and sister, for example, find an outlet in witch and ghost stories. In a striking number of tales and myths, the pursuer who catches a were-animal discovers that the witch is really his own sister or brother. Another common plot in myth and tale revolves around the incestuous attraction between a brother and sister.

The uniformities in the myths of the curing ceremonials are exceedingly revealing. The preoccupation with children is striking. Possibly this could be explained as a device to interest and to educate children or as an unconscious harking back to childhood glories on the part of adult authors and narrators. But the amazing similarity in the human situations dealt with makes another interpretation more plausible. A family situation is always central in the initial episodes. There is a neglected brother or a disobedient nephew or son or a wicked sister. The hero of the tale is often the despised child who overcomes the indulged child. In almost every case, the plot appears to be a symbolic resolution of characteristic intra-familial difficulties among The People which must be repressed or suppressed in actual childhood and life.

The story supplies relief through verbal expression for the shocks and emotional wounds that occur during the training of the Navaho child. That brother and sister are the principal dramatis personae fits neatly alike with the central conflicts in the Navaho child-training process (surrendering the breast and the position as favored child to a younger brother or sister and at the same time coming under the disciplinary authority of an older brother or sister) and with the essentially inevitable tensions of adult life.

The ways in which the myths describe the invention of the curing rites and the relationship of the inventor to his first patient suggest that the man who conducts a ceremonial is the psychological equivalent of an older relative who forgives the patient for his or her guilty wishes. This interpretation is borne out by the fact that the myths prescribe that a "medicine man" and his patient must be considered ever thereafter to be related; they call each other by kinship terms. The "medicine man" may never marry anyone over whom he has sung; if he sings over his own wife they must thenceforth behave to each other as close relatives between whom any sexual contact would be strictly forbidden.

Myths give to women a primarily nurturing and protective role. Sun's wife protects even the children of Changing Woman, who are the proof of her husband's faithlessness. Men are portrayed as less dependable, now kind, now cruel: the Sun is a philanderer; the Hero Twins threaten even their mother if she will not tell them what they want to find out. But Changing Woman is uniformly trustworthy and gratifying. Upon only one point is she obdurate—she refuses to change her residence.

The dominant image of women in the mythology approaches that of Changing Woman. But there are women of other types: shrewish First Woman; the quarrelsome and lascivious women of the preëmergence period whose sins begot the dreadful monsters; the lewd Tooth-Gum Woman of the folk tales. The interesting thing is that in the myths the two kinds of female characters are sharply separated. Women tend to be either unfailingly good or completely bad, while men tend to be consistently mixed.

This mirrors rather exactly the concepts which Navahos today have of the two sexes. The "official" view of women is that they are the stable foundations of society. Under normal circumstances a man will not think of making disparaging statements about his female relatives, and the most that he will let slip against his wife is that "she scolds too much." But dreams and the wild recriminations of drunken men and the pent-up fury released at long last in a quarrel between a man and his wife or sister make it plain that the evil women of myth and tale correspond to a generally suppressed part of the conception of women in real life. The image of woman, though mostly warm, positive, and full of strength, also has a component of distrust and even of hate which occasionally bursts forth. Is this partly because the mother is the one who at first grants everything but at the age of weaning denies, scolds, and beats away the child who wants the breast? Men are always a little undependable. The father is affectionate to the child, but from the very beginning he comes and goes; the child can never really count on his comfort. Man is fickle—but is never thought to be otherwise. Woman is the one who is either all bad or all good. She gives all or denies all.

6. THE SUPERNATURAL: THINGS TO DO AND NOT TO DO

When one first studies Navaho religious belief and practice, he thinks more than once that the Eskimos' description of their religion—"We do not believe; we fear"—would be appropriate for the Navahos as well. As one grows more familiar with The People's ways of thinking and feeling, however, he realizes that, although their religion points out that the world is indeed a dangerous place, religious activity is also a source of positive joys and confidence in life. As suggested in Chapter 4, Navahos working away from their kinfolk find it necessary to go home partly for a renewal of the sense of security that the Sings and the great chants bring. In this chapter we shall try to see how The People deal with their dangerous world, what things Navahos do in order to ward off danger and to place themselves in harmony with the beings and powers which are the source of danger and also of possible aid and benefit. Some of this knowledge and some techniques are a part of the daily life of all The People. Some of them are esoteric, that is, known only to those who have had special training. We shall begin with those things which every Navaho does to safeguard himself and his family, and then go on to those things which must be done, or at least directed, by the smaller group of the esoterically initiated.

THOU SHALT NOT

A very high proportion of all the acts which arise out of convictions about beings and powers are negative in character. Thus lightning-struck trees must be avoided. Coyotes, bears, snakes, and some kinds of birds must never be killed. The eating of fish and of most water birds and animals is forbidden, and raw meat is taboo. Navahos will never cut a melon with the point of a knife. They never comb their hair at night. No matter how crowded a hogan may be with sleeping figures, no Navaho may step over the recumbent body of another. Mother-in-law and son-in-law must never look into each other's eyes. Any kind of sexual contact (even walking down the street or dancing together) with members of the opposite sex of one's own or one's father's clan is prohibited. Most technical processes are hedged about with restrictions: the tanner dare not leave the pole on which he scrapes hide standing upright; the potter and the basket-maker work in isolation, observing a bewildering variety of taboos; the weaver shares one of these, the dread of final completion, so that a "spirit outlet" must always be left in the design. Let these few common examples stand as representative of the literally thousands of doings and sayings which are *báhádzid*, or tabooed.

Most of these "superstitions" seem absurd to white persons, but we should not forget that superstition may be well defined as "what your people believe and mine do not." White fears of sitting down thirteen to a table or of starting a journey on Friday seem ridiculous to a Navaho. It should also be remembered that Navaho fears which seem unrealistic to whites are often connected with very real danger. In a country where rattlers abound and lightning kills livestock and humans and destroys dwellings every summer, it is not unrealistic to fear snakes and lightning. The connection between "realism" and "unrealism" in the taboos is not complete—snakes, for example, are avoided rather than killed—but the danger and the taboo may nonetheless be connected.

Moreover, even though the practice of The People in regard to taboos may seem absurd to white persons, a little reflection shows that some taboos have practical values. Coyotes eat prairie dogs that might otherwise ruin meadows and sown fields. The same may be said of snakes. The taboo against destroying birds helps to control grasshoppers and other insect pests. The outlawing of sexual rivalry within a clan undoubtedly makes for clan solidarity. And it does not seem a farfetched speculation to suggest that preventing intimate contacts between sons-in-law and mothers-in-law has socially useful consequences. This does not mean that Navahos at some past time sat down to talk these matters over and made rational decisions about them. It probably does mean that only those taboos which somehow have value will survive indefinitely.

Avoidances are intensified during critical periods in the life of the individual. A pregnant woman is supposed to observe an enormous number of taboos, and her husband must share some of them lest his wife and unborn child be injured. For the person who has just been a patient in a curing rite, for the adolescent girl, for the menstruating woman, the thou-shalt-nots of daily life are multiplied.

As we have already seen, Navaho fears and avoidance reach a climax in the complex of beliefs and acts connected with death. It is believed that only witches will go near places of burial. There is some avoidance of uttering even the names of dead people.

THOU SHALT

Navahos are brought up to fear many forces in the supernatural world, but they are also taught ways of coping with them. In most cases, there are ways to effect a cure after the threat has struck.

Every adult Navaho has "gall medicine," a preparation of the galls of various animals, which he takes as an emetic if he fears that he has absorbed a witch's "corpse poison." Everyone is particularly careful to carry a little sack of gall medicine on his person when he goes into large gatherings of strangers. In the hogan will be kept plants and other protectives against and remedies for witchcraft. In buckskin pouches in every dwelling will be found herbs, pollen, bits of turquoise and shell, tiny carved images of sheep and horses.

The use of the pollen of corn and other plants is very important in maintaining the proper relationship to the Holy People. In old-fashioned households the day still begins with the sprinkling of pollen from one of the little bags and a brief murmured prayer. After the evening meal the members of the family rub their limbs and say, "May I be lively. May I be healthy." More pollen may be offered and a Blessing Way song sung.

The spectacular ceremonials so capture the imagination that it is easy to forget that, for all their drama, they are quantitatively but a small part of the ritual life of The People. The daily routine of every member of the family is tinged by ceremonial observances as well as avoidances. The weaver uses songs and prayers. The tanner places a turquoise or white shell bead on his pole in order to protect his joints from becoming stiff. A squirrel's tail should be tied to a baby's cradle so that the child will be protected in case of a fall. Every family has a number of "good luck songs" which are believed to bring protection to family members and their property, to aid in the production of ample crops, and to secure increase of flocks and herds. Such songs are regarded as important property which a father or uncle may transmit to son or nephew.

The fundamental principles which underlie most Navaho magical practices are those of "like produces like" and "the part stands for the whole." Take this illustration of the first:

> They say that a child who is born in the summer can be rolled in the snow early in the morning and then the snow will disappear. Two years ago, when there was deep snow up to our waists, our sheep and horses died

and we were very hungry. My sister took her child and rolled it in the snow.

The lore of dreams is complex and much discussed by the folk, for most dreams are thought to have prognostic value. A dream of anything sick or weak or deformed is a cause for anxiety. If bad dreams keep coming, the hogan will be torn down and a new one built some distance away, because the bad dreams are supposed to come from ghosts who are frequenting their old haunts and trying to draw their relatives into ghostland with them.

There are many folk rites connected with travel. There are songs for safe journey and for success on a trip undertaken for love-making or for trading. By the side of old trails all over the country of The People, there can be seen cairns three to five feet high made of stones, twigs, bits of turquoise, and shell. These objects have been deposited by individuals on a journey, uttering a prayer like this:

> Placing rocks, Male One.
> Placing rocks, Female One.
>
> Everywhere I go, myself
> May I have luck.
> Everywhere my close relatives go
> May they have their luck.[1]

When Navahos go near sacred places they will visit the shrines and leave offerings. Some shrines lie on the summits of mountain peaks; others are found deep in canyons, in rock crevices, or by streams or springs. They are located wherever events of great mythological significance are thought to have occurred.

Many ritual practices are an everyday adjunct of agriculture. Seeds are mixed with ground "mirage stone" and treated in a variety of other ways. To prevent early frosts, stones from the sweathouses are planted in the fields or at the base of fruit trees. If the crop is being damaged by wind, the wind is called by its secret name and asked to leave the corn alone. Cutworms are placed on fragments of pottery, sprinkled with pollen, and given other "magical" treatment. When the harvest is stored, a stalk of corn having two ears is placed in the bottom of the storage pit to ensure a healthy crop for the next year.

If there is a long dry spell, a rainmaker may be asked to perform a ceremony of which this song is a part:

I usually walk where the rains fall
Below the east I walk
I being the Talking God
I usually walk where the rains fall
Within the dawn I walk
I usually walk where the rains fall (repeated after each line)
Among the white corn I walk
Among the soft goods I walk
Among the collected water I walk
Among the pollen I walk
I usually walk where the rains fall

By means of the white corn darkness is cast
As I walk where it usually rains (repeated after each line)
Over it dark clouds cast a shadow
Over it male rain casts a shadow
Among it zigzag lightning hangs suspended here and there
Among it straight lightning hangs suspended here and there
Among it is a gentle spray of rain
Among it is the twittering of rain prairie dogs heard
At the tips of its tassels the twittering of the blue ceremonial bird is heard
At its base the whites of water are
As I walk where it usually rains
I being the good and everlasting one
It being pleasant in front of me
It being pleasant behind me

As I walk where it usually rains
As I walk where it usually rains[2]

At intervals while the corn is growing the farmer should go to his field, walk around and through it in a special way, singing the appropriate song. At one stage the song is this:

My corn is arising
My corn is continually arising
In the middle of the wide field
My corn is arising
White Corn Boy he is arising
With soft goods my corn is arising
With hard goods my corn is arising
Good and everlasting ones they are arising[3]

Not every Navaho farmer follows every one of these or the hundreds of other negative or positive agricultural folk rites which could be mentioned, but the writers have not known any Navaho families who do not observe some such simple rituals.

Another lay rite is that of the sweathouse. Men retire there in groups to cleanse themselves, to refresh aching or fatigued bodies, to engage in social conversation, and to discuss serious matters of individual decision or family policy. However, the atmosphere is ritual. An invitation is shouted to the Holy People to join in the bath. Before entering the sweathouse, each bather throws fresh dirt on the roof to prevent poverty. The songs sung within are sacred songs. Though formerly groups of women used to take sweatbaths, the sweathouse is today in most Navaho areas an exclusively male institution. It seems to represent, among other things, a place of sanctuary from sex and from female scolding or interference.

RITES OF PASSAGE

One type of ceremonial participation is, in more than one sense, midway between the rites engaged in by all laymen and the more complex "priestly" ceremonials: the ritual occasions which mark passage of a particular milestone in the individual's life career. While some of them require the presence of a trained ceremonialist, they are relatively simple in character, and all Navahos—not just those who are "sick"—pass through them. (The rites attending a girl's puberty, marriage, and death are described in Chapter 3 of *Children of The People,* by Leighton and Kluckhohn, Harvard University Press, 1947.)

BIRTH

The newborn infant is placed in the ceremonially defined position. It is at first fed only pollen, a ceremonial food. Naming the baby is a ritual act which may occur within a few days after birth or not for several months. The infant's first laugh is occasion for a ceremonial gift-giving.

INITIATION

Boys and girls are made recognized members of The People and are introduced to full participation in ceremonial life by a short initiation ceremony which usually occurs on the next to the last night of a Night Way. This ceremony and the whole of the Night Way are popularly known as Yeibichai, from the principal figures in their initiation ceremony, who represent *yei* divinities.

Two assistants of the "medicine man" wash their hair with yucca suds and go into the ceremonial hogan, where they undress and put on kilts reaching just above the knee, ornaments of various kinds, skins, and the like. Wherever their skin is exposed (on the arms, legs, stomach, and chest), white clay is rubbed. One wears a black mask and the other a white mask; they represent Grandfather of the Monsters and Female Divinity. Each covers his mask with a blanket and walks to a spot three hundred yards or so away, where the participants in the initiation ceremony are waiting. Here a fire is burning. Mothers have brought their children and arranged them in a crescent west of the fire, boys on the north, girls on the south. Each child is covered by a blanket and is told not to look at the "gods." The mothers remain west of the children and the men gather east of the fire. Much joking takes place among the women and among the men.

The boys strip to the breechcloth. They are nervous and self-conscious, frequently feeling for the breechcloth to see that it is hanging properly and keeping their eyes on the ground.

The first boy is led out beside the fire. The figure in the white mask makes a mark on each shoulder with sacred cornmeal. Each time he does this the figure in the black mask utters a particular falsetto cry. Then, using a different falsetto cry, the black-masked figure lightly strikes the cornmeal marks with some reeds bound together. This is repeated for other places on the body, and the one who uses the reeds varies the time interval between touching the boys and uttering his cry, so that its unexpectedness causes the boys to start convulsively. The crowd laughs and jokes over this. There are shouts for hard or light strokes for particular boys, but the masked figure always grants these requests in reverse.

The girls remain seated and clothed with their blankets off. "Foreign" objects—such as store combs—are removed from their persons. The figure with the black mask does not use reeds for the girls, but instead he carries in each hand an ear of corn wrapped in spruce twigs. These he presses simultaneously against the cornmeal marks.

When each child has been treated, the two personators remove their masks and lay them on either side of the fire. Each child in turn is given some pollen from the buckskin bag of the "medicine man." The child is directed to sprinkle the pollen on the masks and then to throw some on each of the personators.

Then the one who wore the black mask places it over the face of each child in turn. When he is certain that the child can see through the mask, he gives his peculiar cry and moves on to the next child. All the children are now told to look up and always remember the Holy People. The reversal of the masks is a very intelligent psychological act, for it allows the child to see that the dread figure is actually someone he knows, or at least a human being, and thus the ritual is robbed of some of its terror. Perhaps too the reversal gives the child a sense of the oneness of the Holy People and the Earth Surface People. The ceremony closes with the admonition to each child not to betray to uninitiates what he has seen.

Theoretically this rite should be undergone at least four different times by each individual, so that he has looked upon four sets of masks, two by day and two by night, but nowadays few persons under middle age have actually completed this requirement. The age of first initiation varies with the accessibility of a Night Way, but initiates must be at least seven and may be as old as twelve or thirteen. At any ceremony, therefore, the persons being initiated may range in age from as young as seven to middle life.

FINDING THINGS OUT

We pass now from those "religious" activities which everyone knows how to do to those which are esoteric, known only by the gifted few. The simplest of these is divination. Although diviners may be instructed in certain details of their rites, they do not acquire the ability itself primarily through long training, as do other Navaho ceremonialists. It is a "gift" which suddenly descends upon them.

Disease, we have seen, is the result of violation of a taboo or of attack by one of the Holy People, a ghost, or a witch.

But in a life where the possibilities of transgression and attack are so multifarious, how is one to discover precisely which possible cause needs to be treated? Sometimes the case seems plain to The People. If one has been bold enough to kill a bear or a snake (or has been under the unfortunate necessity of having to do so) and subsequently develops the symptoms of "bear sickness" or "snake sickness," then both cause and cure are clearly indicated. More often, however, the person who is ill is not sure which of the many things he has left undone which he ought to have done, or the things he has done which he ought not to have done, is responsible. The cause is determined by divination.

Divination is also employed to locate property which has been lost or stolen, to find water in unfamiliar territory, to discover the whereabouts of persons, to determine whether one's wife has been guilty of adultery, and to predict the outcome of a hunting party or (in the past) of a war raid. In short, divination is the Navaho way of finding things out. But its greatest function is that of determining the proper form of ceremonial activity to be employed when any Navaho is in difficulties. By divination the cause is discovered and the whole ritual treatment may be prescribed: the precise ceremonial, the time, the right practitioner to select.

Divination can be carried out through "listening," through stargazing, and through chewing a narcotic plant, but today the form most frequently used is that of "hand-trembling." The hand-trembler, like other ceremonialists, is never sought out directly by the sick or troubled person. This must be done by an intermediary, usually a member of the patient's immediate family, who offers a fee and arranges a time.

When the hand-trembler arrives he sits down beside the patient. Water is brought, and he washes his hands and arms. He then takes pollen and, working from right to left, puts it on the soles of the patient's feet, his knees, palms of the hands, breast, between his shoulders, on top of his head, and in his mouth. The motion with the pollen is downward on the feet, knees, hands, and shoulders, upward on the back and breast. Next he seats himself about three feet to the right of the patient, takes more pollen and, beginning at a vein in the inside of his own right elbow, follows it along the inside of the arm, passes over the thumb and back to the starting place. Then from the starting place he runs pollen down to the tips of the index, middle, ring, and little fingers. As he puts the pollen from elbow to thumb he prays: "Black Gila Monster, I want you to tell me what is wrong with this patient. Do not hide anything from me. I am giving you a jet bead to tell me what the illness of this patient is." This prayer is then repeated for each finger, substituting Blue Gila Monster and turquoise bead for the index finger, Yellow Gila Monster and Haliotis shell bead for the middle and ring fingers, and White Gila Monster and white shell bead for the little finger. The whole performance is repeated three more times. While this takes place, no one may leave or enter the hogan or walk around outside. All those present must be quiet, and no dogs are allowed within.

Then a song invoking Gila Monster, "who gave the song in the beginning," is sung in four verses with variations in the colors mentioned analogous to those in the prayers. As soon as the hand-trembler begins to sing, and sometimes even before, his hand and arm begin to shake violently. The way in which the hand moves as it shakes provides the information sought.

This rite has been described in some (though by no means complete) detail both because of its intrinsic interest and because it provides a simple introduction to recurrent features of Navaho ceremonialism. The use of pollen, of songs and prayers, of offerings of turquoise and shells; the invocation of a particular supernatural; the association of colors and directions in symbolism; the insistence upon a carefully defined ritual order; four repetitions

—all these themes are part of the harmony of every "priestly" rite, and indeed of most folk rituals as well.

In cases other than illness the ceremony is carried on as described, except that no patient is present. When a person is lost, some article of his clothing will be used by the hand-trembler. It is said that the shaking hand will lead the diviner to a thief, grasp him by the shoulder, and shake him. If the thief has fled to a distant point, the Gila Monster will tell the hand-trembler where he is hiding. If the stolen goods have been hidden, if property has been lost, or if water is sought, it is believed that the trembling hand will lead to the right place.

THE WAY OF GOOD HOPE

The rite called Blessing Way is, as English-speaking Navahos are wont to say, "for good hope." In other words, it places the Navahos in tune with the Holy People—particularly Changing Woman—and so ensures health, prosperity, and general well-being. The expectant mother whose pregnancy is proceeding perfectly normally will have Blessing Way sung over her a short time before birth is anticipated. Navahos were given a Blessing Way by their families before they left for the Army or when they returned on furlough. There is a special Blessing Way for newly chosen headmen. The songs sung in the girl's puberty rite and in marriage are from Blessing Way. Blessing Way is thus precautionary, protecting, prophylactic—not a cure.

The People themselves say that Blessing Way, which is the ceremonial held by the Holy People when they created mankind and taught them skills and ritual, is the cornerstone of their whole ceremonial system. Changing Woman gave some of the songs, and the rite in general is most intimately connected with her. Father Berard Haile says the "legends, songs, and prayers are chiefly concerned with the creation and placement of the earth and sky, sun and moon, sacred mountains and vegetation, the inner forms of these natural phenomena, the control of he- and she-rains, dark clouds and mist, the inner forms of the cardinal points and like phenomena that may be considered as harbingers of blessing and happiness."[4]

Blessing Way is given very frequently indeed. Seldom does a family go for six months without having Blessing Way sung at least once in their hogan. It is held to be peculiarly important that every member of the immediate biological family should be present. Despite the sacredness of the ceremonial and the rich, complicated, and beautiful ideas behind it, the rite has the dignity of great simplicity. There are a few songs one night, a ritual bath in yucca suds with prayers and songs the next day, an all-night singing that night. Cornmeal and pollen are prominently used throughout, and drypaintings of these materials and pulverized flower blossoms are sometimes prepared on buckskin spread upon the ground. Only in Blessing Way is Changing Woman ever represented in visible form in a drypainting.

DRYPAINTINGS

Drypaintings are such a characteristic and so famous a feature of Navaho ceremonials that they merit some discussion. Although "sandpaintings" is the familiar term, it is a misleading one. In Blessing Way drypaintings, as just pointed out, the background is of buckskin spread on the ground and the designs are formed of vegetable materials (pollen, meal, crushed flowers). In the curing chants, too, the background is occasionally of buckskin, and the designs are made of charcoal and pulverized minerals—not sand at all in the strict sense. At most, sand forms the background of the drypaintings.

More than five hundred different drypaintings have been recorded, and there is every reason to believe that many others exist. Some are miniatures only a foot or two in diameter; others are so large—twenty feet or more in diameter—that they can be made only in specially constructed hogans. The small ones can be made by two or three people in less than an hour. The largest ones require the work of fifteen men during most of a day. Each drypainting is linked to a particular ceremonial, and the myth prescribes the design and the manner of making the painting. When only an excerpt from a ceremonial is given, only a single drypainting may be made, but a full performance ordinarily calls for a set of four on successive days. When the ceremonial to be used on any given occasion has been decided upon, the Singer consults with the patient and his family and selects from the various drypaintings prescribed for this ceremonial those four that seem most appropriate to the illness and the assumed cause.

Drypaintings are, on occasion, made out of doors, but usually they are made within the hogan where the ceremonial is carried out. Most of them are appropriate to the daytime, but a few are created after dark. Before the drypainting proper begins, charcoal and minerals are ground and placed in bark receptacles. Clean light-colored windblown sand is carried into the lodge and spread over the floor in an even layer from one to three inches thick. On this background the Singer and his assistants kneel or sit to create the design. Colors vary, but the four principal hues—white, blue, yellow, and black—are always present. These colors have symbolic associations with the directions, which vary with the ritual. Most of the color is laid on with the right hand of the artist, who holds the coloring matter against his palm with his closed fingers and lets it trickle out through the aperture between the thumb and flexed index finger. Some parts of the picture are measured by palms and spans; others are drawn freely. Straight lines of any length are made by snapping a cotton string held by two persons. The picture is smoothed off at intervals with the wooden batten used in weaving. Errors are not rubbed out but covered over with the neutral shade of the background. Since the design must not be disturbed, the painters work from the center out, sunwise from left to right.

Designs represent the stories of the Holy People or abstractions of sacred powers. The eight chief figures among the Holy People, other mythological personages such as Big Fly and Corn Beetle, the four sacred plants (corn, beans, squash, and tobacco), other plants such as cactus, stars, lightning, animals of the mountains, the bluebird (symbol of happiness), the Gila Monster and other reptiles, and the sacred arrows or flints often appear in one or more of the four paintings. Frequently the rainbow surrounds the picture on all sides but the east, to protect it from evil influences.

Drypaintings are indeed a form of art, often intricate and strikingly beautiful in color and design, but they are not used as forms of self-expression. The pattern is handed down in memory from one Singer and his assistants to others, and the variations permissible to the individual painter are few and minor, like the design or coloring of the kilts of the holy figures. These highly stylized paintings serve, in somewhat the fashion of medieval glass painting, to make visible and concrete the holy figures and religious concepts of The People. Unlike the windows, they are of only temporary use in connecting gods and men. This use is almost invariably centered in the curing of the sick or the disturbed, as described below in the section on "Curing Chants."

NAVAHO CEREMONIAL MUSIC

The range and complexity of Navaho music are not apparent to white persons, who usually attend only the "squaw dances." (See pp. 222, 228–229 below.) Even these songs require considerable knowledge and study on the part of the hearer if their intricate rhythms and subtle tonal variations are to be appreciated. The verbal improvisations which are a feature of these and other Navaho songs demand quick wit and skill in meeting prosodical requirements.

Helen Roberts provides the following brief technical account of Navaho music:

> . . . a falsetto . . . together with rapid, pulsing, bounding movement, and restless, beautiful melodies with predominant major triad intervals, may be said to characterize many Navaho tunes. In the most beautiful style (which may be heard in the songs of the Yeibichai ceremony), . . . the dominant, speaking in terms of a major diatonic scale, is particularly prominent. It frequently serves as the upper and lower tonal limits, and ground tone, but is associated principally with the tonic and third, rather than with the fourth, second and tonic, as in so much Plains music. These particular Navaho melodies tend to employ even wider intervals than Plains tunes, displaying almost acrobatic feats in bounding back and forth between octaves, while the continual downtrend, so conspicuous in the Plains, is here counteracted by the bold upward leaps. Falsetto, prominent in Navaho music, is rather rare in American Indian music as a whole.[5]

Some songs have as much as an octave range, but many are limited to four or five notes with the melody weaving back and forth between the high and low tones. Halftones and minor tonalities are unusually arranged so that it is difficult to reproduce Navaho music accurately upon a piano or keyed instrument. Where falsetto tones are used, they are primarily an embellishment rather than an essential feature of the melody.

Rhythmic patterns are more complicated than tonal patterns. So involved are the changes of time within a single song that the white listener does not catch them or becomes confused. But the charm of Navaho music consists in these subtle variations more than in any other single feature.

While Navaho music gives more room for individual exhibitionism than does Pueblo music, there are no soloists in the white sense. A Singer will render alone certain passages which no one else present knows. An individual's voice may stand out for a moment at a "squaw dance" while he introduces a new song or variation. But in such cases the individuals are acting as song leaders—not as soloists. The song leader's task is that of setting the pitch and tempo and of keeping the group in unison.

Those who are interested in hearing Navaho music will find certain songs from the Night Chant and the "squaw dance" recorded by Laura Bolton in the Victor series called *Indian Music of the Southwest.*

CURING CHANTS

All chants are curing ceremonials. The chant is given for a patient, and there may be one or more co-patients. There are a large number of distinct chants with innumerable variants, special features, and added ceremonies. The choice of a chant and its specialties is determined by the assumed cause of the trouble (as revealed in divination or as thought to be known from personal experience), by the ability of the patient's family to pay, and by the availability of a Singer. Most chants have two- or three-night forms and five-night forms. There are also short excerpts which may be tried out on the sick person. Separate parts of the chant may be given independently or, more often, two or three may be combined in a rite lasting only a portion of a day or night. If such a brief trial brings some improvement but not a complete cure, the whole chant will then be sung. This should be given a total of four times, usually in alternate five-night and two-night forms. Repetition of the performances may be delayed over many years but should eventually be completed.

A Navaho chant is a framework into which are fitted more or less discrete units ("ceremonies" and "acts and procedures") either as dictated by fixed associations or in accord with the practice of individual Singers, the wishes of the patient or patient's family, the precise nature of the "illness," or other circumstances. The same units are used over and over again in different chants, sometimes with slight modifications. Similarly, while each chant has some distinctive items of equipment, much of the inventory is common to all, or most, chants. There is almost always some kind of a rattle. The Singer or one of his helpers generally uses the "bullroarer" or "groaning stick," a piece of wood from a lightning-struck tree, inlaid with turquoise and abalone shell to give it features, and so shaped that it will make a roaring sound when swung on the end of a buckskin thong. When it is twirled, this device, which was given to the Navahos by the Lightning People, makes a sound like thunder. There are always vessels for administering medicines, the minerals used for paints and in dry-paintings, various aromatic substances which are burned in the "incense" or "fumigant," and pollen, precious stones, and bits of shell used for offering and for tying as a token in the patient's hair, so that afterwards the supernaturals will recognize him as one of their own. The possible combinations and permutations of uses of equipment into acts and procedures, of the order and juxtaposition of acts and procedures into ceremonies, and of the combination of ceremonies into chants have few limitations other than the ingenuity of practitioners. Definite innovations (in the sense of new paraphernalia or new rites), however, although they occur, are viewed with disapproval by the orthodox and only gradually become accepted after their use has had favorable results.

Each chant claims some songs, prayers, and herbal medicines as peculiarly its own. But the greater proportion are shared with one or more other chants or chant groups. Such ceremonies as those of the sweatbath and emetic, the making of prayersticks, the ceremonial bath in yucca suds, the consecration of the hogan, and singing throughout the final night are common to most chants. Some procedures (such as ash-blowing) and ceremonies (such as that of the big hoop, unraveling, arrow-shooting) are more restricted in their appearance. Only a few chants, like Night Way and Mountain Top Way, make provision for public dances (such as the "Yeibichai" and the "fire dance") or exhibitions.

One ceremony which occurs in most Holy Way and Evil Way chants is that of the drypainting. The making and the meaning of drypaintings have been described in a preceding section of this chapter. Here it is appropriate to indicate their use in the curing chants. Regardless of which painting is made or of the particular chant being carried out, the basic procedure is standard. When the painting has been completed to the accompaniment of song and prayer, the patient sits upon it in ceremonially dictated fashion and the treatment begins. The Singer gives the patient an infusion of herbs to drink. He touches the feet of a figure in the painting and then the patient's feet, saying, "May his feet be well. His feet restore unto him." In turn he presses his hands upon the knees, hands, shoulders, breast, back, and head of the figure and the patient, praying for the restoration of each member. When the treatment is finished and the patient has gone outside, the painting is destroyed bit by bit in the order in which it was made. The sand is swept up and carried out to the north of the hogan. When the last picture has been completed and the patient treated in this fashion, his relatives may walk in ceremonial fashion across the painting, treading where the holy figures have trod. Thus not only the sick man but the family as well have come into close communion with the Holy People, and all those present have seen their power.

In all chants there is great stress on the idea of purification. The patient, the Singer, all the central participants must preserve sexual continence. There are restrictions on sleeping and on the places of urinating and defecating.

There is an insistence on "clean thinking" and serious demeanor. The suds bath, the sweatbath, the use of emetics are all based upon this idea, which is one of the most central notions in Navaho thinking. It has been impressed on Navahos from youth, when as growing boys they were told that if they did not take purgatives, emetics, and sweatbaths from time to time, "the first thing that came along would kill them because their systems were filled with ugly things that they should have gotten rid of: they would be quick-tempered, have weak minds, be unable to stand life's hardships and therefore disgrace their families."[6]

Navaho chants fall into a number of groups, differentiated on the basis of mythological association, common rituals, direction against the same or related etiological factors. Thus the Holy Way group of chants deals with troubles which have been traced to lightning, thunder, the winds, snakes, various animals, and other Holy People. If snakes have been offended, Beauty Way is a likely choice from this group of chants, whereas one of the Shooting Way chants is preferred if lightning or thunder is responsible—though these are also used on occasion for "snake sickness." Mountain Top Way is the treatment par excellence for troubles which are believed to have arisen from contact with bears.

Life Way chants are employed in case of bodily injuries. In all of them "life medicine" is administered. Their duration is not fixed as in the case of other chants. The ceremonial continues until relief occurs or until that particular form of treatment is given up as useless.

Evil Way chants are used in curing "ghost sickness." Sickness caused by native ghosts is treated by Moving Up Way and by the Evil Way forms of Shooting Way, Red Ant Way, and others. Sickness arising from molestation by the ghosts of foreigners is treated by Enemy Way, one of the rites formerly used in connection with war but now known to whites as the "squaw dance."

All chants are so powerful they are fraught with potentialities of harm as well as of help. Mistakes either by the patient or by practitioners are dangerous to all concerned. If the Singer has, by an error, endangered those for whom he has assumed responsibility, there are formulas for correction. The whole concept is thus rather mechanical. It is not that the divinities are angered and punish the offenders. Rather, the whole system works automatically according to ineluctable rules. Just as the volition of a divinity is hardly thought of as being involved in the fulfillment of a petition, so also volition is not conceived as causing slips in ritual.

The Navaho notion is that the universe works according to rules. If one can discover the rules and follow them, he may remain safe or be restored to safety—and more. The divinities must themselves bow to the compulsion of ritual formulas. The prayers are usually regarded as the most powerful features of a chant. Reichard describes their emotional tone thus:

> He [the one offering the prayer] does not "count past blessings," nor does he give thanks in prayer. Thanks are not compulsive; all the words of a prayer are. Mortification and humility, opposites of gratitude, are similarly absent. The Navajo is never better than he thinks he is. It would be suicidal to humble himself before his deities for, if he did, why should they identify themselves with him? He does not ask pity, he uses the compulsive technique learned from the gods themselves. Since he never humiliates himself he need not give thanks for the protection or blessings he has received . . . He bows to acknowledge a power superior to his, to recognize defeat not victory.[7]

OTHER RITES

There are minor priestly rites as well as ones of common knowledge for salt-gathering, for trading with foreigners, for gambling. The hunting rites were complex but now, for obvious reasons, are falling into disuse. Deer, antelope, mountain lion, and bear could be hunted only in ceremonial fashion. These rites, like some of the war rites, are continued to some extent with new functions—to prevent or control epidemics, for example.

For victims of witchcraft the treatment most highly valued is one of the several prayer ceremonials. For four days, long prayers are said without singing. There may be the ceremony of the bath, and drypaintings may be made on buckskin.

Enemy Way, though used as a curing ceremonial, has probably enjoyed its continual popularity because of one associated feature, the "squaw dance." The social aspects of this dance will be discussed later, but here it should be pointed out that the curative functions of Enemy Way are in demand for those who, according to the diviner, have received their sickness from non-Navahos. In the old days the prime purpose was to protect warriors from the ghost sickness threatened by ghosts of enemies they had slain. Today the patients are often those who have married into other Indian tribes or have used white prostitutes in Gallup or some other town. Sometimes men or women who have worked in the laundries at Indian agencies, where they handle clothes of white people and of sick people, are advised to have this rite. While whites are often permitted to watch chants in progress, the strictly ritual parts of Enemy Way are almost invariably closed to them. And even though white men are often invited to participate in the "squaw dance" and whites attend this feature more frequently than any other Navaho ceremonial occasion, still an aroma of anti-white feeling is characteristic of the less apparent emotional atmosphere of the Navaho crowd in attendance upon Enemy Way.

Enemy Way has never died out among The People. Most of the other war ceremonials had practically gone out of use before World War II, but since 1941 a number of them have been revived. It is interesting to note certain strange combinations of old Navaho war ceremonials with bits of other rites and even elements of Christian practice.

These revived and combined rites were used to assure the safety of Navaho men in the armed forces. One such ceremonial was held in May 1944 for the well-being of 150 service men, Navahos working in war industries, and members of the Allied armies. Before the ritual began, photographs of the service men for whom the ceremonial was held were piled up in front of the "medicine man." This man, a famous Singer, sang ancient war songs, and Christian Navahos were encouraged to add their prayers to the tribal chants. After the all-night ritual, prayer feathers adorned with turquoise were planted to help assure the warriors' safe return.[8]

7. THE MEANING OF THE SUPERNATURAL

ECONOMIC AND SOCIAL ASPECTS OF CEREMONIALS

THE COST IN TIME

There is good evidence that ceremonials are being performed now more frequently than for many years. This is undoubtedly due in part to the fact that there is more money on the Reservation because of the availability of more jobs for Navahos at higher wages. Without doubt, however, The People's sense of crisis in their economy and their consequent irritability with both whites and their fellow tribesmen also lead them to spend more time in ceremonials. Indeed, in some areas where the facts are known, this heightened participation goes back to the depression years and is almost certainly connected with worry and unrest resulting from white pressure. The following data on individual participation in curing rites are from the immediate prewar period and are thus fairly representative for at least the past decade.

In how many ceremonials has the average individual been a patient during his lifetime? A careful investigation among the Navahos around Ramah shows that the variation among individuals is enormous. One old woman, who was perpetually ailing, had spent nearly 500 days in curing rites, keeping both her immediate and extended families almost continually bankrupt. One of the Singers, on the other hand, had had ceremonials held over him for only

37 days of his life. And one man—presumably about fifty years old—had had but a single three-night ceremonial. Extensive interviewing failed to reveal a single individual over thirty who had not been the patient in at least one ceremonial. Rather typical are the cases of a man and a woman past sixty who were neither rich nor poor by the standards of this community. The woman had spent 83 days as the patient in ceremonials (women are rather more frequently patients than men); the man, 71 days. These represent roughly the mode of about fifty case histories of older people, making allowance for age differences. On the other hand, fully half of those under thirty had never been "sung over."

Of all adult Navaho men past the age of thirty-five today, probably one out of every five or six can do divination or conduct Blessing Way, a chant, or some other rite. Many women are diviners, too, and a few women know other rites. Most Navahos know how to dance in the "squaw dance" or in the dances which close some of the great chants. They also know how to gather plant medicines properly and how to prepare ceremonial foods. All adult men and some women can help with a drypainting and with the singing at a ceremonial.

The amount of time which The People give to ritual activities includes the periods they spend as patients, helpers, and spectators; their trips to summon ceremonialists and to gather plants and other materials; the extra chores in preparing food for practitioners and guests and in hauling larger supplies of water and firewood than usual. Study in the Ramah area indicates that adult men give one-fourth to one-third of their productive time to activities connected with the "priestly" rites; women, one-fifth to one-sixth. This is undoubtedly a higher proportion of time than most white people give to the church, the theatre, and the doctor combined, and it is excellent evidence of the importance of their religion to the Navahos.

THE COST IN MONEY

The values which Navahos derive from ceremonials are literally bought and paid for. A fee is always paid to the Singer, even if he is the patient's own father; otherwise the rite might not be effective. A Singer receives anywhere from five to five hundred dollars in cash or kind for each ceremony. The fee varies with his reputation, the rarity of the ceremonial knowledge involved, the time spent and the distance traveled for the ceremony, and the degree of his relationship to the patient. In addition to fees for conducting ceremonies, a Singer may make and sell ceremonial equipment, and he claims "royalties" on the initial performances of Singers whom he has trained. For most ceremonialists this income is merely a valued supplement to earnings in secular occupations, but a famous Singer earns enough not only to support his immediate family in comparative luxury but also to help out many other relatives. This route to affluence is recognized by The People, and a bright boy with a better-than-average memory is encouraged to apprentice himself to a well-known Singer.

The other ceremonialists besides the Singer are also paid for their services. Those who help with an all-night singing or assist in the bath ceremony or other rites receive gifts of calico, baskets, and the like. Others receive their recompense through the fact that this is part of their training as ceremonialists. Herbalists are paid for the plants they gather, and some rare plants bring quite high prices. Diviners may receive a sheep or a piece of jewelry or cash; the money value of their services ranges from as little as two dollars to as much as twenty.

The fees and gifts to the officiating personnel are but part of the financial burden on the patient's family. Baskets, buckskins, herbs, and other equipment must be purchased. All who attend must be fed. Sometimes, on the final night of one of the great chants, several thousand spectators must be provided with bread, mutton, and coffee.

All ceremonials, therefore, are costly, and some are very expensive indeed. Consequently, poor or only moderately prosperous families are sometimes rendered bankrupt by the need to provide a succession of ceremonials for ailing family members, despite the fact that all family members are obligated to share the cost. So strong is this pressure that, if a man does not help to pay the expenses of a ceremonial for a brother or sister, his refusal is taken as sure proof that he is engaged in witchcraft.

Other obligations to hold ceremonials are strongly felt. Social pressure is put upon the rich to give expensive chants even when no one in their families is obviously ill. Otherwise they are ridiculed as stingy and mean. Thus the system works as a kind of economic leveler: when the rich man has given fifty sheep to a Singer and slaughtered another two hundred to feed the spectators, the economic difference between him and his neighbors is lessened.

Averages of amounts spent for ceremonials are deceptive in that they tend to obscure the great variation from family to family. Still it is instructive to know that in the Ramah area, on the average, 20 per cent of total family income goes into "religion."

We cannot follow out all of the interconnections between the "economic" and the "religious" systems, but it is worth while to point out that the seasons when ceremonials are held are those when time and money are free. While most chants can be held at any time of year, the curing ceremonials which draw the great crowds (Enemy Way, Night Way, Mountain Top Way) are held almost exclusively, in fact if not in theory, during a few months of the year. Enemy Way is almost never given except after the busy time of lambing, planting, and shearing is over and before the heavy work of harvest and getting lambs to market. Night Way and Mountain Top Way cannot be given until after the first killing frost, but in practice performances are virtually limited to November and December. That is, they follow the season of harvest and lamb sales. In short, both types of popular rite follow periods of intensive economic activity when cash and credit are readiest; they offer change and emotional release before settling back into the humdrum of ordinary existence.

COÖPERATION AND RECIPROCITY

A rite calls into action the immediate social organization around the patient. To carry it out properly, the help of many persons is needed: to pay the Singer and his assistants; to gather the plants and other materials; and to carry on the subsidiary activities of preparing food, maintaining the fire or fires, and providing water. The whole system is, of course, founded upon expected reciprocities. A woman helps her sister with the cooking when the sister's daughter is having the girl's puberty rite, but she will expect similar assistance a month later when her husband is having a Life Way chant to cure a sprain caused by being thrown from a horse.

SOCIAL FUNCTIONS: THE "SQUAW DANCE" AS AN EXAMPLE

All Navaho rites have secondary social functions. People are drawn to them not only because they wish to acquire "religious" benefits or because they are under pressure to assist; they come also because the rite offers a chance to see and be seen, to talk and to listen. Increasingly, it must be admitted, ceremonial gatherings are occasions for drinking and violent behavior. This tendency is deplored by most Singers.

In no ceremonial do these secondary motivations loom so large as in Enemy Way. The Girls' Dance ("squaw dance"), at which marriageable girls ask young men to dance, was once only an incidental element in this ceremonial, but today it is the chief attraction for the great crowds which invariably attend. Most of the girls who dance are brought there to announce the fact that they have recently become, or still are, of the right age to marry. Young men come to sing and to hear the singing, and to look over the girls. The crowds gather to watch this public dance each night of the ceremonial and to enjoy the accompanying "sway-singing" of the men, which frequently embodies Rabelaisian quips at the expense of participants and bystanders.

The dance also has its serious side. The parallel to the debutante ball in white society is inescapable. Everyone—particularly members of families who are considering a marriage alliance—dresses as well as possible and appears with his best horse, wagon, or automobile. Putting up a front through borrowed jewelry and other finery is not unknown. Navaho mothers, a trifle franker than is usual among whites, literally push their daughters after a "catch," saying: "Go ask that boy. His mother has two thousand sheep." At last even the shyest girl is induced to choose a man, and the dance goes on until morning.

WHAT MYTHS AND RITES DO FOR THE INDIVIDUAL

PRESTIGE AND PERSONAL EXPRESSION

Skill in all the ceremonial arts—singing, dancing, making drypaintings, telling stories—is highly valued by The People. Experts are richly rewarded in prestige as well as money, and not without reason. Prodigious memory is demanded of the ceremonialist. The Singer who knows one nine-night chant must learn at least as much as a man who sets out to memorize the whole of a Wagnerian opera: orchestral score, every vocal part, all the details of the settings, stage business, and each requirement of costume.

Some Singers know three or more long chants, as well as various minor rites.

But ceremonial life gives opportunity for personal expression to more than the small group of Singers. Lay folk can show their skill in dancing and singing and in making drypaintings. They can win plaudits for their adroitness in helping with the tricks and other "vaudeville acts" which make up a great part of the public performance on the final night of Mountain Top Way. They can show off their good memory and oratorical skill in telling myths.

The giving of a rite—particularly an elaborate one—also confers prestige. It shows not only that the family are doing their duty by one of their number but that they have the wherewithal to pay for it. Hence rites are sometimes given primarily as gestures of affluence rather than because some one of the family is really ill or disturbed. They seem to be the Navaho form of conspicuous spending. To give an unusual ceremonial with elaborate equipment—to summon a famous Singer and invite guests from miles away—is perhaps the best way for a family to show the world that they have "arrived." The analogous situation in white society is the trip to a distant and expensive specialist when the patient is really not very ill so far as anyone else can see; such a trip confers greater prestige than consulting the local doctor.

CURING

It is difficult for many white people to understand why, when the resources of white medicine are available to Navahos in government hospitals and dispensaries, The People continue to patronize "ignorant medicine men." The answer is that native practice brings good results—in many cases as good as those of a white physician or hospital. Admittedly there are types of ailments which must be made much worse by the Singer's treatment. On the other hand, the evidence is good that individuals who obtained no relief from white medicine have been cured by chants.

Some of the help which "sings" give has a perfectly straightforward physical explanation. Massage and heat treatments may be expected to bring the results which white physiotherapy sometimes does. The sweatbath and the yucca root bath probably have effects on the nervous system in some ways similar to those of hydrotherapy. It is possible that some of the herbal concoctions have therapeutic properties.

But there can be no doubt that the main effects are "psychological." There is nothing too mysterious about this. Skillful physicians have long known that the will to get well, the belief that one is going to recover, and other attitudes can be more than half the battle. Moreover, the fact that many "physical" disabilities have "psychic" causes is being increasingly recognized.

In the hospital a Navaho is lonely and homesick, living by a strange routine and eating unfamiliar foods. Illness often gives the sufferer the suspicion that he is disliked or unprotected. During the chant the patient feels himself personally (rather than impersonally) being succored and loved, for his relatives are spending their substance to get him cured, and they are rallying round to aid in the ceremonial.

Then there is the prestige and authority of the Singer assuring the patient that he will recover. In his capacity as Singer, gifted with the learning of the Holy People, he is more than a mortal and at times becomes identified with the supernaturals, speaking in their voices and telling the hearers that all is well. The prestige, mysticism, and power of the ceremonial itself are active, coming directly from the supernatural powers that build up the growing earth in spring, drench it with rain, or tear it apart with lightning. In the height of the chant the patient himself becomes one of the Holy People, puts his feet in their moccasins, and breathes in the strength of the sun. He comes into complete harmony with the universe and must of course be free of all ills and evil. Finally, it is very likely that he has seen the ceremonial work with others and may have had it before himself; in this case there will be an upswing of reawakened memories, like old melodies bearing him on emotional waves to feelings of security.

As well as this powerful reassurance, occupation and diversion are supplied to the patient. He has the sense of doing something about a misfortune which otherwise might leave him in the misery of feeling completely helpless. Although he does not himself actually carry out most of the necessary preparations, his mind is full of the things that have to be done. Arrangements must be made for paying the Singer and getting the food supplies together to feed all who come. Ritual material has to be gathered and people have to be found who will do it. During the actual ceremonial the patient's thoughts are busy following the Singer's instructions, pondering over the implications in the songs and prayers, the speeches and side remarks of the Singer. The period of four days of being quiet and aloof after the ceremonial is a splendid opportunity for rumination and for development of the conviction that the purposes of the chant have been achieved, or are starting to be achieved.

SECURITY

The Navaho, then, finds his "religion" a way of good hope when he is sick or disturbed. But myth and ritual also meet other human needs. Otherwise, the stories of the Holy People and the great chants which embody the myths would have died out or have been supplanted by different beliefs, for sheer repetition in and of itself has never assured the persistence of any habit. It is true that some Navaho myths and rituals have disappeared within the last hundred years, but to say that they became extinct because the last old man who knew them died is a very superficial explanation. Had they not lost their importance as conditions changed for The People, younger men would have taken the trouble to learn them. Conversely, the remarkable staying power of the great body of religious lore and practice and the recent resurgence of religious activity are proof that these beliefs play a definite part in present-day life among the Navahos.

The basic function of religion everywhere is to give a sense of security in a world which, seen in naturalistic terms, appears to be full of the unpredictable, the capricious, the accidentally tragic. Someone has said, "Human beings build their cultures, nervously loquacious, upon the edge of an abyss." In the face of chance and the unexpected, of want, death, and destruction, all humans have a fundamental sense of uneasiness. And so they talk and, by making their talk consistent, they assure themselves that "reality" too is consistent. They mask the vast role of "luck" in human life by telling each other that such and such a thing happened because of something a supernatural being did or said long ago. In a world full of hazards, myths affirm that there is rhyme and reason after all. They give the future the appearance of safety by affirming the unbroken continuity of present and past. So it is with The People. Their mythology gives them a sense of continuity and security which Christianity cannot give them because they do not understand it. Their own beliefs continue to satisfy and to help them in the difficult task of living—as do all mythologies which are really believed.

Their system of beliefs, then, gives Navahos something to hold to. The old stories bring both tellers and hearers a sense of exaltation by renewing their touch with the world of the past and a feeling of security that comes from seeing human life as an unbroken chain of events. Myths guarantee the validity of rites not only by detailing their supernatural origins but also by citing chapter and verse as to who was cured and how and when. They relieve the mind from perplexities by supplying final answers.

This conviction of fixity is the essential element in the psychological value of mythology. One Navaho remarked, "Knowing a good story will protect your home and children and property. A myth is just like a big stone foundation—it lasts a long time." The insistence upon correctness in the small points of Navaho ritual, upon preserving the myth in every detail, reflects the fact that myth and ritual deal with those sectors of experience which do not seem amenable to rational control but where human beings can least tolerate insecurity. Ritual and myth provide fixed points in an existence of bewildering change and disappointments. This is especially important to individuals whose world is changing as fast as that of the Navahos.

Lest the writers be accused of romantic prejudice, it should be stated clearly that Navaho "religious" beliefs, especially the negative practices and the great number of fears they symbolize, do have marked psychological disadvantages. Although the taboos and regulations are in essence a system of avoiding harm and their use makes a Navaho feel at least partially protected, these taboos and regulations work two ways. While they quiet some fears, they pile up additional apprehensions and hazards. The situation is not unlike that of the obsessive patient who attains some comfort and security by his rituals of not touching things or of washing them repeatedly, but at the same time makes life intolerable in other ways because he constantly increases the number of things he may not do and lives in never-ceasing fear of transgression. But despite this sort of danger Navaho beliefs (even those pertaining to witchcraft) do answer many of the deepest needs of human beings and, as we shall see in the following section, they help to keep society on an even keel. It is also true that religious practices constitute, in part, an escape mechanism from pressing realities. This seems to be particularly true of the non-Navaho peyote cult, which is gaining adherents especially in the northern portions of the Reservation, where supplies of the drug are obtained from the Utes.

WHAT MYTHS AND RITES DO FOR THE GROUP

The old beliefs have uses for The People as a tribe, as well as for The People as individuals. Some of these are the functions of "religion" in any group without a written language, but others are specifically Navaho. In both secular and sacred spheres, myths serve as statements of the right way to behave and the reasons therefor, somewhat as the Bible does (or did) in Christian societies. Women must sit with their feet in a certain position because the female Holy People sat that way. When questioned as to why almost anything is done in a particular way, Navahos will usually reply, "Because the Holy People did it that way in the first place." Even when children are asked why they play Navaho games according to certain rules, they almost invariably make this response.

Thus to some degree the myths are The People's code of manners and morals and their law books as well. But myths, legends, and folk tales are also their literature, which serves ends from intellectual and moral edification to simple entertainment.

Because myth and ritual tend to preserve and to carry forward ancient Navaho tradition, they have a significant usefulness as brakes upon the speed of cultural change. As it is, the Navaho way of life is altering so rapidly that an individual keeps his balance with difficulty. Were the old beliefs to be swept away all at once and before Christianity had become understandable enough to serve as a satisfactory substitute, The People would be completely disoriented. Their cosmos would be a chaos, their life would be without meaning.

The People themselves are aware of this stabilizing force of their religious beliefs. Consciously or unconsciously, they act accordingly. The revival of almost forgotten rites and the renewed zeal with which others are being used today are a form of what has been called "antagonistic acculturation." In other words, The People symbolically affirm their resistance to white men's efforts to change their way of life by giving even more importance and attention to their own ceremonials.

Rites also play a significant role in interpersonal relationships among The People. One important contribution of the curing chants to good group relationships comes from the informal chat that goes on between the Singer and the patient and other members of the family. Since the Singer is usually an intellectual, who often knows the habits and tendencies of his clientele in the same manner as the family doctor in white society, it is very likely that, like the family doctor, he often gives sound practical advice based on his knowledge of his people. Probably many personal and interpersonal problems come nearer to adjustment at the time of a ceremonial. Indeed, certain passages in the myths indicate that The People have a more or less conscious realization that the ceremonies act as a cure, not only for physical and mental illness, but also for antisocial tendencies. For example, the myth of the Mountain Top Way chant says: "The ceremony cured Dsiliyi Neyani of all his strange feelings and notions. The lodge of his people no longer smelled unpleasant to him." Today ordinary lay Navahos speak of being "changed" so that they are better men and women in their relations with their families and neighbors. For instance, an English-speaking Navaho who had just completed a jail sentence for beating his wife and molesting his stepdaughter remarked: "I am sure going to behave from now on. I am going to be changed—just like someone who has been sung over."

Any effects in this direction are a contribution to one of the major problems of Navaho society. The People have a great deal of trouble with surrounding whites, but they also have much with each other. This intra-tribal friction is probably one very important reason why The People do not coöperate very long in group projects organized along lines that are not familiar to Navahos, such as the white-sponsored coöperatives. This tendency to work together chiefly in family groups sometimes makes for inefficiency in the use of the uncertain natural resources.

This is not to say that Navahos are by nature more quarrelsome than other human beings. When people live under constant threat from the physical environment, where small groups are geographically isolated and "emotional inbreeding" within the extended family group is at a maximum, interpersonal tensions are inevitably present. The occurrence of illness, which throws increased burdens on the well and strong, is an additional disrupting force. Moreover, as already remarked, the myths and rituals are themselves two-edged swords, relieving anxiety on the one hand but creating it on the other with all the possibilities of calamities and errors of behavior, restrictions, and prohibitions. Worry over white encroachments and the conflict contingent upon rapid culture change add to uneasiness.

An uneasy folk is commonly an aggressive folk. But The People have painfully learned that it does not pay to behave aggressively toward whites. Many of the aggressive impulses within the family circle also are suppressed or repressed, for hostile words or acts toward relatives are strongly disapproved and punished by a society where coöperation between relatives is necessary for survival. Hence many antagonistic feelings go unspoken or do not even rise into consciousness. They may nevertheless cause some individuals to develop chronic anxieties. Such persons feel continually uncomfortable; they say they "feel sick all over" without ever locating a pain definitely. Diviners and other practitioners will say that the patient is sick because he has seen animals struck by lightning, has failed to observe ritual requirements, or has in some other way violated a taboo. In this way a substitute is found for the hostility and guilt that probably caused the symptoms, and the substitute can be treated and eradicated, thus relieving the guilt and perhaps reducing the hostility. The patient's evil feelings were not at fault, the myths say; the trouble was just that he was on hand when lightning struck. The proper rite can straighten this out. Thus ritual resolves social maladjustments that might otherwise upset the stability of the group.

But myths and rituals contribute to the equilibrium of the society in other ways than by "curing" individual members of the society. In the first place, the centering of rites upon disease and upon the individual serves social purposes beyond that of helping individuals adjust more amicably to their relatives and neighbors. Furthermore, to describe the rites of The People as purely "individualistic" and purely for curing is an oversimplification.

The Navaho and the Pueblo Indians live in essentially the same physical environment. The Pueblo rituals are concerned predominantly with rain and with fertility; those of the Navaho primarily with disease. In the absence of fuller supporting facts, this contrast cannot be laid to a lesser frequency of illness among the Pueblo, for it seems well documented that the Pueblo Indians, living in congested towns, have been far more ravaged by endemic disease than the Navahos. The explanation is probably to be sought in terms of the differing historical experience of the two peoples and especially in terms of the contrasting economic and social organizations. To people living in relative isolation and largely dependent (as were the Navahos at no distant date) upon ability to move about hunting and gathering wild food plants, ill health presents a danger much more crucial for group survival than it does to Indians who live in towns with reserve supplies of corn and better integrated social organizations.

That Navaho myths and rituals are focused upon the curing of individuals has, thus, a firm basis in the reality of the external world. But other social ends are served by the ceremonials. It should be remembered that they are merely centered upon individuals. Every rite has also an agricultural overtone. There are prayers for rain and for growth. Other benefits for the whole People and especially for those in attendance are held out. The whole character of Navaho ceremonialism would be quite different were participation less general. If rites were carried on mechanically and apart from the general social life by a special class of priests, the cohesive effects might be negligible. But so many people are involved directly and indirectly and they feel their involvement so warmly that groups are knit more closely together. Performance of the rites heightens awareness that The People have common beliefs, common goals, a common value system. The ceremonials bring individuals together in a situation where quarreling is forbidden. Preparing for and the carrying out of a rite also demands intricately ramified coöperation, economic and otherwise, and doubtless thus reinforces the sense of mutual dependency.

The contrast which anthropologists have for many years been drawing between the ritual preoccupation of Pueblos with rain and of Navahos with healing is, in fact, an oversimplified schematization. First, as has just been indicated, the distinction must be seen as one of emphasis—not in all-or-none terms. Second, though in concrete and specific terms the observer is impressed by differences in the relative frequency of rites oriented mainly to curing and rites oriented mainly to fertility, the underlying philosophy is more complicated. One may express the contrast more adequately at a higher level of abstraction by saying that the Navahos' interest is focused upon restoring the harmony within an individual and between that individual and other persons or supernatural forces, whereas the basic theme in almost all Pueblo ritual is that of restoring harmony in the whole universe. The Navaho outlook is more personal, the Pueblo more impersonal. The individual counts for a very great deal in the Navaho way of thinking, while

Pueblo thought tends to regard any single person as a comparatively incidental portion of an intricate equilibrium of forces.

In sum, myths and rituals jointly provide systematic protection against supernatural dangers, the threats of ill health and of the physical environment, antisocial tensions, and the pressures of a more powerful society. In the absence of a codified law and of an authoritarian chief, it is only through the myth-ritual system that the Navahos can present a unified front to all these disintegrating pressures. The all-pervasive configurations of word-symbols (myths) and of act-symbols (rituals) preserve the cohesion of the society and sustain the individual, protecting both from intolerable conflict.

THE GAIN AND COST OF WITCHCRAFT

We have been talking about practices which have the full support of the society. Let us now turn to those attempts to manipulate the supernatural by word and deed which are done furtively and which come under strong social disapproval. The cost of witchcraft belief is obvious: there is the addition of just that many more things to be feared; there are occasional acts of violence; guiltless individuals are made to suffer mildly or tragically. No one would wish to minimize these socially disruptive trends, but what is not likely to be so easily understood or admitted is the fact that belief in witchcraft, as seen by a dispassionate observer, is not much more completely black or white, all bad or all good, than is any other social institution. Even though The People themselves abhor the deeds which witches are believed to do, still their having these fears and talking about them and acting upon them plays a part in easing the strains in the social structure, in keeping Navaho society a going concern.

There is, of course, no question of defending "witchcraft" upon a moral basis. As a matter of fact, the writers are not even absolutely positive that Navahos try to become witches. There is good reason to believe that a few do, and in this discussion we shall assume that this is the case. However, this is a relatively minor point in understanding the workings of Navaho society. What counts is that belief in witches is universal and that there are deep fears, much gossip, and countless and widely current anecdotes.

These tales are the medium through which witchcraft touches the lives of all The People. Together with the myths about witchcraft, they have the effect of plugging up certain holes in the ideological system. If chants don't work, the Navaho doesn't have to say, "Well, that ceremonial is no good." He is encouraged to say, in effect, "I am certain that that chant is wonderfully powerful, but naturally you can't expect it to prevail against the evil strength of witches." In this and in other ways, witchcraft conceptions supply a partial answer to some of the deeper uncertainties.

But the more personal significance of witchcraft lore comes about through the psychological mechanism of identification. Just as the drab little shop girl can become Hedy Lamar during the two hours of a moving picture or the middle-aged housewife can experience the joys and tribulations of the heroines of "soap opera" on the radio, so the Navaho who listens to, or repeats, or manufactures a witchcraft story can identify himself with the aggressor or the victim. Among other things, this provides a harmless outlet in imagination for impulses which are forbidden in real life. The man who consciously or unconsciously wants to commit incest or other prohibited sexual acts but is restrained by fear of the consequences or by moral scruples perhaps finds some relief through identifying himself for a time with the wicked witch. The crucial question for understanding the psychological outlets which The People get through witchcraft tales is always: does the person see himself as the witch or as the victim? If he imagines himself the witch, presumably he gets hostile impulses out of his system vicariously; if he takes the victim's role, some of his uneasiness is allayed. The main contribution which this complex of acts and ideas makes to the steadiness of Navaho society are in handling the anxiety problem and in serving as a safety valve for and control over aggressive tendencies.

ANXIETY

Under the present conditions of Navaho life it is inevitable that there should be a high anxiety level, a large amount of worry and uneasiness, in the society. One common way of expressing this is to gossip about witches. A more drastic way is to become convinced that one is oneself being "witched." It is not just "any Navaho" who feels himself a victim of witchcraft. There is great variation in the frequency and intensity of such worries, depending upon the individual's place in the social structure, his temporary social situation, and probably also upon his nervous constitution. If, for any reason a person is subjected to unusual frustration or if his tolerance of frustration is low, he must imagine an enemy, an aggressor, a cause of his lack of success. Witchcraft lore provides a means of defining and personalizing his anxiety which will be accepted by others. Beliefs and practices related to witchcraft are thus refuges for those persons who are more under the stress of misfortune than others, or for those who by reason of constitutional or other factors are less able to endure misfortunes, real or imagined.

It is no accident that a high proportion of those who suddenly show symptoms of being bewitched (such as fainting or going into a semi-trance) at "squaw dances" or other large gatherings are women or men who are somewhat neglected or who occupy low social status. In most of these cases it is probably not a matter of consciously capitalizing on the credence of their fellows in order to get the center of the stage for themselves. It is unlikely that Navahos often deliberately complain of the symptoms of witchcraft as a device for getting attention. The process normally takes place at an altogether unconscious level: those whose uneasiness goes beyond a certain point have to do something; and if they are believed to be at the mercy of witches they are likely to get help.

Especially in a society where the social units are small, the disturbance of any person's daily routines constitutes a danger to the smooth functioning of the whole social organization, and Navaho society could ill afford not to support its members who are "witched." The rare references to abandonment of such individuals always specify that the case was hopeless. Being "witched" normally calls forth the very maximum of social support, and the writers know of more than one family impoverished from paying for one "cure" after another.

The expensive prayer ceremonials, demanding the presence of the patient's family and of practitioners who represent the wider social organization, symbolically affirm that the victim is succored by the whole social structure. The importance of the near presence and support of one's fellows as the surest protection against witches is attested by the facts that were-animals are almost always seen by lone individuals and that going about alone at night is considered peculiarly dangerous. Moreover, if exaggerated fear of witches arises in a person partly because he feels aggressive and thus suspects that others feel the same way toward him, witchcraft "illness" is to this extent dependent upon a loss of rapport with the society—the penalty for giving way to feelings the society does not permit. The most efficacious reassurance for victims of witchcraft is provided, therefore, by the unusual, complicated, and costly prayer ceremonials, with many relatives and friends in attendance, lending their help and expressing their sympathy.

The important thing for the adjustment of the individual

is that witchcraft is a focus of anxiety which The People recognize as valid. If a Navaho merely complained or put forward an explanation which might carry weight in white society, the reaction of his family would eventually be indifference or active irritation. For a Navaho to tell his family that he was suffering from lack of vitamins would affect them much as white people would be affected if someone were to tell them that he was ill because last year he had been careless enough to look upon a cow that had been struck by lightning. But wherever a Navaho or his family or a diviner can suggest that a witch is responsible for uneasiness or illness, social support is assured.

In terms of witchcraft a person can justify his being worried without taking any blame himself. In the case of those illnesses which are thought to be due to the breaking of some taboo, to a considerable degree it is the individual's own fault that he is sick. But the Navahos consider the witch victim guiltless, so that if witchcraft can be blamed instead of carelessness or misbehavior, the sick man achieves a good position instead of a poor one in the eyes of his fellows.

Nothing is more intolerable to human beings than to be persistently disturbed without being able to say why or without being able to phrase the matter in such a way that some relief or control is available. Witchcraft belief allows one to talk about his anxiety in terms that are acceptable and which imply the possibility of doing something about it. Much of the tension among The People may actually be traced to the uncertainties of making a living in a difficult environment with the technological means at their disposal. Since the caprices of the environment are not controllable by the society, the worry related to this is attributed to witches who, as living individuals, can be dealt with. A correlation between the amount of fear and talk about witches and the general state of tension prevailing among the Navahos is evidenced by the fact that during the recent difficult years of controversy over the stock reduction program there has been appreciably more witchcraft excitement than for some time past, and a number of murders of supposed witches have occurred. There have also been several well-documented attempts by Navahos to "witch" government employees concerned with stock reduction.

AGGRESSION

Witchcraft patterns supply many releases, direct and indirect, actual and imaginative, for hostile impulses. The most obvious of these is actually becoming a witch. It is quite possible that the kind of temperament which in the old days found an outlet through organizing and leading war parties finds witchcraft the most congenial substitute available today. Direct aggression is also expressed, of course, through attacks upon "witches." These range from hushed gossip to public accusation or even physical assault.

The classes of persons accused and gossiped about most frequently, and the relationships between accused and accusers, constitute a revealing commentary on the stresses in Navaho social organization. Rich people, ceremonial practitioners, "political" leaders, the old—these make up the vast bulk of those whom gossip singles out. Sons-in-law spread stories about their fathers-in-law; nephews permit themselves a sly innuendo in referring to their maternal uncles. A brother will sometimes express doubt about a sister, real or clan; but brothers very seldom gossip about brothers or sisters about sisters, and talk against parents is virtually unknown. Very often the expression of aggression is disguised and indirect. For example, a young man will not name his own actual maternal uncle or even imply that he might be a witch. He will, however, evidence much relish in telling a tale laid in a distant locality where the evil hero just happens to show all sorts of resemblances in age, appearance, and personality traits to his own tyrannous uncle.

More significant than the release of direct aggression is that of displaced aggression. That is, Navahos "take out" on witches by word and by deed the hostility which in fact they feel against their relatives, against whites, against the hazards of life itself. Talk about witches commonly has a violent quality completely out of proportion to the involvement of the speaker in that particular case. The killing of witches is characteristically messy and brutal, even on the part of those who are not avenging some near relative or close friend. Witches, in other words, are scapegoats.

In this very general sense of scapegoats "witches" have probably played some part in all social structures since the Old Stone Age. They may be either a minority within the society or an external group. In contemporary America, for instance, we have the "reds," the "capitalists," the "New Dealers," the "Japs," and many others. It would be too much to say that all societies must necessarily have their "witches," that is, persons whom it is proper to fear and to hate, and under defined circumstances, to behave aggressively toward. Some social systems are much more efficient than others in directing aggression into oblique or socially non-disruptive channels. But there is no doubt that witchcraft is Navaho culture's principal answer to the problem that every society faces: how to satisfy hate and still keep the core of the society solid. Among other things, witchcraft is the Navahos' substitute for the race prejudice of white society in the United States. The People blame their troubles upon "witches" instead of upon "Jews" or "niggers." In place of selecting its scapegoats by skin color or by religious tradition, Navaho culture selects certain individuals who are supposed to work evil by secret supernatural techniques.

SOCIAL CONTROL

Seen from the angle of the survival of the society as a whole rather than from that of the adjustment of the single individual, witchcraft functions in two principal ways: it helps maintain a system of checks and balances, so that the ceremonial practitioners and the rich are kept from attaining too much power; and it is an implied threat against all socially disrupting action, strengthening in various ways social inhibitions consonant with the old native culture.

Gossip against the rich almost always takes the form of implying that they got their start by stealing jewelry and other valuables from the dead. The prevalence of this rationalization acts as a kind of economic leveler. The rich feel pressure to be lavish in hospitality, generous in gifts to needy relatives and neighbors, prodigal in the ceremonials they sponsor. Otherwise they know the voice of envy will speak out in whispers of witchcraft which would make their life in society strained and unpleasant, if not positively dangerous. This trend materially helps in maintaining the coherence of Navaho life and preserving its continuity. Navaho society is in process of transition from a familial structure where the bonds between kinfolk are everything to an individualistic, ruthlessly competitive social organization like that of white Americans. The change may or may not be inevitable, but if it occurs too fast one or more generations of The People will be utterly uprooted and disoriented. There is also the crucial land question. If livestock becomes more and more concentrated in the hands of a few large owners, the majority of the Navahos will be reduced to peonage or to dependence upon relief supplied by the government. So anything which tends to prevent a few from getting rich too fast and sets limits upon the property they may accumulate is, to that extent, useful.

Singers are also often well off, but here another factor

is added. Navaho religion is formalized so that any man of enough intelligence can learn to be a Singer, and the relationship of the practitioner to his power is not altogether personal. For this reason the possessor of ritual is not feared in the same way he is among the Apache tribes, where the power is thought to be completely subject to the shaman's will. Navaho fears are concentrated primarily upon the breaking of ritual formulas, the infraction of taboos, and upon the supernaturals, the Powers themselves. Still, feeling toward Singers always tends to be somewhat two-sided. On the one hand, they have great prestige, are revered for the aid they bring, are much in demand, and may obtain large fees. On the other hand, the border of active distrust that the Singer may have caused the illness in order to be paid for curing it is always close. A Singer must not lose too many patients. He must also be more generous and hospitable than the ordinary Navaho. He must not presume upon his position by overweening behavior. On the contrary, he is expected to affect humility by dressing much less expensively than his income would allow. He must be jovial and good-humored even while he is in charge of a ceremonial.

There is the same kind of check upon the power and authority of "political" leaders, who dare not act the autocrat lest they either be accused as witches or have witchcraft directed against them or members of their families. As a matter of fact, this sanction goes too far for utility because it discourages individuals from assuming the burdens of leadership or frightens them into relinquishing office. On the other hand, the effectiveness of leaders is sometimes increased by the fear that they are witches and that if they are disobeyed they will use witchcraft against those who fail to follow them. While this sometimes doubtless has the consequence of perpetuating bad leadership, it has its good side too in that the anarchistic tendencies of Navaho society make it peculiarly vulnerable when facing a society organized like that of whites. The survival of Navaho groups is favored by any sanctions which help to produce a united front behind leaders of some permanence.

At various crucial times in the history of The People clever leaders have used witchcraft beliefs as a means of keeping down "agitators." During the period after Fort Sumner, for example, some leading headmen took care of advocates of renewed resistance to the whites by spreading the word that these persons were witches. Many were executed within a few days.

There are other respects in which witchcraft belief is an effective sanction for the enforcement of social coöperation. The aged, whether they have claims as relatives or not, must be fed or they will "witch" against one. The disposition to aid brothers or sisters who are ill is reinforced by the realization that their death may give rise to suspicion that a survivor is learning witchcraft. Even the fear of going about at night has social value. One of the principal sources of friction among Navahos is sexual jealousy. Fear of witches at night acts to some slight extent as a deterrent to extra-marital sex relations because nighttime would otherwise provide favorable conditions for secret rendezvous.

In brief, witchcraft lore affirms solidarity by dramatically defining what is bad: namely, all secret and malevolent activities against the health, property, and lives of fellow tribesmen. This sanction is reinforced by attributing to witches all the stigmata of evil: incest, nakedness, cruelty, bestiality, and other kinds of forbidden knowledge and actions. The following extract from notes on a talk with a middle-aged Navaho man shows very clearly how any individual who is observed to be guilty of behavior which the Navahos consider antisocial is likely to have heaped upon his head the additional opprobrium that attaches to those suspected of witchcraft, incest, etc. This passage is also an excellent example of the way Navahos think about these subjects and of how a conversation upon almost any subject may turn to that of witchcraft. Finally it indicates the problems of an anthropologist in getting information from a Navaho.

Sometimes they have a two-headed lamb. [Did you ever see one?] No, but my family did. It was near us but I didn't go over. That is bad luck. The man had that two-night sing. [What made the lamb have two heads?] Well, something going on with that flock, maybe a witch-wolf.

Two years ago I went pinyon-hunting and I got caught with that storm. I hired Tall Boy to herd our sheep and my father-in-law's. He did something to those sheep so I paid him and told him to get out. I was having a two-night sing and in the night we heard a ewe bleating like she was going to have a lamb. My mother-in-law got up and she went out. She found a lamb there with no head. It just had a neck and two small ears. [No eyes?] No. [No mouth?] No. She took it over to where they were cooking and then she called us all. It was my father-in-law's lamb. [Did he have a sing?] No, we were having that sing and the sheep was in our flock. That sing protects everybody in the hogan and all the things around like the sheep and horses. [Was someone in your family sick?] No. [Did someone have a bad dream?] No, nothing was wrong. I just had that sing. I have it almost every year. [Your sing was in the spring?] Yes. [But you went pinyon-hunting in the winter?] Yes. [How did you know that Tall Boy had done anything to your sheep?] Well, I just thought so. [When you came home from pinyon-hunting did you tell him to get out?] Yes. [But you didn't have a sing for three or four months.] Well, I have one [Blessing Way] almost every year. [What could Tall Boy have done to your sheep?] He made [i.e., begot] that lamb without any head. [Yes, I know, but how can he do that?] Well, he did something wrong to those sheep [i.e., committed bestiality]. He is mean, that's why I thought he did something. [Has he any sheep?] No. He chases around. He goes to all the dances. He goes with lots of girls. [Is he married?] Yes, he married two girls. They came from way over there at Canyoncito. But they went home. He was mean to them. Sometimes they used to come over to talk to my wife. He beat them and hurt them. They used to cry a lot. He hit them with his fists and sticks.

One day last winter my horses went away. They always go up a canyon near my hogan. There was about that much snow on the ground [indicates 4 inches with his hand]. I walked up that canyon and I found three of them. There were no tracks anywhere. Then I saw some tracks going across the canyon and I thought well I guess someone is going after his traps. I drove the three horses home, then I came back for my other two horses. They were farther up the canyon. Then I passed those tracks coming back. And I thought well I guess that person is going home but I didn't think any more about it. Then I went to my mare. She is very gentle. You just catch hold of her tail and jump on. You don't need any bridle or any rope around her neck. Then I saw those tracks again. They were all around there and then I looked at them and I saw they were Tall Boy's tracks. I said I guess I will follow them. But then they stopped. I only saw my horse's tracks. I saw where he got on the mare so I followed her tracks. Over there was a tree. It had fallen down and when I got there I saw his tracks where he had stood on that tree [for purposes of committing bestiality] and then I saw his tracks where he had run away. [Were the mare's tracks backed up to that tree?] Yes. So I took the horses home. I said to my wife, "Someone's been doing wrong to my mare." She said, "I guess it's Tall Boy." She knew right away. I didn't tell her. She said, "Well, you had better go over to Slim Man's and take him with you." I went over to his place and I told him someone had been doing wrong to my horse up in the canyon and I said, "Let's go and track him." So Slim Man went with me. Then we followed his tracks and they went back to Slim Man's hogan. I said, "Has Tall Boy been here?" He said, "Yes, he was here this morning. He left just before you came." [How did you know these were Tall Boy's tracks?] He had two pieces of leather across one shoe on the bottom. They got snow stuck to them and made that kind of track.

[You said that lamb without a head was born two years ago. You said that Tall Boy must have done something. But how did you know because he didn't do this to your mare until last winter?] Well, we knew he did those things. He slept with his half-sister. All the time he was married he was sleeping with that sister. Then she had a child. It is crazy. Its head goes all over and its eyes too. It can't go to school. It can't do anything.

These anecdotes indicate how witchcraft gossip may be used in providing sanctions against socially undesirable activities. Belief in witchcraft thus plays a part in the Navaho scheme of things in keeping the society running. If and when these theories and the associated acts are stamped out or disappear among The People, other customs must be developed to serve the same functions. The extent to which Navaho witchcraft does provide an outlet for aggression and anxiety is proved by the fluctuations in witchcraft phenomena in recent years. These vary with economic conditions and with the changing intensities of white pressure in a manner that cannot be adjudged accidental.

8. THE TONGUE OF THE PEOPLE

Thus far in this book the point of view has been very largely that of the outsider who carefully observes an unfamiliar way of life and tries to interpret it as best he can. Only insofar as statements by Navahos have been quoted has there been any attempt to see The People's life from the inside.

This chapter[1] and Chapter 9 will be devoted to trying to get a little way inside the Navaho mind. Since the Navahos, like all other peoples, necessarily think with words, at least a superficial conception of the main peculiarities of the Navaho language must be gained before endeavoring to see the world as it appears to The People. The forms of each language impose upon its speakers certain positive predispositions and certain negative restrictions as to the meanings they find in their experience.

From characteristic types of expressions even an outsider may safely infer some of the assumptions which The People make about the nature of things. For example, the Navahos do not say, "I am hungry" or "I have hunger." They always put it as "hunger is killing me" and "thirst is killing me." Similarly, they prefer the active, personalized "water is killing me" to the English description of the impersonal process of natural forces, "I am drowning." From such examples an immediate insight is gained into the Navaho manner of conceiving such events. To The People, hunger is not something which comes from within but something to which the individual is subjected by an outside force. Indeed if an articulate Navaho is pressed for an explanation of this linguistic idiom he is likely to say, "The spirit of hunger sits here beside me."

From the psychological point of view, there are as many different worlds upon the earth as there are languages. Each language is an instrument which guides people in observing, in reacting, in expressing themselves in a special way. The pie of experience can be sliced in all sorts of ways, and language is the principal directive force in the background. It is a great pity that most Americans have so strong an emotional block against the formal analysis of linguistic structures. They have been made to suffer so much from having to memorize rules and from approaching language in a mechanical, unimaginative way that they tend to think of "grammar" as the most inhuman of studies. Looked at in another way, nothing is more human than the speech of an individual or of a folk. No clues are so helpful as those of language in leading to ultimate, unconscious psychological attitudes. Moreover, much of the friction between groups and between nations arises because in both the literal and the slangy senses they don't speak the same language.

For the Navaho case, Robert Young and William Morgan have well put the basic problems:

> The pattern of Navaho thought and linguistic expression is totally unlike that of the European languages with which we are most commonly familiar. We learn such foreign languages as Spanish, French, Italian, and German with a minimum of difficulty because there exist so many analogies, both with respect to grammar and to words, with our own native English. Moreover, the pattern according to which we conceive and express our thoughts in English and in these common European languages is basically the same throughout. We translate readily from one to the other, often almost word for word. And lastly, similar or very closely related sound

systems prevailing throughout make the words easy to pronounce and to remember.

On the other hand, the Navaho language presents a number of strange sounds which are difficult to imitate, and which make the words very hard to remember at first. Secondly, the pattern of thought varies so greatly from our English pattern that we have no small difficulty in learning to think like, and subsequently to express ourselves like the Navaho. An understanding of the morphology and structure of the language, and an insight into the nature of the thought patterns involved can go far in aiding to solve the puzzle.[2]

The tacit premises that are habitually present in the thinking of Navahos elude the outsider until he actually studies somewhat minutely some native utterances recorded in text and compares them with translations given by several different English-speaking Navahos. Better still, if he learns a little Navaho and tries to express himself—even on very simple matters—he is speedily compelled to realize that the categories in which one classifies experience and tries to communicate it to others are not altogether "given" by the events of the external world. Every language is a different system of categorizing and interpreting experience. This system is the more insidious and pervasive because native speakers are so unconscious of it as a system, because to them it is part of the very nature of things, remaining always in the class of background phenomena. That is, the very fact that Navahos do not stop every time they talk about hunger and say to themselves, "When I talk this way I am personalizing hunger as a force outside myself," makes for difficulty of understanding between whites and The People. They take such ways of thought as much for granted as the air they breathe, and unconsciously assume that all human beings in their right minds think the same way.

It is primarily for this reason that administrators, teachers, missionaries, and others who have to do with the Navahos—or any foreign people—would do well to learn something of the salient features of the linguistic structure. It is also for this reason that anyone who wants to understand the Navahos at all must know something about their language and the way in which it molds thought, interests, and attitudes.

There is no doubt that Navaho is a difficult language, but this is not sufficient cause for throwing up one's hands and avoiding the whole subject like the plague. There is a difference between learning a language and using a language. Few whites have the time or the skill to learn to speak Navaho so well that they can dispense with an interpreter. But mastering the tongue or remaining completely ignorant of it are not the only alternatives. The white person who will make the effort necessary to gain a general orientation to the language will not only find the information intensely interesting but will also discover that he can use even this limited knowledge very effectively. If he will then take the further step of talking a bit, in spite of the mistakes he is certain to make, he will be rewarded for this venture considerably beyond his expectations.

The purpose of this chapter can clearly be neither to give a scientific description of the language nor to provide a manual for learning Navaho. The aim is to sketch some structural features to show the reader how the climate of feeling, reacting, and thinking created by the Navaho language is different from that created by English and other European languages.

NAVAHO SOUNDS

White people despair at learning Navaho not only because of its unfamiliar and difficult sounds but also because Navahos are accustomed to respond to small variations which in English are either ignored or used merely for expressive emphasis. For example, a small clutch of the breath ("glottal closure"), which the speaker of European languages scarcely notices, often differentiates Navaho words. *Tsin*[3] means "log," "stick," or "tree," whereas *ts'in* (the ' representing glottal closure) means "bone." Similarly, *bita'* means "between," but *bit'a'* means "its wing."

The Navahos also distinguish quite separate meanings on the basis of pronouncing their vowels in long, intermediate, or short fashion. For example, the words *bito'* (his water) and *bitoo'* (its juice) are absolutely identical save for the fact that the second vowel in the latter is lingered over.

Finally, the Navahos, like the Chinese, pay very careful attention to the tones of vowels (and of the sound "n" which is sometimes used in Navaho with vowel quantity). Four separate tones (low, high, rising, falling) are differentiated. The only difference between *'azee'* (medicine) and *'azéé'* (mouth) is that the final long vowel of the latter has a high pitch, as indicated by the accent mark. The same thing is true for the difference between *'anaa'* (war) and *'anáá'* (eye). The phonetic variations in the following five words are almost imperceptible to the untrained white ear.

bíni', his mind — *binii'*, his face
bíníí', his nostrils — *bini,* in it
biníí', his waist

Perhaps in the case of most nouns, as in the examples just given, meanings would ordinarily become clear from context. But when we come to verbs, differences in pronunciation so slight as to pass unnoticed by those habituated to tongues of Indo-European pattern make for a bewildering set of variations, many of which would be equally suitable to an identical context. For example:

naash'á, I go around with the round object.
naash'aah, I am in the act of lowering the round object.
násh'ááh, I am in the act of turning the round object upside down (or over).

naash'áah, I am accustomed to lowering the round object.

Any of these expressions might easily be confused with *násh'a,* which means "I am skinning it."

The importance of these minute variations in Navaho cuts both ways in complicating the problems of communication between whites and Navahos. These variations make it difficult for whites to speak Navaho, and they also make it difficult for Navahos to learn English sounds accurately. The very fact that the Navahos themselves are sensitized from childhood to these (and not to other) types of sound patterns and alternations makes the phonetics of English or Spanish hard for them to master.

So far as pronunciation alone is concerned, there are languages whose systems of sounds present more problems to the speaker of European background than does Navaho. There are a number of sounds in Navaho that are not found in English, but there are parallels to almost all (except glottalization) in German, Welsh, Polish, and other European languages. The real difficulty with Navaho rests in the fact that the small phonetic differences of the sort that have been illustrated above cannot be bypassed. There is no leeway. In the language of the Sioux Indians there are also long vowels; one can, however, communicate quite effectively without rendering them very accurately. But there is nothing slouchy about Navaho. Sounds must be reproduced with pedantic neatness. Tones can be ignored in Chinese for the sake of stress. Not so in Navaho. The language of The People is the most delicate known for phonetic dynamics.

A few white persons (children of traders or missionaries) who have learned Navaho as small children, speak "without an accent." A very few other whites have learned as adults to speak fluent and correct Navaho but have failed to acquire certain nuances in the sheer style of speaking. Learners may take comfort against their mistakes and embarrassment from the realization that the only recipe for pronouncing Navaho perfectly is to take the precaution of being born of or among Navahos. The talk of those who have learned Navaho as adults always has a flabby quality to the Navaho ear. They neglect a slight hesitation a fraction of a second before uttering the stem of the word. They move their lips and mouths too vigorously. Native Navaho has a nonchalant, mechanical flavor in ordinary discourse—almost as if a robot were talking.

NAVAHO WORDS

It is often said that the word range of all "primitive" peoples is small and that vocabularies of more than a few thousand words are rare. This is pure mythology. It is impossible to say how many "words" there are in Navaho without the statement's being susceptible of misunderstanding, for everything depends upon the standard adopted as to what constitutes a separate word, a peculiarly acute problem in Navaho. But it may be asserted without qualification that Navaho has a very rich vocabulary. Some suggestion of extent may be given by noting that there are more than a thousand *recorded* names for plants, that the technical terms used in ceremonialism total at least five hundred, that every cultural specialization or occupation has its own special terminology.

The language has shown itself flexible in its capacity for dealing with new objects (the parts of an automobile, for example) and new experiences. But this has been done, for the most part, by making up new words in accord with old patterns rather than by taking over Spanish and English words and pronouncing them in Navaho fashion. "Tomato" is "red plant." An elephant is "one that lassoes with his nose." Many American Indian languages have enlarged their vocabularies by incorporating European words, but Navaho has admitted very few. An automobile is called by one of two terms (*chidí* or *chuggi*) which imitate the sound of a car. "Gasoline" then becomes *chidi bi tó,* "car's water."

Words are very important to The People. They are things of power. Some words attract good; others drive away evil. Certain words are dangerous—they may be uttered only by special persons under specially defined conditions. Hence there are specialized vocabularies known only to those who are trained in a craft or ceremonial skill. Young Navahos who have spent much time away at a boarding school or among whites will often complain of an uncle or grandfather, "He uses hard words. I can't understand him."

Not only are many words differentiated from each other by small sound changes, but there are many actual homonyms, words which have very similar or identical sounds but quite different meanings. The presence of these homonymous words and syllables gives rise to the many puns in which the Navahos delight. For instance, *ha'át'íishą' nílį́* means either "what is flowing?" or "what clan are you?" and The People tell stories with many embellishments about this question's being asked of a man who was standing beside a river. Another favorite pun hangs on the fact that the same verb means either "to decide on the matter" or "to put the round object down." This is often employed to satirize the ponderous dealings of important people or, less kindly, to jibe at the hunched back (round object) of a cripple. Still another worn joke arises from the fact that *hodeeshtał* means equally "I will sing" or "I will kick him." And so there are many anecdotes of this pattern:

"So-and-so has gone over yonder."
"What for?"
"He is going to give one a kick." (i.e., The man [a Singer] will perform a chant.)

Many puns are more subtle than they appear on the surface. To enter fully into their humor requires sensitiveness to no less than three or four changes of linguistic front.

A QUICK GLANCE AT NAVAHO GRAMMAR

Navaho grammar is primarily a matter of the verb. The other parts of speech can, however, be used by the beginner to make himself fairly well understood.

NONVERBAL PARTS OF SPEECH

There are few true Navaho nouns, though the list does include some of the commonest and most basic words in the language. Most words which English speakers are apt to term nouns are really nominalized verbs. Some nouns, in fact, can be conjugated after the fashion of neutral verbs. Adjectives are almost entirely the third-person forms of neuter verbs that denote quality, state, or condition. In the formal sense Navaho has no adjectives. Other parts of speech are: pronouns, postpositions, and particles.

Many pronouns are absorbed in verbs, but they are also used independently or prefixed to nouns and postpositions. Navaho pronouns present features of usage and nuances of meaning which it is hard indeed for the European to grasp. For example, "it" as the object of a verb has several different forms, depending upon whether "it" is thought of as definite or indefinite or as a place. The speaker must also choose between a number of possible alternatives for a third person subject of a verb. One of these, which has been called "the person of preferred interest," makes a nice discrimination that is typically Navaho. This form of "he" designates the hero of the story as opposed to others, a Navaho as opposed to a member of another tribe, and so on.

Independent possessive pronouns have two forms, distinguished only by the length of the final vowel. One form signifies merely the state of possession; the other indicates that the owner just came into possession of the object. In the case of body parts, the Navahos make use of another subtle distinction. Thus, *shibe‘* means "my milk" in the sense of milk which actually came from my breasts, whereas *she‘abe‘* means "my milk" in the sense of milk owned by me.

Postpositions are roughly the Navaho equivalent of our prepositions, except that they follow rather than precede their objects. There are a great variety of these, and their usage is relatively simple. They are a godsend to the foreigner, for by combining nouns and postpositions one may communicate many meanings without venturing into the intricacies of the Navaho verb. For instance, one may dodge the very difficult verb "go" by saying, "Your father, how about him?" and the child will state where the father has gone.

Navaho nouns have no gender and, with a few exceptions, have the same forms for singular and plural. Save for a few subtleties in the use of pronominal possessives, nouns are quite easy to handle. Thus, a white man can say a good deal in Navaho if he learns a few hundred nouns and ten or twenty postpositions.

The particles (numerals, "adverbs," "conjunctions," etc.) are many and varied and bafflingly idiomatic. A few of the directional enclitics will illustrate the idiomatic quality and also the precision that is so characteristically Navaho. By selecting among them, the Navaho divides space into zones and circles or into lines and directions, or indicates many other refinements of these ideas. For example, *kodi* (near me) and *kojí* (nearer me than you) show zones and circles thus:

ńlaáhdi, at a point away from me and from you
ńláahjí, at a point distant from both you and me

They can indicate lines and directions in this fashion:

ńleídi, way over there where he is
nahjí, away from where we are

NAVAHO VERBS

Navaho has a peculiarly intricate construction of verbs which derive quite definite meanings from the assembling of elements that are generalized and colorless in themselves. Indeed, it might be called a chemical language. That is, the basic process is that of utilizing the varying effects of small elements in different combinations. Syntax, to the Navaho consciousness, is locked up, confined within the verb.

In a sense, the conjugation of the verb is primarily a matter of making the proper alterations in the prefixes. The verb stem conveys an image which remains constant. However, this nuclear notion is much more minutely specific than is that of the vast majority of English verbs. Verbs of going, for example, are a great nuisance in all Athabascan languages. The first difficulty is that there are usually entirely different stems when one, two, or three or more persons are involved in the action. Thus one stem for the simplest kind of "going" is *-gháách* in the singular, *-'aash* in the dual, and *-kááh* in the plural.

deeshááł, I shall go.
diit'ash, We (two) will go.
diikah, We (more than two) will go.

The complications are bewildering to a white person:

nił deesh'ash, I'll go with you. (The verb has a singular subject but the dual stem is used because two persons are involved in the action.)

nihił deeshkah, I'll go with the two of you. (The subject is still singular but the plural stem must be used because more than two people are involved.)

On the other hand:

I TO LOWER IT	II TO DROP IT	III TO FALL
‘áál, ‘aah, ‘ą, ‘ááh, ‘áál	łniił, łne‘, łne‘, łniih, łne‘	łts‘ił, łts‘iíd, łts‘id, łts‘i‘, łts‘iíd
jih, jááh, jaa‘, jih, jááh	nił, nííł, nil, ‘nił, nííł	dah, déćh, dee‘, dah, déćh *
ghééł, gheeh, ghį́, géćh, ghééł	ghééł, gheeh, ghį́, géćh, ghééł	łhęsh, łhę́ę́sh, łhęęzh, łhęsh, łhę́ę́sh
łjoł, łjooł, łjool, łjoł, łjooł	łjoł, łjooł, łjool, łjoł, łjooł	joł, jooł, jool, joł, jooł
kááł, kaah, ką́, ką́áh, kááł	łkał, łkaad, łkaad, łka‘, łkaad	kał, kaad, kaad, ka‘, kaad
léél, lé, lá, dlééh, léél	łdił, łdeeł, łdéél, łdił, łdeeł	dił, deeł, déél, dił, deeł
nił, nííł, nil, ‘nił, nííł	nił, nííł, nil, ‘nił, nííł	dah, déćh, dee‘, dah, déćh *
łtééł, łtech, łtį́, łtééh, łtééł	łt‘eeł, łt‘e‘, łt‘e‘, łt‘eeh, łt‘e‘	tłish, tłíísh, tłizh, tłish, tłíísh
tį́įł, tį́įh, tą́, tį́įh, tį́įł	łt‘eeł, łt‘e‘, łt‘e‘, łt‘eeh, łt‘e‘	kǫs, kęęs, kę́ę́z, kǫs, kęęs
tłoh, tłeeh, tłéé‘, tłoh, tłeeh	tłoh, tłeeh, tłéé‘, tłoh, tłeeh	łhęsh, łhęęsh, łhęęzh, łhęsh, łhęęsh
łtsos, łtsóós, łtsooz, łtsos, łtsóós	‘ał, ‘áád, ‘ah, ‘ah, ‘áád	nah, nééh, na‘, nah, nééh

THE PARADIGMS FOR NOS. I & II ABOVE ARE AS FOLLOWS:

Future	*Imperfective*	*Perfective*	*Repetitive*	*Optative*
Ndeesh-	naash-	náá-	ninásh-	naoosh-
ndíí-	nani-	néíní-	ninání-	naóó-
neidoo-	nei-	nayíí-	ninéí-	nayó-
nizhdoo-	nji-	njíí-	ninájí-	njó-
ndoo-	na-	náá-	niná-	naó-
nibidi‘doo-	nabi‘di-	nabi‘doo-	ninábi‘di-	nabi‘dó-
ndii-	neii-	neii-	ninéii-	naoo-
ndooh-	naah-	naoo-	nináh-	naooh-

THE 3RD PERSON FORMS FOR NO. III ARE:

Future	*Imperf.*	*Perf.*	*Repet.*	*Optat.*
ndoo-	naa-	náá-	niná-	naoo-

English TO DROP IT (from one's grasp) is rendered by postposition of -lak‘ee, the (area of the) hand to:

hadoo-	haa-	háá-	haná-	haoo-
hadínóo-	hani-	haníí-	hanání-	hanó-

*The stem *dah* requires the following:

ndínóo-	nani-	naníí-	ninání-	nanó-

de'nohháah, One of you come here (*-noh-* refers to plural "you" but, since only one person is expected to act, the stem is singular).
de'nínáah, Come here (you, singular).
de'nohkáah, Come here (you, plural, in a group).
de'hohkáah, Come here (you, plural, one after another).

In short, where English is loose, Navaho is fussy about the finest shades of meaning, which it expresses by small permutations of verbal elements.

Navaho is compact as well as precise. The last example above shows how with great economy the Navaho language by the simple substitution of a monosyllable conveys ideas which take many words in English. Take two more examples along the same line.

Fig. 5. Partial Paradigm of Three Navaho Verbs
(From Robert W. Young, Window Rock, Arizona)

The accompanying schematic presentation is designed to bring out the relationship existing in the classification of certain concepts, the relationship being illustrated by giving the stem forms which correspond to object class with relation to a given concept. Thus, the stem *'áál* refers to the handling of a bulky roundish object; in conjunction with the derivational prefix *na-*, down, the idea is "to handle it downward." However, in performing this act, the subject of the verb, or the agent of the act retains contact with the object, so the English translation is "to lower it." When the agent of the act does not retain contact with the object, with the result that the object *falls,* a separate set of stems is required in most instances; these still classify the object with reference to shape, size, number and other characteristics, but alter the action concept expressed by the stem. When the object falls of its own accord, the stems may again vary from those in I or II. It will be noted that, in some instances, the same stems are used in I and II; while in several cases the stem employed for the concept "to drop it" is merely the corresponding "to fall" stem rendered causative by the l-classifier. One would not expect to find stem distinctions between the closely related concepts "to drop" and "to fall." "To lose it" and "to knock it over" require the stem forms given under II.

dadiikah, We will each go separately.

hidiikah, We will go one after another, in succession.

Some of these prefixes are difficult to distinguish in English translation. For instance, *ná-* and *náá-* are ordinarily both rendered by "again," but actually there is a significant shade of difference.

deesk'aaz hazlį́į́, It (the weather) got cold.
deesk'aaz náhásdlį́į́, It got cold again.
deesk'aaz nááhásdlį́į́, It got cold again.

But really the third form means "it got cold *back*"; that is, a return to a previous state is specified.

Navaho is likewise very finicky in expressing agency. *Tsinaa'eeł shił ní'éél, tsinaa'eeł shił 'aníł'éél,* and *tsinaa'eeł níł'éél* may all be rendered: "I came by boat." But the first form implies that the boat floats off of its own accord, the second that the movement is caused by an indefinite or unstated subject, the third that the movement of the boat was caused by the speaker.

A great many verbs have alternating stems, depending upon the type of object which is acted upon or is the subject of a positional verb. To give the reader an idea in the concrete of how these stems vary and to show what the paradigm of a Navaho verb looks like we have reproduced a hitherto unpublished communication by Robert Young (Figure 5). This does not show all of the possible class stems and gives only the more commonly used tenses, aspects, and modes. But the chart does illustrate other principles of the classification of experience as enjoined by the Navaho language that are discussed in this chapter. In connection with this figure, the reader should note Figure 10. These class stems embrace such categories as the following: the long-object class (a pencil, a stick, a pipe); the slender-flexible-object class (snakes, thongs, certain pluralities including certain types of food and property); the container-*and*-contents class; the granular-mass class (sugar, salt, etc.); the things-bundled-up class (hay, bundles of clothing, etc.—if they are loose and not compact); the fabric class (paper, spread out leather, blankets, etc.); the viscous-object class (mud, feces, etc.); the bulky-round-object class; the animate-object class; and others.[4] Thus there is no such thing as saying "I give" in Navaho—there are more than twenty different forms, one of which must be chosen to accord with the nature of the object given.

It is really a distortion to say that there is any Navaho verb stem meaning "to give." With greater correctness we might say that "give" in Navaho is the transitive correspondent of "come." You cause something to come to one. "To give A to B" becomes, as it were, in Navaho "to handle such and such an object (the precise stem will depend, of course, upon the class of object) completively to or for such and such a person." To generalize: one cannot decide what stem to use in Navaho on the basis of the nuclear idea in English. The structure is too different. The Navaho language represents an importantly different mode of *thinking* and must be regarded as such.

The inflections of the verb in most European languages perform as one of their principal functions those distinctions between past, present, and future which we call "tense." It is an arguable question whether there are tenses in the European sense in Navaho. The language of The People is interested primarily in the category the grammarians call "aspect."

Aspect defines the geometrical character of an event, stating its definability with regard to line and point rather than its position in an absolute time scale or in time as broken up by the moving present of the speaker. Traces of aspect inflection may be found in modern Greek, German, and Spanish, but only in Slavic languages such as Russian and Polish does it have any systematic importance among contemporary European tongues. Aspect indicates different types of activity. Thus, the momentaneous aspect in Navaho means that action is thought of as beginning and ending within an instant, while the continuative suggests that action lasts. Inceptive, cessative, durative, imperfective, and semelfactive, are some of the other aspects in Navaho—with a different paradigm of every verb stem for each.

Grammarians also consider modes as one of the principal verbal categories in Navaho. Some modes are similar to, but not identical with, the tenses of English. Others indicate the way an act is performed—repeatedly or customarily, etc. For example, *biih náshdááh* (iterative mode) means "time and again I put it on," whereas *biih yíshááh* (usitative mode) means "habitually I put it on." The usitative mode implies the speaker's interest is general, not in a specific event. Often it should be translated "our custom is so and so." It may indeed refer to events that are hypothetical so far as the speaker is concerned. Hence sometimes it must be rendered "if I were to" or "whenever." The iterative, in contrast, refers to actual repetition of acts.

Future, present, and past time may be left unspecified or may be indicated by suffixes, but sometimes they are made clear by the combination of aspect and mode. For instance, *'áásh'łííł* (imperfective aspect, progressive mode) may be rendered "I am (progressively) making it." The imperfective aspect most often conveys a sense analogous to that of English indefinite present. But the primary idea which The People express through this aspect is that of uncompleted action. So far as time is concerned, the act may take place in the past, provided that the act is uncompleted. Or it may refer to the future when one is about to do or in the act of doing something. Depending upon context and upon the mode with which it is combined, therefore, the imperfective must be rendered "I am in the act of" or "I was in the act of" or "I am about to be in the act of," and in a great variety of other ways.

Navahos are perfectly satisfied with what seem to whites rather imprecise discriminations in the realm of time sequences. On the other hand, they are the fussiest people in the world about always making explicit in the forms of the language many distinctions which English makes only occasionally and irregularly, more often than not leaving them vague or to be clarified from context. In English one says "I eat," meaning "I eat something." The Navaho point of view is different. "I eat" means "I eat it." If the object thought of is actually indefinite, then *'a-* ("something") must be expressed. Furthermore, Navaho always specifies through the form of the verb the contrast between status and action. All verbs in Navaho are divided by grammarians into two groups: neutral and active. "Neutral" designates those verbs that do not change their character. "Active" refers to verbs that denote activities or that do change their character. There is, in Navaho, all the difference in the world between the type of idea suggested by English "I am friendly" and that suggested by "I habitually do friendly acts." The English phrases are rendered by distinct Navaho forms. Each type of verb may also be either transitive or intransitive. "To be tall" is neutral-intransitive. "To hold it" is neutral-transitive. "I see it" (in the sense of "I have it visible") is the neutral-transitive form, whereas "I look at it" is neutral-active.

Because so much is expressed and implied by the few syllables that make up a single verb form, the Navaho verb is like a tiny Imagist poem. A free translation of such a microcosm of meaning must normally become a somewhat extended paraphrase before even the main significance can be included. One Navaho word more often than not turns into a whole sentence in English. The single word *shínii'á,* for instance, means "the rigid object (such as a gun) leans against me."

Let us look at some further examples showing the extent of definition required to convey the sense of a Navaho verb:

haadiǹsh‘aa, I hand it over to him by word of mouth.
shíí‘įįd, He gave me a piece of his mind.
shan‘doo‘aał, Would that you might give me back permission to speak.
‘aajíyígháá́h, He is getting to that point there by you.
ní‘ą́, A set of round objects extends off in a horizontal line, or: I brought it.
‘o‘ó‘ááł, Would that the sun (or moon) might set.
híínááł, You are shuffling along sidewise.
‘eeshdéél, I have eaten some berries (apples, buns, or any plural separable objects) one at a time.
náńdįįh, Time and again you (sing.) eat it.
ná‘íldił, You are accustomed to eat plural separable objects one at a time.
haǹłcóós, You take a fabric-like object out of an enclosed space.

The above translations are no more than crude approximations that by no means transmit the total sense of the Navaho. In the first example the "him" is not just any "him" but a person being addressed politely or respectfully. The verb form is a somewhat stereotyped formula used in making certain types of gifts, especially of land. However, in some contexts it must be rendered "I promise it to him," and in others, "I forgive him." The optative form illustrated in the third example may also have the sense of a polite prohibitive, meaning, "Please don't give me back the floor." In the ninth example the form makes it plain that "it" is a definite "it" not "something" (indefinite), which would be a different form (*ná‘idįįh*). The subtle distinctions inherent in the aspect and tense-mode forms used in the Navaho verbs are left completely unexpressed in the English renderings given. In short, it would take literally pages to analyze the full implications of these eleven words.

BY THEIR SPEECH SHALL YE KNOW THEM

Any language is more than an instrument for the conveying of ideas, more even than an instrument for working upon the feelings of others and for self-expression. Every language is also a means of categorizing experience. What people think and feel, and how they report what they think and feel, is determined, to be sure, by their individual physiological state, by their personal history, and by what actually happens in the outside world. But it is also determined by a factor which is often overlooked; namely, the pattern of linguistic habits which people have acquired as members of a particular society. The events of the "real" world are never felt or reported as a machine would do it. There is a selection process and an interpretation in the very act of response. Some features of the external situation are highlighted; others are ignored or not fully discriminated.

Every people has its own characteristic classes in which individuals pigeonhole their experiences. These classes are established primarily by the language through the types of objects, processes, or qualities which receive special emphasis in the vocabulary and equally, though more subtly, through the types of differentiation or activity which are distinguished in grammatical forms. The language says, as it were, "Notice this," "Always consider this separate from that," "Such and such things belong together." Since persons are trained from infancy to respond in these ways they take such discriminations for granted, as part of the inescapable stuff of life. But when we see two peoples with different social traditions respond in different ways to what appear to the outsider to be identical stimulus-situations, we realize that experience is much less a "given," an absolute, than we thought. Every language has an effect upon what the people who use it see, what they feel, how they think, what they can talk about.

As pointed out in the section on grammar, the language of The People delights in sharply defined categories. It likes, so to speak, to file things away in neat little packages. It favors always the concrete and particular, with little scope for abstractions. It directs attention to some features of every situation, such as the minute distinctions as to direction and type of activity. It ignores others to which English gives a place. Navaho focuses interest upon doing —upon verbs as opposed to nouns or adjectives.

Striking examples of the categories which mark the Navaho language are the variations in many of its verb stems according to the types of their subjects or objects. As has been illustrated above, the verb stem used often depends upon whether its subject (or object) is in the long-object class (such as a pencil, a stick, or a pipe), the granular-mass class (such as sugar and salt), the things-bundled-up class (such as hay and bundles of clothing), the animate-object class, and many others.

It must not be thought that such classification is a conscious process every time a Navaho opens his mouth to speak. It would, of course, paralyze speech if one had to think, when about to say a verb, "Now I must remember to specify whether the object is definite or indefinite; whether it is something round, long, fluid, or something else." Fortunately this is no more necessary in Navaho than in English. The Navaho child simply learns that if he is talking about dropping baseballs or eggs or stones he uses a word different from the word he would use if he spoke of dropping a knife or a pencil or a stick, just as the English-speaking child learns to use different words (herd, flock, crowd) in mentioning a group of cows, sheep, or people.

The important point is that striking divergences in manner of thinking are crystallized in and perpetuated by the forms of Navaho grammar. Take the example of a commonplace physical event: rain. Whites can and do report their perception of this event in a variety of ways: "It has started to rain," "It is raining," "It has stopped raining." The People can, of course, convey these same ideas—but they cannot convey them without finer specifications. To give only a few instances of the sorts of discrimination the Navaho must make before he reports his experience: he uses one verb form if he himself is aware of the actual inception of the rain storm, another if he has reason to believe that rain has been falling for some time in his locality before the occurrence struck his attention. One form must be employed if rain is general round about within the range of vision; another if, though it is raining round about, the storm is plainly on the move. Similarly, the Navaho must invariably distinguish between the ceasing of rainfall (generally) and the stopping of rain in a particular vicinity because the rain clouds have been driven off by wind. The People take the consistent noticing and reporting of such differences (which are usually irrelevant from the white point of view) as much for granted as the rising of the sun.

Navaho is an excessively literal language, little given to abstractions and to the fluidity of meaning that is so characteristic of English. The inner classification gives a concreteness, a specificity, to all expression. Most things can be expressed in Navaho with great exactness by manipulating the wide choice of stems in accord with the multitudinous alternatives offered by fusing prefixes and other separable elements in an almost unlimited number of ways. Indeed Navaho is almost overneat, overprecise. There is very little "give" in the language. It rather reminds one of a Bach fugue, in which everything is ordered in scrupulous symmetry.

The general nature of the difference between Navaho thought and English thought—both as manifested in the language and also as forced by the very nature of the linguistic forms into such patterns—is that Navaho thought is prevailingly so much more specific, so much more concrete. The ideas expressed by the English verb "to go" provide a nice example. To Germans the English language seems a little sloppy because the same word is used regardless of whether the one who goes walks or is transported by a train or other agency, whereas in German these two types of motion are always sharply distinguished in the two verbs *gehen* and *fahren*. But Navaho does much more along this line. For example, when one is talking about travel by horse, the speed of the animal may be expressed by the verb form chosen. The following all mean "I went by horseback."

łį́į́ shił níyá, (at a walk or at unspecified speed).
łį́į́ shił yíldloozh, (at a trot).
łį́į́ shił neeltą́ą́ʻ, (at a gallop).
łį́į́ shił yílghod, (at a run).

When a Navaho says that he went somewhere he never fails to specify whether it was afoot, astride, by wagon, auto, train, or airplane. This is done partly by using different verb stems which indicate whether the traveler moved under his own steam or was transported, partly by naming the actual means. Thus, "he went to town" would become:

kintahgóó ʻííyá,	He went to town afoot or in a nonspecific way.
kintahgóó bił ʻiʻííbą́ą́z,	He went to town by wagon.
kintahgóó bił ʻoʻootʻaʻ,	He went to town by airplane.
kintahgóó bił ʻiʻííʻéél,	He went to town by boat.
kintahgóó bił ʻoʻooldloozh,	He went to town by horseback at a trot.
kintahgóó bił ʻoʻooldghod,	He went to town by horseback at a run (or perhaps by car or train).
kintahgóó bił ʻiʻnooltą́ą́ʻ,	He went to town by horseback at a gallop.

Moreover, the Navaho language insists upon another type of splitting up of the generic idea of "going" to which German is as indifferent as English. The Navaho always differentiates between starting to go, going along, arriving at, returning from a point, etc., etc. For instance, he makes a choice between:

kintahgi níyá,	He arrived at town.
kintahgóó 'íiyá,	He went to town and is still there.
kintahgóó naayá,	He went to town but is now back where he started.

Let us take a few more examples. The Navaho interpreter, even though his behavior or side comments may make it perfectly apparent that he feels there is a difference, will translate both *háájísh 'íiyá* and *háágósh 'íiyá* as "where did he go." If you say to him, "The Navaho sounds different in the two cases and there must be some difference in English meaning," the interpreter is likely to reply, "Yes, there is a difference all right, but you just can't express it in English." Now this is not literally true. Almost anything which can be said in Navaho can be said in English and vice versa, though a translation which gets everything in may take the form of a long paraphrase which sounds strained and artificial in the second language. In the case of the examples given above, the nearest equivalents are probably: "in what direction did he leave" and "for what destination did he leave."

In English one might ask, "Where did he go" and the usual answer would be something like, "He went to Gallup." But in Navaho one would have to select one of eight or ten possible forms which, if rendered exactly into English, would come out something like this: "He started off for Gallup," "He left to go as far as Gallup," "He left by way of Gallup," "He left, being bound for Gallup (for a brief visit)," "He left, being bound for Gallup (for an extended stay)," etc.

The People are likewise particular about other differentiations, similar to some of those discussed earlier in this chapter:

kin góne' yah 'iikai,	We went into the house (in a group).
kin góne' yah 'ahiikai,	We went into the house (one after another).

or:

chizh kin góne yah 'íínil,	I carried the wood into the house (in one trip).
chizh kin góne yah 'akénil,	I carried the wood into the house (in several trips).

It is not, of course, that these distinctions *cannot* be made in English but that they *are not* made consistently. They seem of importance to English-speakers only under special circumstances, whereas constant precision is a regular feature of Navaho thought and expression about movement.

The nature of their language forces The People to notice and to report many other distinctions in physical events which the nature of the English language allows speakers to neglect in most cases, even though their senses are just as able as those of the Navaho to register the smaller details of what goes on in the external world. For example, suppose a Navaho range rider and a white supervisor see that the wire fence surrounding a demonstration area is broken. The supervisor will probably write in his notebook only: "The fence is broken." But if the range rider reports the occurrence to his friends he must say either *béésh 'alc'ast'i* or *béésh 'alc'aat'i;* the first would specify that the damage has been caused by some person, the second that the agency was nonhuman. Further, he must choose between one of these statements and an alternative pair—the verb form selected depending on whether the fence was of one or several strands of wire.

Two languages may classify items of experience differently. The class corresponding to one word and one

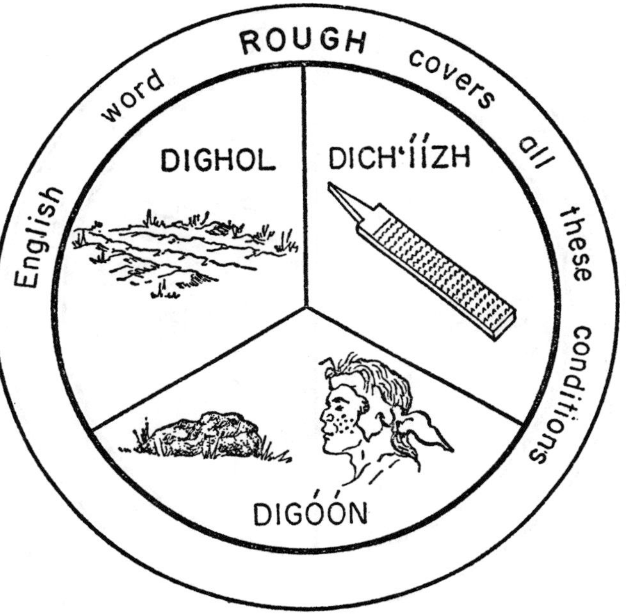

Fig. 6.

In this case Navaho distinguishes more kinds of roughness than does English.

thought in Language A may be regarded by Language B as two or more classes corresponding to two or more words and thoughts.[5] For instance, where in English one word "rough" (more pedantically, "rough-surfaced") may equally well be used to describe a road, a rock, and the business surface of a file, Navaho finds a need for three different words which may not be used interchangeably (see Figure 6). While the general tendency is for Navaho to make finer and more concrete distinctions, this is not invariably the case. The same stem is used for "rip," "light beam," and "echo," ideas which seem diverse to white people. One word is used to designate a medicine bundle with all its contents, the skin quiver in which the contents

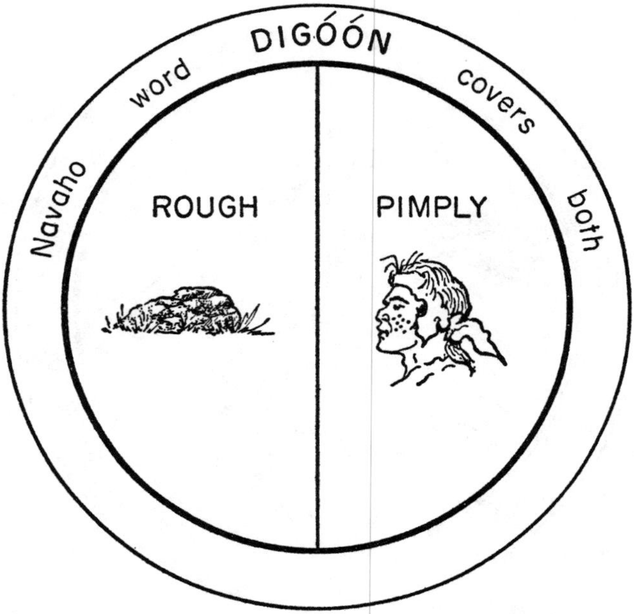

Fig. 7.

Here English will generally use two different words rather than the same one for both conditions.

are wrapped, the contents as a whole, and some of the distinct items of the contents. Sometimes the point is not that the images of Navahos are less fluid and more delimited but rather just that the external world is dissected along different lines. For example, *digóón* may be used to describe both a pimply face and a nodule-covered rock. In English a complexion might be termed "rough" or "coarse" but a rock would never, except facetiously, be described as "pimply." Navaho differentiates two types of "rough rock"—the kind which is rough in the manner in which a file is rough, and the kind which is nodule-encrusted. In these cases (see Figure 7) the difference between the Navaho and the English ways of seeing the

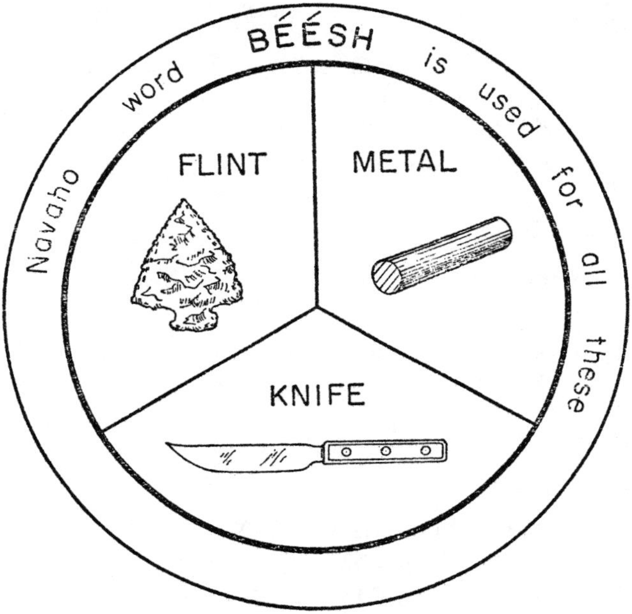

Fig. 8.

These are all one sort in the Navaho view—mostly because metals and knives came to them at the same time to take the place of flint.

world cannot be disposed of merely by saying that Navaho is more precise. The variation rests in the features which the two languages see as essential. Cases can even be given where Navaho is notably less precise: Navaho gets along with a single word for flint, metal, knife, and certain other objects of metal (see Figure 8). This, to be sure, is due to the historical accident that, after European contact, metal in general and knives in particular largely took the place of flint. But in the last analysis most linguistic differentiations, like other sorts of cultural selectivity, rest upon the historical experience of the people.

How the Navaho and English languages dissect nature

differently perhaps comes out most clearly when we contrast verbal statements. Take a simple event such as a person dropping something. The different "isolates of meaning" (thoughts) used in reporting this identical experience will be quite different in Navaho and in English (see Figure 9). The only two elements which are the

Fig. 9. "I drop it."

ENGLISH specifies

1. Subject: *I*
2. Type of action: *drop*
3. Time of action: while speaking or just before

NAVAHO specifies

1. Subject: *sh*
2. Direction of action: downward—*Naa*
3. Definite or indefinite object: (verb form)
4. Type of object: (verb stem) here a bulky, roundish, hard object—*Naa*

5. Amount of control of subject over process:

in act of lowering

in act of letting fall

6. From area of the hand: *-lak'ee*

Naash'aah lak'ee

(I am in the act of lowering the definite, bulky, roundish, hard object from my hand.)

Naashne' lak'ee

(I am in the act of letting the definite, bulky, roundish, hard object fall from my hand.)

same are "l" and "sh," both of which specify who does the dropping. A single image "drop" in English requires two complementary images (*naa* and *'aah*) in Navaho. English stops with what from the Navaho point of view is a very vague statement—"I drop it." The Navaho must specify four particulars which the English leaves either unsettled or to inference from context:

1. The form must make clear whether "it" is definite or just "something."
2. The verb stem used will vary depending upon whether the object is round, or long, or fluid, or animate, etc., etc.
3. Whether the act is in progress, or just about to start, or just about to stop or habitually carried on or repeatedly carried on must be rigorously specified. In English, "I drop it" can mean once or can mean that it is customarily done (e.g., in describing the process of getting water from my well by a bucket). All the other possibilities are also left by English to the imagination.
4. The extent to which the agent controls the fall must be indicated: *naash'aah* means "I am in the act of lowering the round object" but *naashne'* means "I am in the act of letting the round object fall."

To make the analysis absolutely complete, it must be pointed out that there is one respect in which the English is here a bit more exact. "I drop it" implies definitely (with the exception of the use of the "historical present") that the action occurs as the speaker talks or just an instant before, while the two Navaho verbs given above could, in certain circumstances, refer either to past or to future time. In other words, Navaho is more interested in the type of action (momentaneous, progressing, continuing, customary, etc.) than in establishing sequences in time as related to the moving present of the speaker.

Many other sorts of difference could be described, some of which are illustrated in Figures 10–12. A full technical treatment would require a whole book to itself. The widest implications have been beautifully phrased by one of the great linguists of recent times, Edward Sapir:

> Language is not merely a more or less systematic inventory of the various items of experience which seem relevant to the individual, as is so often naïvely assumed, but is also a self-contained, creative symbolic organization, which not only refers to experience largely acquired without its help but actually defines experience for us by reason of its formal completeness and because of our unconscious projection of its implicit expectations into the field of experience. In this respect language is very much like a mathematical system which, also, records experience in the truest sense of the word, only in its crudest beginnings, but, as time goes on, becomes elaborated into a self-contained conceptual system which previsages all possible experience in accordance with certain accepted formal limitations . . . [Meanings are] not so much discovered in experience as imposed upon it, because of the tyrannical hold that linguistic form has upon our orientation in the world. Inasmuch as languages differ very widely in their systematization of fun-

Fig. 10. "It bent."

Yiitaaz

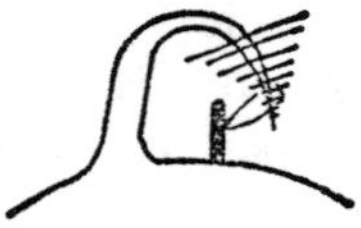

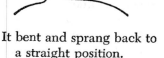

It bent and stayed that way.

'Ahą́ą́h niijool

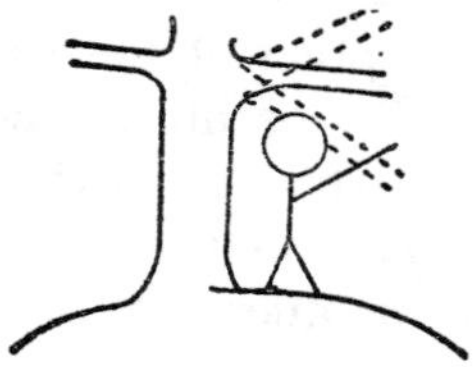

It bent and sprang back to a straight position.

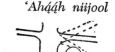

damental concepts, they tend to be only loosely equivalent to each other as symbolic devices and are, as a matter of fact, incommensurable in the sense in which two systems of points in a plane are, on the whole, incommensurable to each other, if they are plotted out

Fig. 11. "He went to town."

ENGLISH

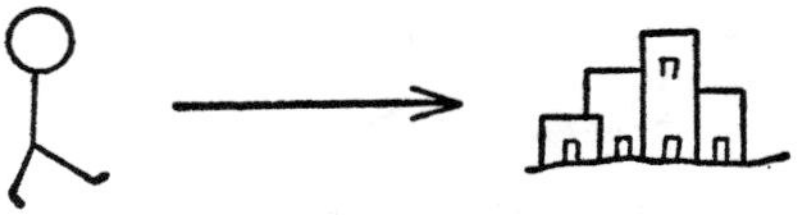

He went to town.

NAVAHO

a. *Kintahgóó ʻííyá*

b. *Kintahgóó bił ʻoʻooldloozh*

c. *Kintahgóó bił ʻi̒nooltą́ą́ʻ*

d. *Kintahgóó bił ʻi̒íbą́ą́z*

e. *Kintahgóó bił ʻoʻootʻaʻ*

f. *Kintahgóó bił ʻi̒í̒éél*

The verb here implies *means of locomotion* because, for example, b. and c. would be used mostly of a horse, d. of something that rolls, e. of something that flies. In b. and c. *speed of locomotion* is also indicated.

with reference to differing systems of coördinates . . .

In many ways the Navaho classifications come closer to a freshly objective view of the nature of events than do those of such languages as English or Latin.[6]

Fig. 12. "I kicked him."

1. *Sétał:* I kicked him.

2. *Néishtał:* I gave him a kick on repeated occasions.

3. *Nánéétáál:* I gave him repeated kicks on the same occasion.

---

4. *Nínáníshtał:* I gave him repeated kicks on repeated occasions.

WHY BOTHER ABOUT THE LANGUAGE?

The problems faced by The People in adjusting to white society, and especially the problems faced by the Navaho child in school, must be viewed within the framework of the differences between the English and the Navaho languages. Whites who have tried to learn Navaho have a lively realization of how difficult it is, but they often fail to comprehend that it is equally hard for Navahos to master English. English sounds are so different from Navaho and so indistinct by comparison that they are hard for The People to learn. Most Navahos actually feel that their own language is easier because they sense the function of each element, whereas English is difficult for them because the proportion of sheer idiom is so much greater and the underlying conceptual bases of idiom are so different.

Other more specific problems for the Navaho learner of English arise from technical differences in the structure of the two languages. For example, there is no gender in Navaho verbs, so Navaho youngsters use "he" and "she" interchangeably or say "he" for "she" to the end of time. Similarly the English practice of expressing plurality in nouns by an internal vowel change (goose, geese) is completely unfamiliar to Navahos and baffles them.

Because of the structure of their language The People are bound to have mental processes that are, in some significant senses, different from those of English-speaking peoples. The one fact that Navaho is a verb language, whereas English is mainly a noun-adjective language, of itself implies a different order of thought habits.

All study of the Navahos and all administrative communication with them are complicated by these differences in linguistic and thinking habits. This was painfully true of the program of giving Navaho children psychological tests described in *Children of The People*, by Leighton and Kluckhohn (Harvard University Press, 1947). Even where the child spoke enough English so the tests could be administered without an interpreter, it is doubtful whether the English words used really conveyed the same meaning to the Navaho child as they would have to a white child of similar age and temperament. Likewise, there were created for the investigators many puzzles in interpreting the English phrases used by the child in reply.

ESTABLISHING GOOD RELATIONS

At least some understanding of Navaho ways of speech and thought is essential to the teacher, the government official, or any other white person who needs or wants to understand The People. Part of its usefulness lies in indicating the good will of the white person, in paying Navahos the implied compliment of making the effort necessary to learn something about their language, and in establishing the friendly relation that arises between the earnest novice and the expert. To American Indians, whose language has usually been ignored or ridiculed by whites, there is satisfaction in the spectacle of the white man taking the trouble to study their tongue. His very difficulties and mistakes tend to promote good feeling toward him. Indians have seldom had the opportunity of laughing at a white man to his face with impunity. If they can smile and joke freely when one tries haltingly to pronounce words or speak a sentence, their hostile impulses toward him are diminished.

Using the language even a very little helps to build up easy and confident relations with Navahos. With skill or luck, the white man may win for himself a place as a person who is not always in the superior role, as a potential friend who may sometimes be laughed at or with, rather than just another member of a distrusted or even hated race, to whom taciturnity, sullenness, suspicion, or active hostility are the usual responses. A few words of greeting and farewell, a face not blank or troubled but lighting with comprehension when a daily commonplace is uttered in Navaho, sometimes mean the difference between being regarded as a foreign intruder or as a sympathetic visitor.

DEALING WITH INTERPRETERS

We have seen in this chapter enough of the differences between Navaho and English to realize that any translation from one to the other is a difficult business and requires sensitivity and skill. Few indeed are the individuals who are prepared for this demanding task. Not many Navahos have a quick command of fluent, idiomatic English. Of those who do, a large proportion speak only "schoolboy" Navaho, missing much that should be rendered into English and often foundering completely when the more involved Navaho constructions are used.

The interpreter's lot is not a happy one. He is under pressure from both the Navaho and the English-speaker to translate quickly, and so does not have time to think out the full implications of what he is saying in either language. Old Navahos are exasperated when the interpreter asks them to repeat or re-phrase some verb form that has baffled him. Whites become impatient at the amount of time consumed. Both sides blame the interpreter if they sense that effective communication is not being established. At the same time they too frequently trust the translations, believing that their own meanings have been transmitted intact and without essential distortion. Most Navahos and whites alike assume naïvely that an interpreter can or ought to be able to work with the precision of a machine. The interpreter deserves sympathy for his almost impossible job, for it is too much to expect one man to take the whole responsibility for bridging the gulf between worlds that are as different as their languages.

To turn a sentence from English into Navaho or from Navaho into English involves a great deal more than choosing the proper word for word equivalents from a dictionary. Bewildered by the lack of structural correspondences between the two tongues, most interpreters succumb to one or both of two temptations: either they leave out a great deal in passing from Navaho to English (or vice versa); or they translate all too freely, projecting their own meanings into the sentences they "translate." Sometimes difficulties arise because the interpreter tries to stick too closely to the literal text of the English. For example, at a Navajo Council meeting within the last few years there was a discussion of how to develop mineral and gas resources on the Reservation. The white speaker from Washington who introduced the matter used the phrase "hidden beneath the ground." When translated literally into Navaho this had the sense of "secreted beneath the ground." The Council got the sense that there was some skulduggery in the whole business and got so worked up that certain measures which should have been passed in the interests of the war had to be held over until the next meeting.

A Navajo Agency interpreter may take a speech that an official has couched in conciliatory and expository English, and by his compression and by the Navaho forms he selects, may give the Navaho audience the impression that a brusque order has been issued. The official meant to present a policy for discussion, or to explain and win the assent of the Navaho group to a policy that had been decided upon. But the English nuances which imply courtesy and interest in Navaho opinion are too difficult to get over (at least without long thought in advance), so The People get the sense that they are being told to do thus and so without any if's, and's, or but's. On the basis of detailed examination of certain cases that are probably all too typical, it can be asserted without any doubt whatsoever that the resentment and resistance that occurred at certain points during the stock reduction program might have been avoided, or at least much mitigated, if communication had not been so faulty from inaccurate interpreting.

One should not expect too much from interpreters, but one should expect the right things. Some whites, realizing that the interpreter is omitting a good deal of the Navaho, adopt the wrong corrective. They demand that the interpreter give a translation of each Navaho syllable. This is a mistake because only the most sophisticated Navahos can break even a majority of words into their elements, and then usually only after considerable reflection and discussion. (How many English-speakers can, offhand, break down "parliament," "stethoscope"—or even a word of Anglo-Saxon derivation such as "enthralled"—into their smallest meaning units?) In any event, there is enough idiom in Navaho to make a literal etymological translation meaningless in many cases. For instance, *náhookǫs* (north) translates literally as "one stiff slender object makes a revolution" (from the constellation of the dipper which revolves about the North Star). For purposes of conveying meaning the etymology does not matter, and such a rendering would merely compound confusion—to say the least—save for the purposes of the scientific linguist.

This is not to say that etymology is irrelevant to all the nuances of communication. While it would be absurd to pretend that the whole etymology of *náhookǫs* is present to the consciousness of a Navaho every time he says the word, still the sheer formal nature of the verb as well as the meanings of its separable elements must carry with them a background of association and connotation that is altogether lacking in the English noun "north." Something is lost of the flavor of the Navaho just as when the English words "thinker" and "ratiocinator" are indiscriminately translated into French as *penseur*. However, this whole problem of word flavor as contingent upon formal etymology is but one rather minor instance of the important generalization that the meanings expressed in one language can never be transmuted into another language without some loss or change. The wise Italian proverb: *Traditóre, traduttóre* ("The translator is a betrayer"), is even truer for Navaho than for most languages.

But this is a counsel of wisdom—not of despair. The white teacher or administrator who is aware that translation can never achieve mechanical perfection will keep his expectations realistically modest. If he has knowledge of the peculiar difficulties of Navaho, he will have a healthy respect for the problems faced by his interpreters. This will lead him, on the one hand, to have more patience and thus bolster the interpreter's confidence and produce better feeling toward the white, both of which will promote greater efficiency. On the other hand, the white will know that, at best, a perfect job cannot be done, and will make allowances in his behavior for partial failure of communication. He will be less easily moved to harmful or futile anger at "broken promises," for he will realize that, in many cases, his understanding of an agreement or a situation diverged in important particulars from that of the Navahos with whom he was dealing.

In many specific ways a white person can put even a smattering of knowledge about the Navaho language to useful and highly practical purposes. If he catches even an occasional Navaho word that the interpreter does not translate, he can question the interpreter about it. Experience shows that this procedure results in much greater care in translation. When the interpreter is aware that there is any chance at all of his being checked up on, both pride and the fear of losing his job result in more alertness and precision. The white may actually know fewer than a hundred words, but if they are common words one or more will eventually enter into any conversation. Navahos who discover that a white man knows any Navaho at all usually tend to exaggerate this knowledge, and this tendency can be exploited to the fullest in controlling interpreters.

Realization that most Navaho verbs need to be rendered by at least several English words (cf. p. 269) and that, in general, any Navaho utterance has to be translated by a correspondingly longer English remark constitutes a practical basis for suspecting that an interpreter is taking the easy way out by omission and selection. Whenever a white official knows at least enough Navaho to sense where the interpreter is going wrong or likely to go wrong, he can save himself and the Navahos much grief and waste effort by insisting on repetitions or fuller translations at the right moment and by phrasing his own remarks with due consideration for the precision and specificity of the language into which they are to be translated. Awareness of characteristic differences in idiom and construction are especially helpful to this end.

Young and Morgan's words on this subject of translation arise from long practical experience and are sufficiently cogent to be worth quoting at length:

> Too often White speakers employ phraseology, idiomatic expressions, similes and allegories in delivering discourses which must be extemporaneously translated, that baffle and confuse the native interpreter. The result is that he either misinterprets due to misunderstanding, or says something entirely at random to avoid embarrassment to himself.
>
> Use of abstractions, similes, allegories and idiomatic expressions in speaking should be minimized, and entirely avoided, if at all possible. Instead of saying "incidence of tuberculosis on the Navaho reservation reached a new high in 1942, after which a sharp decline was reported. In view of this turn of events, a reduced medical staff will suffice to maintain the Navaho population in 'tip-top' condition for the duration," the White speaker would be better understood, and a better interpretation would result if he said something like, "one year ago a great many people in the Navaho country had tuberculosis. Before then there were less people with tuberculosis, and since then there are not as many people with tuberculosis, it is said. Because there are not very many people with tuberculosis now, less doctors can take care of the whole Navaho people and keep them well until the war is ended."

It is true that it is not considered good oratorical form to use "choppy," childishly simple, and to the orator, monotonous phraseology bristling with repetitions, as in the above modified form. However, such simple and lucid statements can be quickly and easily translated with a maximum of accuracy, whereas the orator using the first example would no doubt be horrified to find his vaunted oratory replaced by a translation distorting beyond recognition the point he was trying so euphoniously to convey; or perhaps he would find that he had lost his interpreter at the end of the first phrase, and that the latter had quoted him as saying "he says that a lot of you people have tuberculosis, and you must come to the hospital, but because they are fighting a war, there are not enough doctors to keep you well now," or perhaps "he says that it has rained a lot this year, and the roads are so muddy he cannot go out over the Navaho country to help you until after the war."

Such renditions of otherwise excellent and valuable speeches are far too common. Too often council members vote without knowing, or without fully understanding, that for or against which they are declaring themselves.

The more knowledge one has of the Navaho language, in this instance, and the pattern according to which the Navaho conceives and expresses his thoughts, the better will one be able to express himself in English of a type that can be translated and accurately conveyed to his audience—and the better will one be fitted to teach English to Navaho children in terms which they can comprehend.

The ideal would be to give all speeches to the interpreter beforehand, and require him to make a written translation at his leisure—or to teach English in terms of Navaho but these ideals cannot always be achieved.

It is quite obvious that the Navaho language is not a primitive tool, inadequate for human expression, but a well developed one, quite as capable of serving the Navaho people as our language is of serving us. The mere fact that translation of English into Navaho is difficult does not prove, as some believe, that the Navaho language is a poor one, any more than difficulty of translation from Navaho to English proves English to be poor.[7]

GETTING THE NAVAHO VIEWPOINT

More important, however, than the use of the language to establish rapport or to ask questions, give instructions, or otherwise make official communications, is the usefulness of knowing some Navaho in helping the white person to see things as the Navahos see them. The meanings which the events of a Navaho's life have to the Navaho will always remain somewhat opaque to the white man unless he has given a certain minimum of attention to the language, and thus obtained entrance to this foreign world whose values and significances are indicated by the emphases of native vocabulary, crystallized in the structure of the language, and implicit in its differentiations of meaning. All this does *not* mean that the administrator or teacher or anyone else who wants to know Navahos must speak the language like a native, though this would certainly be ideal. What is needed is merely enough study and thought to make the white person aware of habitual differences in ways of thinking characteristic of those who think in Navaho. Even a few days of intelligent study will do more than any other investment of the same time to unlock the doors of the world in which Navahos live, feel, and think, for it will show that the lack of equivalences in Navaho and English is merely the outward expression of inward differences between two peoples in premises, in basic categories, in training in fundamental sensitivities, and in general view of the world.

9. THE NAVAHO VIEW OF LIFE

In our survey of The People's way of life, the least tangible but by no means the least important subject has been reserved for the last. The problems the Navahos face and the techniques they have developed for coping with them—their material technology and their ways of handling human relations and of dealing with superhuman forces—have been considered. Through the survey of their language in the last chapter, the view of life which lies behind the special character of the Navaho adaptation was partially revealed. This subject must now be further amplified in more direct and explicit terms.

Adjustments and adaptations are always selective. Almost always more than one solution is objectively possible. The choices which a people make and the emphasis they give to one problem at the expense of others bear a relationship to the things they have come to regard as especially important. All people have to eat to survive, but whether they eat to live or live to eat or live *and* eat is not fixed by uncontrollable forces. Even if they live to eat, there will be choices as to what they eat. No society utilizes all the foods present in the environment which can be handled by the available technology. For example, neither Navahos nor white people commonly eat snake flesh although it is perfectly nutritious. The external facts—important though these always are—are not the only determinants of what people do.

The way of life which is handed down as the social heritage of every people does more than supply a set of skills for making a living and a set of blueprints for human relations. Each different way of life makes assumptions (and usually somewhat different assumptions) about the ends and purposes of human existence, about what human beings have a right to expect from one another and from the gods, about what constitutes fulfillment or frustration. Some of these assumptions are made explicit in so many words in the lore of the folk; others are tacit premises which the observer must infer by finding consistent trends in deed and word.

All of the specific things which The People approve or disapprove cannot be mentioned. Many of these have already been stated or implied. But the central directions of Navaho goals and values need to be indicated. It must, however, always be remembered that in this respect also The People are in a transitional stage. They are torn between their own ancient standards and those which are urged upon them by teachers, missionaries, and other whites. An appreciable number of Navahos are so confused by the conflicting precepts of their elders and their white models that they tend, in effect, to reject the whole problem of morality (in the widest sense) as meaningless or insoluble. For longer or shorter periods in their lives their only guide is the expediency of the immediate situation. One cannot play a game according to rule if there are sharp disagreements as to what the rules are. The incipient breakdown of any culture brings a loss of predictability and hence of dependability in personal relations. The absence of generally accepted standards of behavior among individuals constitutes, in fact, a definition of social disorganization.

A stable social structure prevails only so long as the majority of individuals in the society find enough satisfaction both in the goals socially approved and in the institutionalized means of attainment to compensate them for the constraints which ordered social life inevitably imposes upon uninhibited response to impulse. In any way of life there is much that to an outside observer appears haphazard, disorderly, more or less chaotic. But unless most participants feel that the ends and means of their culture make sense, disorientation and amorality become rampant. Synthesis is achieved partly through the overt statement of the dominant conceptions and aspirations of the group in its religion and ethical code, partly through unconscious apperceptive habits, habitual ways of looking at the stream of events.

In this chapter an attempt will be made to describe not only Navaho ethics and values but also some of those highest common factors that are implicit in a variety of the doings and sayings of The People. In the not distant past these recurrent themes, these unstated premises, gave a felt coherence to life in spite of social change, in spite of the diversity of institutions, in spite of differences in the needs and experiences of individuals. These distinctly Navaho values and premises still do much to regulate group life and to reconcile conflicts and discrepancies. But the basic assumptions of The People are now under attack from a competing set of assumptions. The majority of Navahos no longer feel completely at home and at ease in their world of values and significances, and an appreciable minority are thoroughly disoriented. This chapter will portray the Navaho view of life in its integrated form as still held by most older people and many younger ones, for probably no Navaho alive today is completely uninfluenced by this set of conceptions of the good life, of characteristic ways of thinking, feeling, and reacting, although it should be remembered that many younger people partly repudiate some of these notions and find themselves in an uneasy state between two worlds.

NAVAHO "ETHICS"

In no human group is indiscriminate lying, cheating, or stealing approved. Coöperation is of course impossible unless individuals can depend upon each other in defined circumstances. Societies differ in how they define the conditions under which lying or stealing is forgivable or tolerable or even perhaps demanded. In their general discussions The People make virtues of truth and honesty, much as white people do. In the advice fathers give their children, in the harangues of headmen at large gatherings, these two ideals never fail to be extolled.

The difference in the presentation of these ideals by whites and Navahos lies in the reasons advanced. The Navaho never appeals to abstract morality or to adherence to divine principles. He stresses mainly the practical considerations: "If you don't tell the truth, your fellows won't trust you and you'll shame your relatives. You'll never get along in the world that way." Truth is never praised merely on the ground that it is "good" in a purely abstract sense, nor do exhortations ever take the form that the Holy People have forbidden cheating or stealing. Certain other acts are commanded or prohibited on the basis that one or more of the Holy People did or did not behave in similar fashion, but never in the modes which would seem "natural" to Christians: "Do this to please the Holy People because they love you," or "Don't do this because the Holy People punish wrong-doing." The Navahos do most definitely believe that acts have consequences, but the nature of the consequence is not wrapped up in any intrinsic "rightness" or "wrongness" of the act itself. In the matters of truth and honesty, the only appeal to the sentiments (other than those of practicality and getting along with relatives and neighbors) which Navaho "moralists" permit themselves is that of loyalty to tradition. The old Navaho way was not to lie, to cheat, or to steal. The prevalence of such vices today, they say, is due to white corruption. So much for theory.

When it comes to practice, it is harder to put the finger on the differences between Navaho and white patterns. One gets the impression that Navahos lie to strangers with fewer qualms than the average well-socialized white adult would feel. (However, the white adult's easy acceptance of "white lies" must not be overlooked.) There are also occasions on which stealing seems to be condoned "if you can get away with it." Again, though, a qualification must be entered; in many parts of the Navaho country, one can leave an automobile containing valuable articles unlocked for days and return to find not a single item missing. Thefts occur chiefly in the areas under strongest white influence, especially at "squaw dances" frequented by ne'er-do-well young men who are souls lost between the two cultures. There is undoubted evidence that white contact brings about—at least in the transitional generations—some breakdown in the moralities. This much, however, seems to be a distinctive part of the native attitude: a Navaho does not spend much time worrying over a lie or a theft when he is not found out; he seems to have almost no "guilt" feelings; but if he is caught he does experience a good deal of shame.

Offenses more strongly condemned are those which threaten the peaceful working together of The People. Incest and witchcraft are the worst of crimes. Murder, rape, physical injury, and any sort of violence are disapproved and punished, but some of the penalties seem relatively light to white people. By Navaho custom, murder, for instance, could be compounded for by a payment of slaves or livestock to the kin of the victim. To this day the Navaho way of dealing with violent crimes against the person is not ordinarily that of retaliation or even of imprisonment of the offender but of levying a fine which is turned over, not to "the state," but to the sufferer and his family to compensate for the economic loss by injury or death—a custom bearing marked resemblance to the old Teutonic wergild, or "blood money."

The positive behaviors which are advocated center on affectionate duty to relatives, pleasant manners to all, generosity, self-control. It has already been pointed out that the widest ideal of human conduct for The People is "to act to everybody as if they were your own relatives." A courteous, nonaggressive approach to others is the essence of decency. Polite phrases to visitors and strangers are highly valued. If an English-speaking Navaho wishes to speak approvingly of another Navaho with whom he has had a chance encounter, he is likely to say, "He talks pretty nice." Generosity is uniformly praised and stinginess despised. One of the most disparaging things which can be said of anyone is, "He gets mad like a dog." Women will be blamed for "talking rough" to their children. The Navaho word which is most often translated into English as "mean" is sometimes rendered "he gets mad pretty easy." In short, one must keep one's temper; one must warmly and cheerfully do one's part in the system of reciprocal rights and obligations, notably those which prevail between kinfolk.

NAVAHO "VALUES"

Health and strength are perhaps the best of the good things of life for The People. If you aren't healthy, you can't work; if you don't work, you'll starve. Industry is enormously valued. A family must arise and be about their tasks early, for if someone goes by and sees no smoke drifting out of the smokehole it will be thought that "there is something wrong there; somebody must be sick." In enumerating the virtues of a respected man or woman the faithful performance of duties is always given a prominent place. "If you are poor or a beggar, people will make fun of you. If you are lazy people will make fun of you."

By Navaho standards one is industrious in order to accumulate possessions—within certain limits—and to care for the possessions he obtains. Uncontrolled gambling or drinking are disapproved primarily because they are wasteful. The "good" man is one who has "hard goods" (turquoise and jewelry mainly), "soft goods" (clothing, etc.), "flexible goods" (textiles, etc.), and songs, stories, and other intangible property, of which ceremonial knowledge is the most important. An old Navaho said to W. W. Hill, "I have always been a poor man. I do not know a single song." The final disrespect is to say of a man, "Why, he hasn't even a dog."

A good appearance is valued; while this is partly a matter of physique, figure, and facial appearance, it means even more the ability to dress well and to appear with a handsome horse and substantial trappings.

However, as Adair[1] says:

> This display of wealth is not a personal matter as much as it is a family matter. It is not "see how much money I have," but "see how much money we have in our family."

Thus possessions are valued both as providing security and as affording opportunities for mild ostentation. But to take the attainment of riches as the chief aim of life is universally condemned. This is a typical pronouncement by a Navaho leader:

> The Navaho way is just to want enough to have enough to eat for your family and nice things to wear sometimes. We don't like it when nowadays some of these young men marry rich girls for their money and waste it all right away. The old people say this is wrong. You can't get rich if you look after your relatives right. You can't get rich without cheating some people. Cheating people is the wrong way. That way gets you into trouble. Men should be honest to get along.

Many skills carry prestige. We have spoken of the ability to dance, to sing, to tell stories. Skill at speaking is important and is expected of all leaders. "He talks easy" is high praise. Conversely, "He doesn't talk easy. He just sits there," is a belittling remark. Training in certain occupations is emphasized: a man will spend all the time he can spare from subsistence activities in order to learn a ceremonial; grandmothers and mothers are expected to teach young girls to weave. Knowledge is power to Navahos as to other peoples, but the kinds of knowledge which are significant to the Navaho are naturally limited by his technology and his social organization. The skillful farmer or stockman is admired. So also is he who excels at cowboy sports, but the runner comes in for his meed of praise too, even though this skill is today of minimal social utility.

Personal excellence is thus a value, but personal "success" in the white American sense is not. The Navaho lack of stress upon the success goal has its basis in childhood training but is reinforced by various patterns of adult life. A white man may start out to make a fortune and continue piling it up until he is a millionaire, where a Navaho, though also interested in accumulating possessions, will stop when he is comfortably off, or even sooner, partly for fear of being called a witch if he is too successful. This statement represents tendency rather than literal fact, for a few Navahos have in this century built up fortunes that are sizable even by white standards. The attitudes of the Navaho population generally toward these *ricos* are very mixed. Envy, fear, and distrust of them are undoubtedly mingled with some admiration. But there is almost no disposition for parents to hold these individuals up as models to their children. No elder says, "If you work hard and intelligently you might get to be as rich as Chee Dodge."

Navaho ideas of accumulation are different from those of whites. Riches are not identified so much with a single individual as with the whole extended family and "outfit." Indeed the social pressure to support and share with relatives has a strong leveling effect. The members of a well-off family must also spend freely, as in the white pattern of "conspicuous consumption." But all wealth is desired for this purpose and for security rather than as a means of enhancing the power and glory of specific individuals. The habit of whites in the Navaho country of attributing full control of the incomes of *rico* families to the male head of the family is a falsification, a projection of white ways. As a practical matter, he does not have the same freedom as a white millionaire to dispose of his fortune.

That individual success is not a Navaho value is reflected also in the avoidance of the types of leadership which are familiar in white society. To The People it is fundamentally indecent for a single individual to presume to make decisions for a group. Leadership, to them, does not mean "outstandingness" or anything like untrammeled power over the actions of others. Each individual is controlled not by sanctions from the top of a hierarchy of persons but by lateral sanctions. It will be remembered that decisions at meetings must be unanimous. To white persons this is an unbelievably tiresome and time-wasting process. But it is interesting to note that experiments with "group decision" in war industry have shown that the greatest increases in production have been attained when all workers in a unit concurred. Majority decisions often brought about disastrous results. (In passing it may be remarked that these experiments offer perhaps another lesson for the government in its dealings with The People: when the groups of workers were allowed to set their own goals, far more was achieved than when they were asked to strive for goals set by management.)

Some personal values which bulk large among whites have a place among The People which is measured largely by the degree of white influence. Cleanliness, for instance, is an easy virtue where there is running water, but where every drop must be hauled five miles washing is an expensive luxury. Navaho social and economic life is not geared to fine points of time scheduling. If a Singer says he will arrive "about noon," no one takes it amiss if he appears at sundown, though an arrival a day or more late would call for explanation. Work is not, as it is in our Puritan tradition, a good thing in itself. The Navaho believes in working only as much as he needs to.

In sum, the Navaho concept of "goodness" stresses productiveness, ability to get along with people, dependability and helpfulness, generosity in giving and spending. "Badness" means stinginess, laziness, being cruel to others, being destructive. The concept of value stresses possessions and their care, health, skills which are practically useful. Concerning all of these topics The People are fully articulate. Such sentiments are enunciated again and again in the oral literature, in formal addresses, and in ordinary conversation.

SOME PREMISES OF NAVAHO LIFE AND THOUGHT

To understand fully the Navaho "philosophy of life" one must dig deeper. The very fact that The People find it necessary to talk about their "ethical principles" and their values suggests that not everybody lives up to them (any more than is the case in white society). But many characteristically Navaho doings and sayings make sense only if they are related to certain basic convictions about the nature of human life and experience, convictions so deep-going that no Navaho bothers to talk about them in so many words. These unstated assumptions are so completely taken for granted that The People take their views of life as an ineradicable part of human nature and find it hard to understand that normal persons could possibly conceive life in other terms.

PREMISE 1. LIFE IS VERY, VERY DANGEROUS

This premise is of course distinctive only in its intensity and its phrasing. All sensible human beings realize that there are many hazards in living; but to many whites, Navahos seem morbid in the variety of threats from this world and from the world of the supernatural which they fear and name. Of course this is largely a point of view. To some detached observers it might seem more healthy to worry about witches than about what you will live on when you are old or about the dreadful consequences of picking up some germ. Whites also tend to personify evil forces. They found relief in "discovering" that World War I was all due to J. P. Morgan. All human beings doubtless have the tendency to simplify complex matters because this gives the gratifying illusion of understanding them and of the possibility of doing something about them.

However, while this is clearly not a matter of black or white, The People do have a more overwhelming preoccupation than whites with the uncertainty of life and the many threats to personal security. The great emphasis laid upon "taking care of things," upon the industry and skills necessary for survival, and upon the ceremonial techniques bear witness to this. There are five main formulas for safety.

Formula 1: Maintain orderliness in those sectors of life which are little subject to human control. By seeming to bring the areas of actual ignorance, error, and accident under the control of minutely prescribed ritual formulas, The People create a compensatory mechanism. As we saw in Chapter 5, these prescriptions are partially negative and partially positive. The Navaho conceives safety either as restoration of the individual to the harmonies of the natural, human, and supernatural world or, secondarily, as restoration of an equilibrium among nonhuman forces.

This is achieved by the compulsive force of order and reiteration in ritual words and acts. The essence of even ceremonial drama is not sharp climax (as whites have it) so much as fixed rhythms. The keynote of all ritual poetry is compulsion through orderly repetition. Take this song which the Singer of a Night Way uses to "waken" the mask of each supernatural supposed to participate in the rite.

He stirs, he stirs, he stirs, he stirs.
Among the lands of dawning, he stirs, he stirs;
The pollen of the dawning, he stirs, he stirs;
Now in old age wandering, he stirs, he stirs;
Now on the trail of beauty, he stirs, he stirs.
He stirs, he stirs, he stirs, he stirs.

He stirs, he stirs, he stirs, he stirs.
Among the lands of evening, he stirs, he stirs;
The pollen of the evening, he stirs, he stirs;
Now in old age wandering, he stirs, he stirs;
Now on the trail of beauty, he stirs, he stirs.
He stirs, he stirs, he stirs, he stirs.

He stirs, he stirs, he stirs, he stirs.
Now Talking God, he stirs, he stirs;
Now his white robe of buckskin, he stirs, he stirs;
Now in old age wandering, he stirs, he stirs;
Now on the trail of beauty, he stirs, he stirs.
He stirs, he stirs, he stirs, he stirs.[2]

The song goes on like this for many verses. To white people it has a monotonous quality, but infinite repetitions in an expected sequence seem to lull the Navaho into a sense of security.

Formula 2: Be wary of non-relatives. This is, to some extent, the obverse of the centering of trust and affection upon relatives. If one feels thoroughly at home and at ease when surrounded by one's kin, it is natural that one should distrust strangers. In white society (and probably in all others) there is a distrust of strangers, members of the "out-group." But the Navaho fears also the other members of his own people who are not related to him. Hence anti-witchcraft protection must always be carried to a "squaw dance" or any other large gathering. This tendency to be ill at ease when beyond the circle of one's relatives is a truly "primitive" quality and is characteristic, to varying degrees, of most nonliterate folk societies.

This formula is closely related to the preceding one; if one wins security by reducing the uncharted areas of the nonhuman universe to familiar patterns, it is natural that unfamiliar human beings should be regarded as threats.

Formula 3: Avoid excesses. Very few activities are wrong in and of themselves, but excess in the practice of any is dangerous. This is in marked contrast to the puritanical concept of immorality. To Navahos such things as sex and gambling are not "wrong" at all but will bring trouble if indulged in "too much." Even such everyday tasks as weaving must be done only in moderation. Many women will not weave more than about two hours at a stretch; in the old days unmarried girls were not allowed to weave for fear they would overdo, and there is a folk rite for curing the results of excess in this activity. Closely related is the fear of completely finishing anything: as a "spirit outlet," the basketmaker leaves an opening in the design; the weaver leaves a small slit between the threads; the Navaho who copies a sandpainting for a white man always leaves out something, however trivial; the Singer never tells his pupil quite all the details of the ceremony lest he "go dry." Singers also systematically leave out transitions in relating myths.

This fear of excess is reflected also in various characteristic attitudes toward individuals. There is, for example, a folk saying: "If a child gets too smart, it will die young." The distrust of the very wealthy and very powerful and the sanctions and economic practices which tend to keep men at the level of their fellows have already been mentioned.

Formula 4: When in a new and dangerous situation, do nothing. If a threat is not to be dealt with by ritual canons, it is safest to remain inactive. If a Navaho finds himself in a secular situation where custom does not tell him how to behave, he is usually ill at ease and worried. The white

American under these circumstances will most often overcompensate by putting on a self-confidence he does not in fact have. The American tradition says, "When danger threatens, *do* something." The Navaho tradition says, "Sit tight and perhaps in that way you may escape evil."

Formula 5: Escape. This is an alternative response to Formula 4, which The People select with increasing frequency when pressure becomes too intense. Doing nothing is not enough: safety lies in flight. This flight may take the form of leaving the field in the sheer physical sense. Navahos have discovered that they don't get very far by trying to resist the white man actively; so they scatter. The white man then cannot deal with them as a group—he can't even locate and exhort or admonish or punish them as individuals. Escape may be this sort of passive resistance or it may be simple evasion, as when a Navaho woman, who was otherwise fairly happy in a government hospital, left it rather than ask for one kind of food which she desperately missed. Had she asked, it would have been given her, but she found it simpler to leave. Flight also takes the even more unrealistic form of addiction to alcohol or of indiscriminate sexuality. In effect, the Navaho says, "My only security is in escape from my difficulties."

These types of behavior in the face of danger are documented by the following episode related by a fifth-grader in one of the boarding schools.

> We look down to the river, we saw a lot of cows at the river. My brother said, "I am not scared of those cows that are at the river." Soon the cows were going back up the hill. We just climb up on a big tall tree and sit there. The cows come in closer and closer. We stay on the tree. Soon they come under the tree. My brother and I were so scared that we just sit there and not move. Soon my brother start crying. When the cows go away we laugh and laugh. My brother said, "The cows were scared of me." I said, "They are not scared of

you." We say that over and over. Soon my brother got angry, then we fight in the sand. After we fight we go home.

PREMISE 2. NATURE IS MORE POWERFUL THAN MAN

Navahos accept nature and adapt themselves to her demands as best they can, but they are not utterly passive, not completely the pawns of nature. They do a great many things that are designed to control nature physically and to repair damage caused by the elements. But they do not even hope to master nature. For the most part The People try to influence her with various songs and rituals, but they feel that the forces of nature, rather than anything that man does, determine success or failure of crops, plagues of grasshoppers, increase of arroyos, and decrease of grass. If a flood comes and washes out a formerly fertile valley, one does not try to dam the stream and replace the soil; instead one moves to a floodless spot. One may try to utilize what nature furnishes, such as by leading water from a spring or stream to his fields, but no man can master the wind and the weather. This is similar to the attitude toward sex, which is viewed as part of nature, something to reckon with, but not a thing to be denied.

Many white people have the opposite view; namely, that nature is a malignant force with useful aspects that must be harnessed, and useless, harmful ones that must be shorn of their power. They spend their energies adapting nature to their purposes, instead of themselves to her demands. They destroy pests of crops and men, they build dykes and great dams to avert floods, and they level hills in one spot and pile them up in another. Their premise is that nature will destroy them unless they prevent it; the Navahos' is that nature will take care of them if they behave as they should and do as she directs.

In addition to all the other forces which make the acceptance of the current program of soil erosion control and limitation of livestock slow and painful, this premise plays an important and fundamental part. To most Navahos it seems silly or presumptuous to interfere with the workings of nature to the extent that they are being told to do. Besides, they believe it won't bring the benefits the white people promise. If anything is wrong these days, it is that The People are forgetting their ways and their stories, so of course anyone would know that there would be hard times. It has nothing to do with too many sheep.

PREMISE 3. THE PERSONALITY IS A WHOLE

This assumption also must be made explicit because white people so generally think of "mind" and "body" as separable units. The whole Navaho system of curing clearly takes it for granted that you cannot treat a man's "body" without treating his "mind," and vice versa. In this respect Navahos are many generations ahead of white Americans, who are only now beginning to realize that it is the patient, not the disease, which must be treated. Successful physicians who understood "human nature" have acted on this premise always, but it has found verbal expression and acceptance only recently; at present it is receiving the most publicity in the specialty known as "psychosomatic medicine."

PREMISE 4. RESPECT THE INTEGRITY OF THE INDIVIDUAL

While the individual is always seen as a member of a larger group, still he is never completely submerged in that group. There is an area of rigidity where what any given person may and may not do is inexorably fixed, but there is likewise a large periphery of freedom. This is not the "romantic individualism" of white tradition, but in many respects the Navaho has more autonomy, more opportunity for genuine spontaneity than is the case in white society. Rights of individuals, including children, over their immediately personal property, are respected to the fullest degree, even when their wishes run counter to the obvious interests of the family or extended family. White people seeking to purchase a bow and arrow that they see in a hogan are surprised to have the adults refer the question to the five-year-old who owns the toy and whose decision is final. If a youngster unequivocally says he does not want to go to school or to the hospital, that is, in most families, the end of it. Husbands and wives make no attempt to control every aspect of the behavior of the spouse. Although individuals are not regarded as equal in capacity or in all features of the treatment that should be accorded them, still the integrity of every individual is protected from violation at the hands of more powerful people.

Where survival is held to depend on coöperation, the subordination of the individual to the group is rigorously demanded. Such interdependence is felt to exist in all sorts of ways that are not, from the white point of view, realistic. Success in hunting is thought to depend as much upon the faithful observance of taboos by the wife at home as upon the husband's skill or luck in stalking game. The individualism which expresses itself in social innovation is disapproved as strongly as is that which expresses itself in too obtrusive leadership. The following quotation (which, incidentally, is also a nice illustration of Navaho logic) brings out the Navaho feeling exactly.

> You must be careful about introducing things into ceremonies. One chanter thought that he could do this. He held a Night Chant. He wanted more old people so he had the dancers cough and dance as old people. He also wanted an abundance of potatoes so he painted potatoes on the dancers' bodies. He desired that there should be a great deal of food so he had the dancers break wind and vomit through their masks to make believe that they had eaten a great deal. They surely got

their reward. Through the coughing act a great many of the people got whooping cough and died. In the second change many of the people got spots on their bodies like potatoes only they were measles, sores, and smallpox. In the part, where they asked for all kinds of food, a lot died of diarrhea, vomiting and stomach aches. This chanter thought that he had the power to change things but everyone found out that he was wrong. It was the wrong thing to do and today no one will try to start any new ceremonies. Today we do not add anything.[3]

On the other hand, where autonomy does not seem to threaten the security of established practices or the needful coöperative undertakings, individuality is not only permitted but encouraged. Men and women feel free to vary their costumes to suit their temperaments, to experiment with variations in house style and other technological products, to break the day's routine with trips and other diversions spontaneously decided upon, while displays of jewelry, saddles, and horses bring admiration more than disapproval. He who makes up a new secular song or coins a new pun or quip wins many plaudits. Unity in diversity is the Navaho motto.

PREMISE 5. EVERYTHING EXISTS IN TWO PARTS, THE MALE AND THE FEMALE, WHICH BELONG TOGETHER AND COMPLETE EACH OTHER

With the Navaho this premise applies to much more than biology. The clear, deep, robins-egg-blue turquoise they call male, and the stone of a greenish hue they call female. The turbulent San Juan River is "male water," the placid Rio Grande "female water." The mountains of the north where harsh, cold winds blow are "male country," the warm open lands of the south "female country." There are male rains and female rains, the one hard and sudden, the other gentle; there are male and female chants; male and female plants are distinguished on the basis of appearance, the male always being the larger. The supernaturals, as seen in the sandpaintings or mentioned in the songs and prayers, are nearly always paired, so that if Corn Boy appears, one can be sure that Corn Girl will soon follow.

PREMISE 6. HUMAN NATURE IS NEITHER GOOD NOR EVIL—BOTH QUALITIES ARE BLENDED IN ALL PERSONS FROM BIRTH ON

The notion of "original sin" still lurks in white thinking. But the premise that children are "born bad" and have to be beaten into shape seems completely absent from the Navaho view. On the other hand, white "liberals" act upon the assumption that human beings can be educated into almost complete perfection, that if ignorance is removed people will act in full enlightenment. Similarly, at least some Christian groups hold that "grace" can permanently transform the wayward into paragons of virtue. The Navaho assumption is that no amount of knowledge and no amount of "religious" zeal can do more than alter somewhat the relative proportions of "bad" and "good" in any given individual.

PREMISE 7. LIKE PRODUCES LIKE AND THE PART STANDS FOR THE WHOLE

These are two "laws of thought" almost as basic to Navaho thinking as the so-called Aristotelian "laws of thought" have been in European intellectual history since the Middle Ages. Of course, *similia similibus curantur* has been important in the thinking of most human groups since the Old Stone Age or earlier; but among whites this principle is now largely relegated to the realm of folk belief, whereas among The People it still dominates the thought of the most sophisticated members of the society.

Let a few examples do for many. Because the juice of

the milkweed resembles milk it is held to be useful in treating a mother who cannot nurse her infant. Since the eagle can see long distances, the diviner who does star-gazing must rub a preparation which includes water from an eagle's eye under his own eyelids. Witchcraft performed over a few hairs from an individual is as effective against the owner of the hairs as if done upon his whole person. In chants small mounds of earth stand for whole mountains.

PREMISE 8. WHAT IS SAID IS TO BE TAKEN LITERALLY

As has been pointed out in the last chapter, the easy ambiguities, the fluidities of English speech are foreign to the Navaho. There is little "reading between the lines," little exercise of the imagination in interpreting utterances. A student was asking about a girl who was said by a white person to be feeble-minded. He asked, "Can so-and-so's daughter speak?" The Navaho replied very positively, "Yes." Observation showed that the girl uttered only unintelligible sounds. When this was later thrown back at the original informant he countered, "Well, she *does* speak—but no one can understand her." And this was said without a smile or even a twinkle in the eye.

Similarly, a Navaho will seldom take it upon himself to attribute thoughts or sentiments to others in the absence of very explicit statements on their part. White workers among The People find it irritating when they ask, "What does your wife (or brother, etc.) think about this?" and get the reply, "I don't know. I didn't ask her." Their supposition is that spouses or close relatives or intimate friends have enough general knowledge of each other's opinions to answer such questions with reasonable accuracy even if there has been no discussion of this precise point. But the Navahos do not see it this way.

PREMISE 9. THIS LIFE IS WHAT COUNTS

Because the Christian tradition is so prevalent in white society, it is necessary to bring this premise out explicitly. The People have no sense whatsoever that this life is a "preparation" for another existence. Indeed, except for the (by no means universally accepted) view that witches and suicides live apart in the afterworld, there is no belief that the way one lives on this earth has anything to do with his fate after death. This is one reason why morality is practical rather than categorical. While the Navaho feels very keenly that life is *hard*, his outlook is quite foreign to that of "life is real, life is earnest, and the grave is not the goal." White life is so permeated with the tradition of Puritanism, of "the Protestant ethic," that much Navaho behavior looks amoral or shiftless.

Another reason would seem to be that Navahos do not need to orient themselves in terms of principles of abstract morality. They get their orientations from face-to-face contacts with the same small group of people with whom they deal from birth to death. In a large, complex society like modern America where people come and go and where business and other dealings must be carried on by people who never see each other, it is functionally necessary to have abstract standards which transcend an immediate concrete situation in which two or more persons are interacting.

SEEING THINGS THE NAVAHO WAY

To most people most of the time, the habitual ways of speaking, acting, feeling, and reacting to which they have been accustomed from childhood become as much a part of the inevitables of life as the air they breathe, and they tend unconsciously to feel that all "normal" human beings ought to feel and behave only within the range of variation permitted by their own way of life. Then, however, when they have to deal with other groups who have been brought up with a somewhat different set of unquestioned and habitual assumptions about the nature of things, they all too often label the other group as "ignorant" or "superstitious," "stupid" or "stubborn." Many teachers and administrators of the Navajo Agency have very unrealistic expectations as to the capacities of Navahos to think and respond in white terms, forgetting that the median schooling of the Navaho adult is nine months!

Difficulties arise largely because, on both sides, the premises from which thought or action proceeds are unconscious—in the simple sense of unverbalized. Teachers, for example, urge Navaho children to strive for what the teachers want most in life without stopping to think that perhaps The People want quite different things. If a teacher who has had great success in teaching white children does not get comparably good results with Navaho children, she thinks this is because the Indian children are less bright. As a matter of fact, the trouble is often that the incentives which have worked beautifully to make white children bestir themselves leave Navaho children cold, or even actively trouble and confuse them.

For instance, the teacher holds out the hope of a college education with all that this implies for "getting on" in the white world; to at least the younger Navaho child, this means mainly a threat of being taken even further from home and country. The teacher reads or posts a complete set of grades for her class. To her, this is a way of rewarding the students who have done well and of inciting those who have not done so well to more strenuous efforts. Her students, however, may feel quite differently about the matter. Those at the top of the list may find it embarrassing to be placed publicly ahead of their contemporaries, and the list may seem cruel ridicule to those who have lagged behind. The whole conception that individuals can be rated on a scale from 0 to 100 is foreign to The People.

Or suppose a primary teacher sets both boys and girls to making pottery. From her point of view this is an interesting and worthwhile class activity, for white people do not make a sharp distinction between what six-year-old boys and girls should do. Yet this is as grievous a humiliation to a Navaho boy as a ten-year-old white boy would feel if he were made to appear at school in lace petticoats. A high-school teacher tries to induce a boy and a girl to fox-trot together; when they refuse, she says: "They acted like dumb animals." But they are from the same clan, and the thought of clan relatives having the type of physical contact involved in white social dancing gives Navahos the same uncomfortableness the teacher would feel if the manager of a crowded hotel demanded that she and her adult brother share the same bed. There is nothing "reasonable" —or "unreasonable"—about either attitude. They are just different. Both represent "culturally standardized unreason."

The People have only "object taboos" as regards sex, none of the "aim taboos" which are so marked a development of western culture. That is, Navahos do feel that sexual activity is improper or dangerous under particular circumstances or with certain persons. But they never regard sexual desires in themselves as "nasty" or evil. In school and elsewhere, whites have tended to operate upon the premise that "any decent Navaho" will feel guilty about a sexual act which takes place outside of marriage. This attitude simply bewilders Navahos and predisposes them to withdrawal of coöperation in all spheres. To them sex is natural, necessary and no more or no less concerned with morals than is eating.

The Navaho and the white administrator may see the same objective facts, and communication may be sufficiently well established so that each is sure the other sees them. Naturally, then, there is mutual irritation when the same conclusions are not reached. What neither realizes is that all discourse proceeds from premises and that premises (being unfortunately taken for granted by both) are likely, in fact, to be very divergent. Especially in the case of less sophisticated and self-conscious societies where there has not been much opportunity to learn that other peoples' ways of behaving and of looking at things differ from their own, the unconscious assumptions characteristically made by most individuals of the group will bulk large.

Let us put this in the concrete. A wealthy man dies and leaves considerable property. He has a widow but no children by her. There are, however, two sons by another woman to whom the deceased was never married in either white or Navaho fashion. He left, of course, no written will, and it is agreed that he gave no oral instructions on his deathbed. These are the facts, and there is no dispute about them between the Navaho and the white administrator.

Nevertheless the prediction may safely be made that before the estate is settled the white man will be irritated more than once and some Navahos will be confused and indignant at what seems to them ignorance, indifference, or downright immorality. The white man will unconsciously make his judgments and decisions in terms of white customs. Navahos will take Navaho customs as the standard except in so far as some may deliberately try to get a share, or more than their rightful share, by insisting upon the application of the white man's law. But the main difficulties will arise from the fact that the premises are never brought out into the open and discussed as such.

The Indian Service administrator is likely to take white customs and legal system for granted as "part of human nature" and to act upon the unstated assumptions in the following left-hand column. Navahos, unless they happen to be familiar with and to want to take advantage of white patterns, view the situation in the light of the very different principles in the right-hand column.

WHITE	NAVAHO
1. Marriage is an arrangement, economic and otherwise, between two individuals. The two spouses and the children, if any, are the ones primarily involved in any question of inheritance.	1. Marriage is an arrangement between two families much more than it is between two individuals.
2. A man's recognized children, legitimate or illegitimate, have a claim upon his property.	2. Sexual rights are property rights; therefore, if a man has children from a woman without undertaking during his lifetime the economic responsibilities which are normally a part of Navaho marriage, the children—however much he admitted to biological fatherhood—were not really his: "He just stole them."
3. Inheritance is normally from the father or from both sides of the family.	3. Inheritance is normally from the mother, the mother's brother, or other relatives of the mother; from the father's side of the family little or nothing has traditionally been expected.
4. As long as a wife or children survive, no other relatives are concerned in the inheritance unless there was a will to that effect.	4. While children today, in most areas, expect to inherit something from their father, they do not expect to receive his whole estate or to divide it with their mother only; sons and

daughters have different expectations.

5. All types of property are inherited in roughly the same way.

5. Different rules apply to different types of property: range land is hardly heritable property at all; farm land normally stays with the family which has been cultivating it; livestock usually goes back (for the most part) to the father's sisters and maternal nephews; jewelry and other personal property tend to be divided among the children *and* other relatives; ceremonial equipment may go to a son who is a practitioner or to a clansman of the deceased.

The white administrator would be likely to say that the *only* heirs to *any* of the property were the wife, children, and perhaps the illegitimate children. Such a decision would be perplexing or infuriating to the Navaho. To say in the abstract what disposal would be proper at the present complicated point in Navaho history is hardly possible. But it is clear that a verdict which seemed so "right" and "natural" to a white person as to require no explanation or justification would probably appear equally "unjust" and "unreasonable" to the Navaho involved.

The pressure of such double standards is highly disruptive. Just as rats that have been trained to associate a circle with food and a rectangle with an electric shock become neurotic when the circle is changed by almost imperceptible gradations into an ellipse, so human beings faced with a conflicting set of rewards and punishments tend to cut loose from all moorings, to float adrift and become irresponsible. The younger generation of The People are more and more coming to laugh at the old or pay them only lip service. The young escape the control of their elders, not to accept white controls but to revel in newly found patterns of unrestraint.

The introduction of the white type of individualism without the checks and balances that accompany it leads to the failure of collective or coöperative action of every sort. The substitution of paid labor for reciprocal services is not in and of itself a bad thing. But there is not a commensurate growth of the white sort of individual responsibility. There tends to be a distortion of the whole cultural structure which makes it difficult to preserve harmonious personal relationships and satisfying emotional adjustments. Widespread exercise of escape mechanisms, especially alcohol, is the principal symptom of the resultant friction and decay. Human groups that have different cultures and social structures have moral systems that differ in important respects. The linkage is so great that when a social organization goes to pieces morality also disintegrates.

Instead of a patterned mosaic, Navaho culture is becoming an ugly patchwork of meaningless and totally unrelated pieces. Personal and social chaos are the by-products. The lack of selective blending and constructive fusion between white and Navaho cultures is not due to low intelligence among The People. They are perfectly capable of learning white ways. But when the traits of another culture are learned externally and one by one without the underlying values and premises of that culture, the learners feel uncomfortable. They sense the absence of the fitness of things, of a support which is none the less real because difficult to verbalize.

For every way of life is a structure—not a haphazard collection of all the different physically possible and functionally effective patterns of belief and action but an interdependent system with all its patterns segregated and arranged in a manner which is *felt,* not *thought,* to be appropriate. If we wish to understand The People in the world today, we must remember that, like ourselves, they meet their problems not only with the techniques and the reason at their disposal but also in terms of their sentiments, of their standards, of their own hierarchy of values, of their implicit premises about their world.

Let us not hastily dismiss as "illogical" their views. If we do, we are probably just reacting defensively to the fact that their views and ours often fail to coincide. If "romantic love" plays a very small part in their lives, if women find plural marriage tolerable and sometimes even invite their husbands to marry a younger sister, it is not that The People are "unnatural." As a matter of fact, so far at least as "romantic love" is concerned they are acting the "normal" way, in the statistical sense that this sort of love is the accepted tradition among only a few groups of human beings.

Nor must we say: "Yes, the Navahos are different. I grant that. But they are *so* different that I can't see how any effective communication is possible." No, The People are also human beings. Like us, they must eat and have shelter and satisfy sexual urges. And they must do this with the same biological equipment and in a physical world where heat and cold, summer and winter, gravity and other natural laws set limits as they do for us. In a certain ultimate sense the "logic" of all peoples is inescapably the same. It is only the premises which are different. When we discover the premises we realize that the phrase "a common humanity" is full of meaning.

ACKNOWLEDGMENTS

This book is the product of a coöperative undertaking. Though the writers must bear full responsibility for the form in which all information and ideas finally appear, so many persons have made valuable and indeed indispensable contributions to this study that it is in an important sense a falsification for us to claim authorship.

In the first place, we are naturally dependent upon the Navahos, too numerous to mention, who have shared their lives and thoughts with us. For the most part they have been patient with our demands upon their time, tolerant of our intrusion into their personal lives, good-humored about the questions (impertinent, stupid, or at least meaningless to them) with which we have constantly badgered them. We have done our best to protect them from any embarrassment resulting from revelation of their identities in any quotations. We hope we have managed to convey some sense of the deep pleasure our relationship with them has brought to us. Some of the happiest times we have known have been in the Navaho country, and many Navahos we count among our closest friends. We also trust that our respect for the Navaho way of life and our admiration for many Navaho customs have been apparent in these pages. In short, we hope that the Navahos will feel that this is their book more than ours—as indeed it is.

Our work would have been infinitely more arduous and less pleasant had it not been for the kindnesses shown us throughout the years by many white traders, ranchers, missionaries, and government employees. If we have sometimes found it necessary to comment unfavorably upon the activities of these groups in relation to The People, this does not mean that we are unaware of the difficulties of their position or that we forget how many splendid persons in each of these categories have given us their friendship and the benefit of their knowledge.

Our obligations to our professional colleagues are also extremely heavy. We are particularly grateful to David F. Aberle, John Adair, Flora L. Bailey, Beatrice Blackwood, Helen Bradley, Janine Chappat, Malcolm Carr Collier, Margaret Fries, Willard W. Hill, J. C. Kelley, John Landgraf, Josephine Murray, T. Sasaki, C. C. Seltzer, Katherine Spencer, Harry Tschopik, Jr., Leland C. Wyman, Robert W. Young, and the anonymous authors of numerous government reports for the aid we have obtained from their unpublished manuscripts and field notes. We thank Dr. Ward Shepard for allowing us to use his illuminating manuscript, "Toward a Self-Propelled Navaho Society." We have profited directly and indirectly from work connected with the human problems of soil conservation initiated and directed by Dr. John Provinse and Dr. Solon Kimball, and we have been much influenced by the point of view developed in their studies. Our obligations to all of these persons are not made as clear in detail as would have been proper in a more technical publication, because to have indicated each idea, sentence, or part of a sentence which was directly borrowed would have created a maze of footnotes, tedious and distracting to the lay reader.

We have received much help from Indian Service personnel, though the views expressed in this book are those of the authors and are not necessarily endorsed by the Indian Service. The Honorable John Collier, former commissioner, gave us the benefit of much frank discussion and aided us in many ways. The whole Indian Education Research Project was inspired by him; all social scientists owe Mr. Collier an immense debt for his imaginative statesmanship. Dr. Willard Beatty, Director of Education, readily answered many requests for information and other assistance, such as the making of maps. We have to thank many members of the Navajo Agency, and especially Superintendent James M. Stewart, Director of Education George Boyce, and former Field Representative F. W. LaRouche, for enthusiastic coöperation and for preparing and assembling useful memoranda. Dr. Laura Thompson, coördinator of the Indian Education Research Project, gave generously of her energy and intelligence. The volume has been greatly enriched by the maps provided by E. H. Coulson of the Office of Indian Affairs in Chicago.

The book embodies in part researches carried on or directed by Dr. Kluckhohn over a number of years. These studies have been supported by the Division of Anthropology, the Peabody Museum, and the Milton Fund of Harvard University, the Carnegie Corporation of New York, the Viking Fund, the Social Science Research Council, and the American Philosophical Society. Officers of these organizations have also provided moral as well as financial support and valued advice. In particular, Dr. Kluckhohn is under the deepest obligations to Professor Alfred Tozzer (himself the first anthropologically trained student of the Navahos), Professor Donald Scott, and Professor Earnest Hooton of Harvard University; to Mr. Charles Dollard of the Carnegie Corporation; to Dr. Donald Young of the Social Science Research Council; to Dr. Paul Fejos of the Viking Fund. He also owes much to the late Professor Edward Sapir of Yale University, to Father Berard Haile, O.F.M., and to Professor Gladys A. Reichard of Barnard College for assistance in his studies of the Navaho language. He is also grateful to his senior colleagues in Navaho research, notably Father Berard, Dr. Wyman, Dr. Hill, Dr. Reichard, and Mr. Van Valkenburgh, for the benefits of many letters and oral discussions. It has been a great pleasure to work in a field in which such a coöperative spirit has prevailed.

The substance of this book was delivered in Boston in

February, 1944, as a series of Lowell Lectures by Dr. Kluckhohn. He expresses his gratitude to the Trustee of the Lowell Institute for this opportunity and the stimulus it afforded.

Dr. Leighton is particularly obligated to Dr. Adolph Meyer, Professor Emeritus of Psychiatry at Johns Hopkins University, for inspiring an interest in studying individuals in their society. This interest was encouraged and facilitated by the Social Science Research Council and by Dr. John C. Whitehorn, Professor of Psychiatry at Johns Hopkins University.

We must thank Dr. George Boyce, Miss Helen Bradley, Professor Phillips Bradley, Dr. Janine Chappat, Commissioner John Collier, Mrs. Malcolm Carr Collier, Dr. Elizabeth Colson, Dr. Willard W. Hill, Dr. Solon Kimball, Mr. and Mrs. John Kirk, Dr. Florence Kluckhohn, Dr. Alexander Leighton, Professor Arthur Nock, Dr. and Mrs. Adolph Meyer, Professor Donald Scott, Dr. Ward Shepard, Miss Katherine Spencer, Superintendent James M. Stewart, Dr. Laura Thompson, Dr. Esther Goldfrank Wittfogel, and Dr. Leland C. Wyman for reading all or part of the typescript and offering many useful suggestions and criticisms. Mrs. Kirk reviewed the book in an especially intensive way and supplied certain new materials. We are also most grateful to Professor Scott for the interest he took in the publication of the book. Mrs. Roma McNickle, editor of the Indian Education Research Project, did much more for the manuscript than we can express in a sentence. We also thank her (and Katherine Spencer) for helping us with the proofs.

Finally, we express our appreciation to John Adair, Flora L. Bailey, Walter Dyk, Father Berard Haile, Willard W. Hill, Harry Hoijer, William Morgan, Gladys A. Reichard, Richard Van Valkenburgh, Benjamin L. Whorf, Leland C. Wyman, Robert W. Young, and to the American Museum of Natural History, Harcourt Brace and Company, the Northern Arizona Society of Science and Art, the University of Oklahoma Press, and the Yale University Press for permission to quote from published materials.

The index was prepared by Katherine Spencer.

CLYDE KLUCKHOHN
DOROTHEA LEIGHTON

NOTES AND REFERENCES

INTRODUCTION: "THE PEOPLE" AND THIS STUDY

1. Tewa languages are spoken by various town-living Indians in the general neighborhood of Santa Fe, New Mexico. It should be remembered that many different languages and a number of distinct language stocks or families are found among the American Indians. There is, for example, less resemblance between the tongues of the Tewa Pueblo Indians of New Mexico and the Hopi Pueblo Indians of Arizona than between English and Russian; and Tewa and Hopi have not been found to have even a remote connection with the Navaho language.

1. THE PAST OF THE PEOPLE

1. "Villages" on mesas undoubtedly made sense at this period in terms of protection. That Navahos ceased to live in small, compact communities is probably due in large part to two factors: the end of warfare and the increase of sheep. However, a third factor may be of equal significance. Accelerated erosion may, by gullying the valleys, have made floodwater irrigation impossible on a scale large enough to support even a small community.

2. LAND AND LIVELIHOOD

1. Data for the prewar years are from the 1940 *Statistical Summary, Human Dependency Survey,* listed in the bibliography. Data for the period between 1940 and 1958

are from *The Navajo Yearbook*, edited by Robert W. Young, Navajo Agency, Window Rock, Arizona, 1958.

2. Arthur Woodward, *A Brief History of Navajo Silversmithing*, Museum of Northern Arizona, Bulletin No. 14 (Flagstaff, Arizona: Northern Arizona Society of Science and Art, 1938), p. 47.

3. This and the many similar quotations from field notes which follow represent records made at the time of utterance or shortly thereafter of what Navahos said to one of the writers. So far as possible, the transcription is literal and there has been no editing. The English of interpreters and of English-speaking Navahos has been preserved. Statements made in Navaho have been freely translated into idiomatic English. Bracketed materials are questions or remarks interpolated by the interviewer.

4. In each statement the first figure is the average for the years 1930, 1931, and 1932. The final figure is the average for 1942 and 1943. The goals for stock reduction have now been attained (1945) in fifteen of the eighteen Navaho districts.

5. See *Newsweek* (May 29, 1944) for story and pictures.

3. LIVING TOGETHER

1. Flora L. Bailey, "Navaho Motor Habits," *American Anthropologist*, XLIV (1942), p. 210.

2. Willard W. Hill, *Navaho Humor*, General Series in Anthropology, No. 9 (Menasha, Wis.: George Banta Publishing Co., 1943), p. 7.

4. THE PEOPLE AND THE WORLD AROUND THEM

1. In recent times such a land dispute with the Hopi has been taken to the white man's court. In past years

this would be settled by an arbitrary decision of the Indian Service, and prior to that by open hostilities.

2. Many of the difficulties encountered by the Navajo Agency are strikingly similar to those met by County Extension Agents in dealing with rural whites during the early years of this century.

3. A word of caution should be entered that Navaho morbidity data are even rougher than those for white persons the country over. Even death rates are estimates at best.

4. *The Navaho Door* (listed in the Bibliography) represents a project in research and communication toward this end.

5. This quotation is verbatim. Since the employee was a high-school graduate, the document is also an effective comment on the linguistic situation.

5. THE SUPERNATURAL: POWER AND DANGER

1. Gladys A. Reichard, *Prayer: the Compulsive Word* (New York: J. J. Augustin, 1944), p. 21.

2. Reichard, *Prayer: the Compulsive Word,* p. 33.

3. Leland C. Wyman, Review of "The Story of the Navajo Hail Chant" by Gladys A. Reichard, *The Review of Religion* (May, 1945), pp. 380–384.

4. Washington Matthews, "The Mountain Chant: A Navajo Ceremony," *Fifth Annual Report of the Bureau of Ethnology to the Secretary of the Smithsonian Institution, 1883–'84* (Washington: U. S. Government Printing Office, 1887), p. 393.

6. THE SUPERNATURAL: THINGS TO DO AND NOT TO DO

1. Richard F. Van Valkenburgh, "Sacred Places and Shrines of the Navajos," *Plateau,* XIII (1940), p. 8.

2. "Rain prairie dogs" are a kind of small bird; "whites of waters" are the froth of flood waters. For the source of this translation, see Willard W. Hill, *The Agricultural and Hunting Methods of the Navaho Indians,* Yale University Publications in Anthropology, No. 18 (New Haven: Yale University Press, 1938), pp. 75–77. The translation of lines 24 and 25 has been slightly altered by Kluckhohn.

3. Hill, *The Agricultural and Hunting Methods of the Navaho Indians,* p. 65.

4. Berard Haile, "Some Cultural Aspects of the Navajo Hogan" (Mimeographed, 1937), pp. 5–6.

5. Helen H. Roberts, *Musical Areas in Aboriginal North America,* Yale University Publications in Anthropology, No. 12 (New Haven: Yale University Press, 1936), p. 33.

6. Willard W. Hill, *Navaho Warfare,* Yale University Publications in Anthropology, No. 5 (New Haven: Yale University Press, 1936), p. 7.

7. Reichard, *Prayer: the Compulsive Word,* pp. 17–18.

8. For further details, see *Gallup* (New Mexico) *Gazette* (May 25, 1944).

8. THE TONGUE OF THE PEOPLE

1. The writers are very grateful for the criticisms, materials, and suggestions provided by Robert Young, specialist in the Navaho language, of the Education Division, U. S. Office of Indian Affairs. Their greatest obligation is to the late Edward Sapir, who instructed Kluckhohn in Navaho, and whose published and unpublished materials have been drawn upon. Kluckhohn is also indebted to Dr. Gladys Reichard for the benefit of many discussions and access to her unpublished materials.

2. Robert W. Young and William Morgan, *The Navaho Language* (United States Indian Service, Education Division, 1943), p. 40.

3. Since Navaho was not a written language, various white linguists have developed sets of standard conventions for symbolizing Navaho sounds. The system used in the bilingual readers mentioned in Chapter 4 and now standard in all government publications is followed here. The concordance with English sounds is explained in Young and Morgan (see above) and in the various bilingual primers and readers.

4. Since this chapter was written, Harry Hoijer has published a scientific account of some features of these verbal classes in his article, "Classificatory Verb Stems in the Apachean Languages," in the *International Journal of American Linguistics,* XI (1945), 13–23. He considers the most frequently occurring classificatory forms to be: round object, long object, living being, set of objects, rigid container with contents, fabric-like object, bulky object, set of parallel objects, a mass, wool-like mass, rope-like object, mud-like mass. In the above-mentioned article he makes the following generalization: "The Athabascan languages frequently employ verb stems that refer not to a characteristic type of event, such as *stand* or *give* or *fall,* but to the class of object or objects conceived as participating in such an event, whether as actor or goal. Thus in all Apachean languages there is no simple verb *to give,* but a number of parallel verb themes consisting of a certain sequence of prefixes plus a classificatory verb stem. The sequence of prefixes is the same for each theme, but the stem varies with the class of object referred to."

5. The first two sentences of this paragraph and one or two phases in this and the following paragraph are taken almost verbatim from Benjamin L. Whorf's article, "Science and Linguistics," in *Technology Review,* XLII (1940), 229–231, 247–248. This article also suggested the type of drawing used here.

6. Edward Sapir, "Conceptual Categories in Primitive Languages," *Science,* LXXIV (1931), 578.

7. Young and Morgan, *The Navaho Language,* pp. 113–114.

9. THE NAVAHO VIEW OF LIFE

1. John Adair, *The Navajo and Pueblo Silversmiths* (Norman, Okla.: University of Oklahoma Press, 1944), p. 98. By permission of the publisher.

2. Washington Matthews. *The Night Chant, a Navaho Ceremony,* Memoirs of the American Museum of Natural History, VI (1902), 110–111.

3. Willard W. Hill, "Stability in Culture and Pattern," *American Anthropologist,* XLI (1939), 260.

BIBLIOGRAPHY

1: THE PAST OF THE PEOPLE

For publications prior to 1940 which deal with Navaho archaeology and history, see Clyde Kluckhohn and Katherine Spencer, *A Bibliography of the Navaho Indians* (New York: J. J. Augustin, 1940). Articles on the history are scattered, but those listed on pp. 5–22 give an idea of the character and variety of sources. The following articles on Navaho history and archaeology give new materials and also summarize most of the earlier work:

Hall, Edward T., Jr., "Recent Clues to Athapascan Prehistory in the Southwest," *American Anthropologist*, XLVI (1944), 98–106.

Hoopes, Alban W., "The Indian Rights Association and the Navajo, 1890–1895," *New Mexico Historical Review*, XXI (1946), 22–47.

Huscher, Harold A., and Betty H. Huscher, "Athapaskan Migration via the Intermontane Region," *American Antiquity*, VIII (1942), 80–88.

—"The Hogan Builders of Colorado," *Southwestern Lore*, IX (1943), 1–92.

Keur, Dorothy L., *Big Bead Mesa*, Memoirs of the Society for American Archaeology, No. 1 (Menasha, Wis.: 1941).

—"A Chapter in Navaho-Pueblo Relations," *American Antiquity*, X (1944), 75–86.

Lindgren, Raymond E., "A Diary of Kit Carson's Navaho Campaign, 1863–4," *New Mexico Historical Review*, XXI (1946), 226–247.

Reeve, Frank D., "A Navaho Struggle for Land," *New Mexico Historical Review*, XXI (1946), 1–22.

2: LAND AND LIVELIHOOD

Publications prior to 1940 which deal with Navaho lands, economy, and technology are listed in Kluckhohn and Spencer, *A Bibliography of the Navaho Indians*, pp. 38–43. Recent publications and others referred to in this chapter include the following:

Adair, John, *The Navajo and Pueblo Silversmiths* (Norman, Okla.: University of Oklahoma Press, 1944).

Creamer, Daniel, and Charles F. Schwartz, "State Income Payments in 1942," *Survey of Current Business*, XX (1943), 10–22.

"General Statement of Conditions in the Navajo Area" (Mimeographed, Window Rock, Ariz.: Navajo Agency, 1941).

Goldfrank, Esther S., "Irrigation Agriculture and Navaho Community Leadership," *American Anthropologist*, XLVII (1945), 262–278.

"Individual Income—Resident Population, 1942" (Processed, Chicago: U. S. Office of Indian Affairs, 1943).

Kluckhohn, Clyde, "The Navahos in the Machine Age," *Technology Review*, XLIV (1942), 178–180, 194–197.

National Resources Committee, *Consumer Incomes in the United States: Their Distribution in 1935–36* (Washington: U. S. Government Printing Office, 1938).

"1940 Statistical Summary, Human Dependency Survey, Navajo Reservation and Grazing District 7" (Mimeographed, Window Rock, Ariz.: Navajo Agency, 1941).

Tschopik, Harry, Jr., *Navaho Pottery Making*, Papers of the Peabody Museum of American Archaeology and Ethnology, Harvard University, XVII (Cambridge, Mass.: The Museum, 1941).

Woodward, Arthur, *A Brief History of Navajo Silversmithing*, Museum of Northern Arizona, Bulletin No. 14

(Flagstaff, Ariz.: Northern Arizona Society of Science and Art, 1938).

3: LIVING TOGETHER

Publications prior to 1940 which deal with Navaho physique and human biology are listed on pp. 31–33 of Kluckhohn and Spencer, *A Bibliography of the Navaho Indians*. Materials on social organization and kinship are listed on pp. 43–45. Recent publications on subjects discussed in Chapter 3 and other publications quoted include the following:

Bailey, Flora L., "Navaho Motor Habits," *American Anthropologist*, XLIV (1942), 210–234.

Hill, Willard W., *Navaho Humor*, General Series in Anthropology, No. 9 (Menasha, Wis.: George Banta Publishing Co., 1943).

—"Some Aspects of Navajo Political Structure," *Plateau*, XIII (1940), 23–28.

Kimball, Solon T., and John H. Provinse, "Navajo Social Organization in Land Use Planning," *Applied Anthropology*, I (1942), 18–25.

Spencer, Katherine, *Reflection of Social Life in the Navaho Origin Myth*, University of New Mexico Publications in Anthropology, No. 3 (Albuquerque, N. Mex.: University of New Mexico Press, 1946).

Steggerda, Morris, "Physical Measurements of Negro, Navaho, and White Girls of College Age," *American Journal of Physical Anthropology*, XXVI (1940), 417–431.

4: THE PEOPLE AND THE WORLD AROUND THEM

Publications prior to 1940 which deal with Navaho relations with whites are listed in Kluckhohn and Spencer, *A Bibliography of the Navaho Indians*. Materials on health are listed on pp. 31–33. Recent publications on these subjects include the following:

Kluckhohn, Clyde, "Group Tensions: Analysis of a Case History," *Approaches to National Unity* (New York: Harper and Brothers, 1945), pp. 222–241.

Leighton, Alexander H., and Dorothea C. Leighton, *The Navaho Door* (Cambridge, Mass.: Harvard University Press, 1944).

Shepard, Ward, "Toward a Self-Propelled Navaho Society" (Ms.).

5–7: THE SUPERNATURAL

More recent publications and others quoted in Chapters 5–7 are listed by subject below:

CEREMONIALISM AND MYTHOLOGY

Aberle, David F., "Mythology of the Navaho Game Stick-Dice," *Journal of American Folk-Lore*, LV (1942), 144–155.

Haile, Berard, "Navaho Upward-Reaching Way and Emergence Place." *American Anthropologist*, XLIV (1942), 407–421.

–*Origin Legend of the Navaho Flintway*, University of Chicago Publications in Anthropology, Linguistic Series (Chicago: The University of Chicago Press, 1943). See particularly p. 8.

–"Some Cultural Aspects of the Navajo Hogan" (Mimeographed, 1937).

Hill, Willard W., *The Agricultural and Hunting Methods of the Navaho Indians*, Yale University Publications in Anthropology, No. 18 (New Haven: Yale University Press, 1938).

–*Navaho Warfare*, Yale University Publications in Anthropology, No. 5 (New Haven: Yale University Press, 1936).

Hill, Willard W., and Dorothy W. Hill, "The Legend of the Navajo Eagle-Catching Way," *New Mexico Anthropologist*, VI–VII (1943), 31–36.

Matthews, Washington, "The Mountain Chant: A Navajo Ceremony," *Fifth Annual Report of the Bureau of Ethnology to the Secretary of the Smithsonian Institution, 1883–'84* (Washington: U. S. Government Printing Office, 1887), pp. 379–467.

—"Navaho Night Chant," *Journal of American Folk-Lore*, XIV (1901), 12–19.

Morgan, William, "The Organization of a Story and a Tale," *Journal of American Folk-Lore*, LVIII (1945), 169–195.

Oakes, Maud, recorder, *Where The Two Came to Their Father* (New York: Pantheon Books, Inc., 1943).

Reichard, Gladys A., *Navajo Medicine Man; Sandpaintings and Legends of Miguelito* (New York: J. J. Augustin, 1939).

—*The Story of the Navajo Hail Chant* (New York: Published by the author, 1944).

—"Distinctive Features of Navaho Religion," *Southwestern Journal of Anthropology*, I (1945), 199–220.

Van Valkenburgh, Richard F., "Sacred Places and Shrines of the Navajos. Part II: Navajo Rock and Twig Piles," *Plateau*, XIII (1940), 6–10.

Wheelwright, Mary C., recorder, *Navajo Creation Myth* (Santa Fe, N. Mex.: Museum of Navajo Ceremonial Art, 1942).

Wyman, Leland C., and Flora L. Bailey, *Navaho Upward-Reaching Way: Objective Behavior, Rationale, and Sanction*, University of New Mexico Bulletin, No. 389 (Albuquerque, N. Mex.: University of New Mexico Press, 1943).

—"Two Examples of Navaho Physiotherapy," *American Anthropologist*, XLVI (1944), 329–337.

Wyman, Leland C., and Stuart K. Harris, *Navajo Indian Medical Ethnobotany*, University of New Mexico Bulletin, No. 366 (Albuquerque, N. Mex.: University of New Mexico Press, 1941).

FOLK TALES

Hill, Willard W., and Dorothy W. Hill, "Navaho Coyote Tales and Their Position in the Southern Athabaskan Group," *Journal of American Folk-Lore,* LI (1945), 317–344.

Sapir, Edward, and Harry Hoijer, *Navaho Texts* (Iowa City, Iowa: Linguistic Society of America, 1942).

MUSIC

Roberts, Helen H., *Musical Areas in Aboriginal North America,* Yale University Publications in Anthropology, No. 12 (New Haven: Yale University Press, 1936).

GHOSTS

Wyman, Leland C., Willard W. Hill, and Iva Osanai, *Navajo Eschatology,* University of New Mexico Bulletin, No. 377 (Albuquerque, N. Mex.: University of New Mexico Press, 1942).

WITCHCRAFT

Kluckhohn, Clyde, *Navaho Witchcraft,* Papers of the Peabody Museum of American Archaeology and Ethnology, Harvard University, XXII (Cambridge, Mass.: The Museum, 1944). Anecdotal material published in Chapters 5 and 7 above does not duplicate any published in this monograph. A few details which were omitted from it are included in Chapters 5 and 7.

SOCIAL AND PSYCHOLOGICAL ASPECTS OF RELIGION

Kluckhohn, Clyde, "Myths and Rituals: A General Theory," *Harvard Theological Review,* XXXV (1942), 45–79.

Leighton, Alexander H., and Dorothea C. Leighton, "Elements of Psychotherapy in Navaho Religion," *Psychiatry,* IV (1941), 515–524.

—*The Navaho Door* (Cambridge, Mass.: Harvard University Press, 1944).

—"Some Types of Uneasiness and Fear in a Navaho Indian Community," *American Anthropologist,* XLIV (1942), 194–210.

Reichard, Gladys A., *Prayer: the Compulsive Word* (New York: J. J. Augustin, 1944).

Wyman, Leland C., Review of "The Story of the Navajo Hail Chant" by Gladys A. Reichard, *The Review of Religion* (May, 1945), pp. 380–384.

8: THE TONGUE OF THE PEOPLE

Publications prior to 1940 on the subject of Navaho linguistics are listed on pp. 33–36 of Kluckhohn and Spencer, *A Bibliography of the Navaho Indians.* More recent publications and others referred to in this chapter include the following:

Haile, Berard, *Learning Navaho,* Vols. I and II (Saint Michaels, Ariz.: St. Michaels Press, 1941 and 1942).

Hoijer, Harry, "Classificatory Verb Stems in the Apachean Languages," *International Journal of American Linguistics,* XI (1945), 13–23.

–*Navaho Phonology,* University of New Mexico Publications in Anthropology, No. 1 (Albuquerque, N. Mex.: University of New Mexico Press, 1945).

Reichard, Gladys A., "Linguistic Diversity among the Navaho Indians," *International Journal of American Linguistics,* XI (1945), 156–168.

Reichard, Gladys A., and Adolph Dodge Bitanny, *Agentive and Causative Elements in Navajo* (New York: J. J. Augustin, 1940).

Sapir, Edward, "Conceptual Categories in Primitive Languages," *Science,* LXXIV (1931), 578.

Whorf, Benjamin L., "Science and Linguistics," *Technology Review,* XLII (1940), 229–231, 247–248.

Young, Robert W., and William Morgan, *The Navaho Language* (United States Indian Service, Education Division, 1943).

9: THE NAVAHO VIEW OF LIFE

Adair, John, *The Navajo and Pueblo Silversmiths* (Norman, Okla.: University of Oklahoma Press, 1944).

Dyk, Walter, recorder, *Son of Old Man Hat; A Navaho Autobiography* (New York: Harcourt, Brace and Company, 1938).

Hill, Willard W., "Stability in Culture and Pattern," *American Anthropologist,* XLI (1939), 258–260.

Kluckhohn, Clyde, "Covert Culture and Administrative Problems," *American Anthropologist,* XLV (1943), 213–227.

—"A Navaho Personal Document," *Southwestern Journal of Anthropology,* I (1945), 260–283.

Matthews, Washington, *The Night Chant, A Navaho Ceremony,* Memoirs of the American Museum of Natural History, VI (1902).

Reichard, Gladys A., "Human Nature as Conceived by the Navajo Indians," *Review of Religion,* VII (1943), 353–360.

—*Prayer: the Compulsive Word* (New York: J. J. Augustin, 1944).

INDEX